The Place Names
of Yorkshire

Cities, Villages,
Hills, Rivers and Dales
some Pubs too, in praise
of Yorkshire Ales

Paul Chrystal

© 2017 Paul Chrystal
First Published in the United Kingdom, 2017
Stenlake Publishing Limited
54-58 Mill Square, Catrine, KA5 6RD
01290 551122
www.stenlake.co.uk
ISBN 978 1 84033 590 3

Printed by
Berforts,
17 Burgess Road
Hastings,
TN35 4NR

Contents

Preface

A toponym is the name we give for a place or geographical entity. In *The Place Names of Yorkshire* it can be a city, a hamlet, a river, a mountain or, more loosely, a street or even a pub.

This book lists many such places, specifically as they relate to Yorkshire, and it gives etymologies, or definitions, for them – answering the essential questions: how did it come to be called that or, what does the name tell us about the place.

The book covers the whole extent of Yorkshire and uses the county boundaries that existed before local government reorganisation in 1974 – so included are places which once were in Yorkshire but are now in Cleveland such as Middlesbrough, Stockton and Redcar and their surrounding villages. If it was ever in Yorkshire it qualifies for inclusion here.

We visit odd and interestingly-named places such as Wham, Booze, Wass, Whaw, Follifoot, Swine, Spacey Houses, Blubberhouses and Hubberholme; Cosh, Rash, Crackpot, Humble Jumble and Diggle. We recount the fantastic stories of Lake Gormire, the Gallant Band of Five, the Hand of Glory and the Swastika Stone. We scale mountains and hills, we cross lakes, waterfalls and rivers and plunge into dales, down caves, all of which do much to shape and describe the surrounding regions and places in them. So, we encounter such fascinating places as Boggle Hole, Jingling Pot, Samson's Toe, the Fryup Dales, the Valley of Desolation, the River Jordan of England, the Worm village, Hogwart's Castle, Crunkley Gill and Troller's Gill. There are intriguing characters such as the Cottingley Fairies, the Sultan of Zanzibar, the Maharajah of the Punjab, Fat Betty and the Flying Man of Pocklington. We stroll down the Land of Green Ginger, Grapecunt Lane, Waterbag Lane, Footless Lane, Lurk Lane, Elbow Lane, Mad Alice Lane and Mucky Peg Lane, visit Bitchdaughter Tower and follow in the footsteps of Dickens, the Brontës, Sir Walter Scott, Wordsworth and JMW Turner.

No place is complete without a pub, so a selection of more interesting Yorkshire pub names is included with details on their origins and how they reflect the places, cities, towns and villages they serve. So, for example, we pass time at Nellie's, Major Tom's, The Squinting Cat, The Snickelway Inn, The Push Inn, The Just Peter Inn, The Triangle Inn. As if that was not enough, we call in at the Gote Gate Inn, the Gaping Goose, the Zoological, the Portman and Pickles, the Morley Dashers, the Hark to Rover, the Original Alfed Moodies and the Jack and Gill.

Paul Chrystal, York October 2016

Introduction

Place names are invaluable, and essential, signposts to our history. They provide enduring and reliable evidence about a specific place or region, reaching back well before the invasion and settlement of the British Isles by the Romans in the 1st century BC. For any settlement the name can tell us who owned the land, that it was at the site where a river was forded or bridged, that it was under or on top of a hill, the nature of the land, or the flora or fauna that flourished there. In the case of Yorkshire, much of it, pre-Roman, was populated by a Celtic tribe known as the Brigantes who spoke a hybrid form of Celtic made up of what we might call British – roughly centred on England and Wales – and Gaelic from Ireland. The Celtic language is today confined to modern Wales, but around 400 AD variants of the language would have been spoken in Yorkshire.

Places were given names, of course, to differentiate them from all other places and to make them accessible and reachable as destinations. Some also were named to proclaim that this place or that was owned by a particular person: it was his land, his property, his territory. Yockenthwaite (Yoghan's or Eoghan's clearing) or Embsay (Embe's enclosure or hill) are good examples. The most ancient of names are usually those of hills and rivers because these geographical features were always of most significance to the local population as places to live, farm, fish, cultivate, hunt and shelter. Folklore and religion played their parts: Grimwith is named after the wood haunted by a ghost or goblin; and Worton echoes the herb or vegetable garden there.

And that is why old British is particularly dominant in the names of mountains, hills and rivers, for example Pen-y-ghent, Penhill and Pendle where *penno* is a hill, and Nidd ('brilliant'), Wharfe ('winding'), and Ure ('strong').

When the Romans came and then left some four centuries later, nothing much had changed in the meantime but they have left us with early forms of Catterick, Doncaster and Acaster Malbis. Perhaps this suggests that the use of Latin was confined to the larger towns and camps and that the average inhabitant just got on with life in the vernacular. 'Chester' and 'caster' as prefix or suffix or just on its own indicate a Roman fort or fortified town as in Manchester and Doncaster; anything with 'street' in it probably signifies the presence of a Roman road nearby as in Adwick le Street near Doncaster and possibly Streethouses and Ossett Street near Wakefield.

The word 'wic' has a Roman provenance; it means a settlement and originates in the Latin word *vicus*, which originally described a settlement which grew up around a military camp or fort but, in time, came to mean an ordinary village. Examples include East Keswick, Eldwick, Heckmondwike and Wyke.

After the Romans left, much of Yorkshire was then settled by the Angles who became Angel-cynn, the English people, and whose Germanic language was the *lingua franca* of the day. The Northumbrian dialect was the language spoken in Yorkshire and had a vocabulary of 30,000 words, 80% of which have survived into modern English. This linguistic shift was accompanied by a surge in the number of new place names.

The impact of the Anglo-Saxons was to erase many of the Celtic and Roman names and replace them with their own. Old English gradually took over and most of the ancient Celtic words disappeared from our language. We have the Anglo-Saxons to thank for the development of hamlets and villages which typically grew from farmsteads: 'tun' or 'ton'; examples in Yorkshire are legion and include Adwalton, Ackton, Allerton, Beeston, Carlton, Clayton, Cleckheaton, Clifton, Dalton, Deighton, Drighlington, Flockton, Heaton, Horton, Kirkheaton, Ledston, Lepton, Litton, Menston, Middleton, Netherton, Normanton (which confusingly means farmstead of the Norwegians not Normans), Oulton, Poppleton, Sharleston, Swillington and Upton. Homesteads were designated by the word 'ham' (Clapham, Bramham, Kirkleatham) while a settlement in a clearing in the woods is indicated by 'leah' or 'ley' as in Leyburn and

Wensley; 'stan' (stone) tells us that local stone was in used as a building material – Stanningley and Stanwick are examples of this.

'Ing' often means either 'belonging to the people of' or 'belonging to' so frequently is found with a personal name. Addingham, for example, means the farmstead of Adda's people or simply Adda's farm. Other examples are Manningham and Collingham.

The Old English 'walh' means a Welsh speaker and survives in a number of places called Walton, the second part of which, 'tun' meaning a settlement, so giving us the settlement of the Welsh speakers. Other examples are Walsden (valley of the Welsh speakers) and Walshaw (copse of the Welsh speakers). Similarly, Brettas (Britons) and Cumba (Welsh) survive in West Bretton and Cumberworth. Eccles is another prominent Old English place name in various manifestations; it is derived from the English version of a British word for a church and can be seen in Eccleshill in Bradford, Exley in Southowram and Exley Head in Keighley.

A similar linguistic cleansing was carried out by the Scandinavian invaders in the 8th and 9th centuries. The Viking invaders, Danes and Norwegians, had a huge impact. Their Old Norse bore resemblances to Old English and the names they bestowed account for two thirds of all place names in the British Isles. Viking words which infiltrated place names include 'scale' (shieling – a rough and ready hut used while out pasturing animals; pasture), 'gill' (ravine), 'foss' (waterfall), 'slack' (hollow), 'thwaite' (clearing) – originally 'thveit', and 'keld' (spring) found today in Keld (near Muker) and Threkeld. To these we can add beck, fell and –sett as in Appersett, Marsett, Countersett and Bursett – all of which were Norse summer pastures in Wensleydale. Old Norse named a number of rivers too: the Bain (straight), Skirfare (bright), Rawthey (red) and Greta (stony) among them.

Indeed, some Old English names elided into Old Norse - for example, Skipton originally Shipton meaning 'sheep farm', and Austwick, originally Eastwick or 'east dairy farm'. Examples of thwaites are Linthwaite and Slaithwaite in the upper Colne Valley. Then there is 'toft': denoting the site of a house or building as in Toft Green in York and Langtoft. Ness is a headland while kirk is a church, as in Oswaldkirk, also in York, and Felixkirk. The Norwegian 'k' was the equivalent of Old English 'ch', as in kirk/church.

The Danes came from the east and settled in the east of England; the Norwegians arrived from Ireland, the Isle of Man and the Hebrides, settling in the Dales. This is clearly demonstrated by the fact that in the West Riding, only 13% of place names are of Viking origin while in the Dales the number is 65%. Their language not surprisingly contained elements of Old Irish. Norwegian-Irish words include cross, crag and -erg (shieling); Yockenthwaite, Melmerby, Carperby and Feizor derive from this Irish-Norwegian hybrid. The provenance of the Danes explains the comparative rarity of 'thorpe' in the Dales, although it is common in other parts of Yorkshire.

Naturally, over time, there was considerable synthesis in the languages spoken in Yorkshire, one of the results of which was a phenomenon called a Grimston Hybrid. An example is found in Flockton, the first part of which is a Viking personal name Floki, while the second part 'ton' is an English word. This fusion of languages suggests that the Vikings adopted Old English but spoke it with a pronounced Scandinavian accent while retaining some of their own words. There are 50 'Grimston hybrid' names in Yorkshire, including Wigginton, near York. Today's Yorkshire dialect eventually emerged from this.

The Old Norse suffix '-by' indicates a town or village but more often a farmstead, for example Sowerby, Haxby, Grimsby ('Grimr's town') or Wetherby ('sheep's town' – 'wether' today still refers to a 'castrated ram'). There are 210 '-by' place names in Yorkshire as well as Danish place names, such as Brondby and Lyngby. 'Thorpe' is the Old Norse word for village or farmstead, surviving in Scunthorpe along with 154 other place names ending in '-thorpe' in Yorkshire including Alverthorpe, Gawthorpe, Kirkthorpe, and Kettlethorpe, all near Wakefield, and Copmanthorpe near York.

After 1066 it was the abbeys which had the greatest influence, rather than the beneficiaries of the land-grab by supporters of William the Conqueror. Roger de Poitou, who took on Craven, the Scropes of Bolton Castle, the Nevilles of Middleham, the Metcalfs of Nappa, Count Alan of Richmondshire and the Cliffords of Skipton Castle made little impression when it came to naming or renaming places in Old French. Fountains Abbey ('founteins' meant springs), Furness, Rievaulx, Jervaulx ('Valley of the Ure' or Wensleydale) each bear a French influence while Mastiles Lanes on Malham Moor, Fountains Fell, Abbotside, Prior's Rake and Grange all have an early ecclesiastical origin, often related to the grazing and transportation of sheep in the lucrative woollen trade. One notable example of French influence was at Richmond where the early name 'Hindrelac' adopted 'Richemont' - strong hill.

The *Domesday Book* reveals much about the density of Viking settlements in Yorkshire. In parts of North Yorkshire the number of *Domesday Book*-listed place names of Viking origin is over 60% of the total number of place names. However, in parts of West Yorkshire the totals are much lower with the former Viking administrative district (wapentake) of Morley around 12%, and in the wapentake of Skyrack (around modern Leeds) the percentage of Viking place names is as low as 4%. Villages with Viking place names are frequently sited in less desirable locations than English named settlements, less desirable in terms of drainage, accessability and quality of land. This suggests that the Viking settlers of the late 10th and early 11th centuries were arriving in places already settled and where the best locations were already taken. Accordingly, they will have moved on to pastures new, accounting for the low levels of Viking settlement.

The division of the county into three Ridings originated around the 11th century. 'Riding' comes from the Viking word for a 'third' (*thrithjungr* or *thridjung*) and explains why the ancient county of Yorkshire had only a North, East and West Riding, but no South. The *Domesday Book* has them down as *Est*, *Nort* and *West Treding*. The Ridings themselves were sub-divided into smaller administrative units called 'wapentakes'. This word, from *vapnatak*, means 'taker –up of a weapon', the right to bear arms and the badge of a free man who was consulted on issues of local government at civic meetings and who would make clear his assent by brandishing his weapons. Some of these wapentakes, such as Agbrigg (Wakefield) and Skyrack are still reflected in local place names. Two wapentake names suggest that the meetings were held outside, near trees: Barkston Ash (to the east of Leeds) and Skyrack (Shire Oak). This Shire Oak at Headingley lasted until 1941; the administrative centre for the wapentake of Morley was at Tingley: the 'ting' in 'Tingley' derives from the Viking word for council. Wapentakes bore similarities to hundreds in other parts of England.

Viking influence obviously extended to the naming of streets. York is a city where 'gates' are streets and 'bars' are gates. The Vikings, therefore, are responsible for the Briggates, Kirkgates, and Westgates, the Monkbars and the Micklegate Bars to name but a few in, for example, Leeds, Hull, Beverley, York and Scarborough.

More specifically, some names come from historical events or the influence of history. In the Yorkshire Dales, the lead miners introduced the name 'Hush' to Swaledale and Arkengarthdale as in Turk Moor Hush and Bunton Hush. The marauding Scots led to 'beacons' on the hills, for example at Beamsley and on Shunner Fell.

Villages and towns were often distinguished from one another by prefixing a personal name or nickname. For example Haxby north of York; Keik which means 'bent backwards' and is found in Kexby (meaning Keik's farmstead); likewise Sleng means 'idler', but was a man's name as well, and is found, for example, in Slingsby, which would mean Sleng's Settlement (or the idler's village).

Words describing features of the landscape are also all around: Langthwaite means 'long clearing', Selby means 'the Village with Willows', and Ellerton means 'farmstead near alder trees'. The unique limestone landscape of the Dales leaves us with names comprising gill, scar, foss and pot; moss describes the boggy land associated with millstone grit. Others are Blubberhouses (the houses by the bubbling brook) and Redmire (the pool covered with reeds), Arncliffe is under the eagle's cliff and Hebden means the valley where the wild roses and brambles grow. Redcar is a hybrid made up of either the place by the red marsh from the Old English 'rēad' (red) and Old Norse 'kjarr' or Old English 'hrēod', a reed, meaning "reedy marshland".

Other famous Viking named places include Sheffield: field by the River Sheaf; Harrogate: place at the road to the cairn; Whitby: white farm; and Scarborough: the stronghold of Skarthi.

Sources for place names are various and, in terms of spelling, of varying reliability. Invaluable as it is, the *Domesday Book* was written in 1086 by Frenchmen with little or no knowledge of Anglo Saxon or of the Viking dialect which influenced that language. Their English geography must have been minimal. The charters of the great abbeys dating from the 12th century and parish registers from the 16th century also add massively to our knowledge. Wills and deeds and other legal documents are crucial, as are old maps, census returns and gravestone inscriptions. However, all of these primary sources have one thing in common: they all manifest with varying spellings: it was only with the establishment of the Ordnance Survey and its mapping in 1791 and the proliferation of road and street signs in the 20th century that anything like consistency began to emerge.

The Place Names of Yorkshire A-Z

ABDY

Abdy is a village in near Rotherham; its name comes from Old French *abadie* from the Latin *abbatia* meaning "land belonging to an abbey", in this case Monk Bretton Priory or Roche Abbey. Other forms include Abedi, Abdy and Abdi.

ACASTER MALBIS

Five miles south of York. Acaster is part-derived from the Latin for camp (*castra*), and is the site of a Roman fort which was later aquired by an Anglo-Saxon called Aca. After 1066 the manor became the property of the Malbis family. The *Domesday Book* mentions it as "Acastre". 'Malbis' is from the Norman Malbysse, or De Malebys, family. Malbis was a Norman personal name which means "very swarthy".

ACKLAM

Now a suburb of Middlesbrough, Acklam is Old English for 'at the oak woodland' or 'oak clearings'. The name is a plural form of Acley, the original name for Aycliffe in Durham, also meaning the oak clearing. Acklam is listed as "Aclun" in the *Domesday Book*. There is another Acklam about twelve miles north east of York and one six miles south of Malton with the same derivation.

ACOMB

Acomb, a suburb of York, derives from the Anglo Saxon Akum which means oaks, '-um' is an Anglo-Saxon plural. Acomb pre-dates the Norman Conquest and was owned by the Dean and Chapter of York Minster. In the *Domesday Book*, the name appears as both Achum and Acum; later variants include Achu, Acun, Akum and Acham. In the 13th century, we find Acome, Acorn and Akome; Akam and Acombe turn up in the 15th century. There is another Acomb near Hexham.

AINDERBY QUERNHOW

East of the A1, five miles west of Thirsk. Ainderby is Scandinavian, and means the village belonging to Eindrithi, a Viking whose name meant 'sole-ruler'. Quernhow also appears as Whernhowe and Whernou means mill-hill; the etymology of the first part derives from the Old Norse Kvern, a mill stone. How or Howe, was an old word for a hill and is common in Yorkshire place names. The Quernhow is a hillock on the nearby Roman road which was the boundary between the parishes of Ainderby and Middleton Quernhow. Count Alan of Britanny took it over after the Conquest. Ainderby Mires and Ainderby Steeple are also in the district, the latter refers to the local church spire, the former to marshy bogs.

AINTHORPE

A small Viking farm or 'thorpe', that was isolated, on its own. The name means one thorpe or 'lonely farm'. It is just south of Danby and twelve miles west of Whitby in the Esk Valley. Ainthorpe is well-known for its 15th century Fox & Hounds Inn.

AIRE, THE

In 1218 it is Air. It is related to Swiss Aar, German Ahr and Scottish Ayr. The names probably come from a pre-Celtic word meaning river.

AIRMYN

A village at the confluence of the Aire and the Ouse. The *Domesday Book* has it as Ermenie and Ermenia. In 1379 it is Harmyn. It means mouth of the Aire from Old Norse minne – the confluence of two streams. The confluence of the Nidd and Ouse is Nidderminne.

AIREYHOLME

Originally called Erghum. Holme usually means island or meander but not in this case: -'holme' should be 'hum'. Erghum means 'at the shielings', from the Old Irish word 'erg' brought to Yorkshire by Vikings from Ireland. Pre-conquest Erghum means high or summer pasture. Around 1745 James Cook, the father of Captain Cook, was employed as farm bailiff here by Thomas Scottowe. The Cooks lived on Aireyholme Farm.

AISGILL

Aslak's, or oak ravine with the rushing stream. The village is at the head of Mallerstang Dale, near the boundary between Cumbria and North Yorkshire. The Settle-Carlisle Railway climbs to its highest point at Aisgill Summit – 1,168 feet.

There have been three rail crashes on this stretch of line. The first was the Hawes Junction crash which occurred on Christmas Eve 1910, between Hawes Junction and Aisgill, when twelve people lost their lives, some of whom were trapped in the wreckage and were burned to death. This was also the scene of the Ais Gill rail accident in 1913 when two trains collided and caught fire: fourteen people in the first train died at the scene and two passengers later died of their injuries. Thirty-eight passengers in the second train were seriously injured. In 1995 a class 156 Super-Sprinter was derailed near here by a landslide and was subsequently run into by a train travelling in the opposite direction. The conductor of the first train died in the collision.

AISKEW

Aiskew is derived from Eiki Skogr and means oak wood. It is more or less a part of Bedale now. The *Domesday Book* has it as Echescol.

ALDBOROUGH, NEAR BOROUGHBRIDGE

The Old Norse suffixes borough, brough or burgh, usually indicate an ancient fortified settlement or manor and have little to do with the modern word borough. As with Aldbrough St. John near Darlington, Aldborough near Boroughbridge is Anglo-Saxon and means 'old burgh' – an old fortified site. In pre-Saxon times both places were strongholds of the Brigantes. Isurium Brigantum is the Latin name for the Roman town of Aldborough, established in the middle of the 2nd century AD and one of the northernmost settlements in the Roman Empire. Isurium may have been the headquarters of the Roman Legio VIIII Hispana and was strategically situated on Dere Street, the Roman road from York to the Antonine Wall via Corbridge and Hadrian's Wall.

The Brigantum part of the name refers to the native British tribe, the Brigantes, who dominated much of northern England before the Romans arrived. Isurium is probably the British name for the River Ure. Most of the town still awaits excavation but a part of the walls and two mosaic pavements can be seen at the museum. The famous star or flower mosaic is *in situ*, while the fine Romulus and Remus mosaic is in Leeds City Museum.

ALDBROUGH, NEAR HULL

A village about 12 miles north east of Hull on the Holderness coast which is gradually being eaten away by coastal erosion. The parish register for 1823 tells us that Aldbrough was a parish in the Wapentake and Liberty of Holderness. The population, which included East and West Newton, was 998 and included fourteen farmers, two blacksmiths (one of whom was a farrier), a joiner who doubled as an auctioneer, four wheelwrights, four grocers, five shoemakers, four tailors, two butchers, a hairdresser, a common brewer, and the landlords of The George and The Bricklayer's Arms public houses; the parish vicar and the curate, three yeomen, two schoolmasters, two surgeons, a bailiff, an excise officer, a gentleman and a gentlewoman. Five carriers plied between Aldbrough and Hull twice a week.

ALDBROUGH ST JOHN

The fort of Stanwick near Aldbrough St. John was a key fortress of the Brigantes. When the Brigantian

Queen, Cartimandua, betrayed the British rebel Caractacus to the Romans in AD 51 her husband Venutius was so incensed that he captured the stronghold and rebelled against the Romans. The Romans forced the Brigantes out of the fort in AD 73. To police the area the Romans built the town of Isurium. In Norse language Aldbrough means "Old Burh" or fortified stronghold. John Leland in 1540 tells us that Aldbrough St. John once had a "small castle": *"There appere great ruines of a howse or litle castel at Albruch village, and thereby rennith a bekke. It standith a 2 mile south from Perse Bridg on Tese"*

ALDWARK

On the River Ouse about fourteen miles from York, its name derives from the Old Saxon, ald weorc, meaning old fort and may refer to the Roman fort at the ferry crossing on the Roman road to York that passed through here. In the *Domesday Book* it is Adewera and belonged to Ligulf in the Bulford Hundred, only to be handed over to Count Robert of Mortain in 1086. There is also an Aldwarke in Rotherham. A street in York shares the same name. Newark and Southwark are similar.

ALDWARKE

A village near Rotherham. Like its namesakes near and in York, Aldwark, the name means old earthworks.

ALLERTHORPE, NEAR POCKLINGTON.

Allerthorpe's most famous son is Thomas Cooke (1807–68). After two years of schooling the money ran out and so Thomas taught himself maths and navigation with a view to a career in exploration. However, he took up the post of schoolmaster instead and started making lenses, which led to him opening an optometrist's in York's Coney Street in 1829 where he made his first telescope. He soon built a reputation for instruments of the highest quality and in 1856 went on to found the company that became the world-famous Cooke, Troughton & Simms in Bishophill, York, which was taken over by Vickers in 1915. Of the many telescopes he made, one was for a Gateshead millionaire: the telescope tube was 32 feet long and the whole instrument weighed 9 tons – the biggest telescope in the world at the time.

ALLERTON

Yorkshire boasts eight variations on Allerton, whose name is made up of the alder tree, and ton, town. They are: Allerton, a suburb of Bradford; Allerton Bywater on the edge of Leeds; Allerton Mauleverer, a parish between Harrogate and York and Allerton Castle; Allerton wapentake; Chapel Allerton and Moor Allerton both in Leeds; and Northallerton.

The Bradford Allerton is down in the *Domesday Book* as Wilsden-cum-Allerton; locally it is pronounced as 'Ollerton' – 'Ol' rather than 'Al'.

ALLERTON MAULEVERER

The name originally meant "Aelfweard's farm/settlement" a farm held by the Mauleverer family in the 12th century. Claims by the Mauleverers to have come over with William I were revealed to have been fraudulent. Mauleverer is Norman for 'bad harrier'. During the Second World War, Allerton Castle, the home of Lord Mowbray, was the Headquarters of Six Group of RAF Bomber Command, made up of squadrons of the Royal Canadian Air Force.

ALNE

Four miles from Easingwold the *Domesday Book* reveals the village to be part of the Bulford Hundred and owned by the church of St. Peter, York (later the Minster). The name comes from the Latin word *alnus* – alder, the village being surrounded by these trees. The church here is St. Mary the Virgin (not to be confused with St. Mary Magdalen at Great Alne, Warwickshire) notable for its Norman doorway with unique carved animals (taken from the medieval, largely Bible-based Bestiary) and the 14th century effigy in the Lady chapel, which is described movingly as follows: '*The broken figures at her head are angels waiting to catch her soul in a veil and take it to heaven*'.

AMPLEFORTH

The ford where ampre (sorrel) grew. The Abbey of St. Laurence at Ampleforth is Britain's biggest Benedictine community; seventy-eight men live here according to the Rule of St. Benedict under an Abbot. Ampleforth has its origins in the monastery re-established in Westminster Abbey by Mary Tudor, although this was dissolved for a second time (after Henry VIII) by Elizabeth I. At the end of the 18th century Fr. Anselm Bolton, former chaplain of Lady Anne Fairfax at Gilling Castle, moved into Ampleforth Lodge which Lady Anne had built for him. In 1802 Fr. Anselm gave the house over to a number of Benedictines who had fled Dieulouard in Lorraine after the Revolution; this was to be their new monastery; in 1803 the new monastery school opened.

ANGRAM

There are two Angrams: one near Muker in the Dales, the other near Harrogate. Angr is an old word for grazing land. The original name would have been Angrum, plural form of Angr. Angram Reservoir is the first of three reservoirs you come to on the River Nidd in Upper Nidderdale; the others are Scar House Reservoir and Gouthwaite Reservoir. Angram is at OS map reference SE040759 and is a popular tourist attraction attracting, with the other two, around 150,000 visitors a year. The name comes from Angram, a settlement in the township of Stonebeck Up which was submerged when the reservoir was built.

APPLETON-LE-MOORS

Appleton-le-Moors is a village in the Ryedale district in the North York Moors National Park, and is near to Pickering and Kirkbymoorside. It features in the *Domesday Book* and retains its classic mediaeval layout as a croft and toft (back garden) village. Flint tools, Roman coins and a mediaeval oven have been excavated here. John Betjeman called the famous Grade I listed 19th century church "the little gem of moorland churches", notable for its beautiful west-facing rose window similar to the White Rose of York Minster. One of the village's earlier names was Dweldapilton which was revived by the former hotel here on the site of Dweldapilton Hall, built by a wealthy whaler, Joseph Shepherd.

APPLETON ROEBUCK

Appleton signifies an Anglo-Saxon farm where apples grew. Roebuck derives from Rabuk, the name of a man who owned the village in the 14th century. It lies nine miles south west of York. In the 12th century a nunnery was established at nearby Nun Appleton, founded by Adeliza, or Alice de St. Quintin, in the reign of King Stephen. One of the two local pubs is named The Roebuck.

APPLETON WISKE

Quite simply, Appleton Wiske literally means an 'apple farm on the River Wiske' which runs nearby. Appleton Wiske is a small village between Northallerton and Yarm in the Vale of York. It was known as Apletona in the *Domesday Book*. The road out of the village to the west runs up a small hill known locally as Cheesecake. William the Conqueror gave the parish to Robert de Brus of Skelton, an ancestor of Robert the Bruce. De Brus's son in turn gave it to St. Mary's Abbey, York, along with Hornby.

APPLETON-LE-STREET

More apple farms, this one near a Roman Road. It is close to Malton, and mentioned in the *Domesday Book* as "Appletun", part of the Maneshou Hundred. In 1066 it belonged to Cnut, son of Karli, but was duly surrendered to William I. The church is Saxon and is dedicated as All Saints.

APPLETREEWICK

Appletreewick, pronounced 'Aptrick', literally means the farm where apple trees grew. Wick, farm, may be Anglo-Saxon or Viking. It is twelve miles north east of Skipton. The Tudor-style High Hall was restored by Sir William Craven, Appletreewick's own Dick Whittington, who became Sheriff and Lord Mayor of London in the early 17th century. Apparently in 2009, an AA study of rural driving awarded

Appletreewick the title of 'Britain's Friendliest Town to Drive Through' – based on data monitoring road rage, driver communication, average speeds and hand wave acknowledgments of courteous driving.

ARKENGARTHDALE
Arkengarthdale is a dale on the east side of the Pennines running north west to south east, and is the northernmost of the Yorkshire Dales, Arkengarthdale means Arkle's enclosure in the valley, Arkle being a common Viking personal name. Garth is Viking for an enclosure; the dale is formed by the Arkle Beck and is the source of some wonderful names: from Reeth the unclassified road there crosses a number of other becks such as Great Punchard Gill, Roe Beck, Annaside Beck, and William Gill. It passes through Raw, Arkle Town, Langthwaite (from where a back road leads to Booze), Eskeleth and Whaw.

The 1851 census records 1283 people living in the dale, 1073 of which were born there. Males comprised 659; 254 were lead miners and a further 42 worked in smelting, construction and transportation. Eighteen women and children washed the ore. There were seven coal miners in William Gill and 49 farms employing 64 men and women. Of the fourteen trades counted there were four dressmakers, one knitter and one tailor. Fifty one of the 294 boys under the age 15, and 40 of the 247 girls attended school. Thirty-seven men from Arkengarthdale served in the First World War, three of whom were killed. 1921 was the first year in which anyone in the dale owned a car, a Ford.

ARKLE TOWN
Close to Langthwaite. Arkle, as noted above, is a Norse personal name and probably came here with settlers during the 10th century. It once had a parish church, inn and workhouse. In the 19th century a lead ingot stamped with the name Hadrian (the Roman emperor from AD 117 to 138) was found, at Hurst, to the east of the dale. This, combined with records of the Romans at Richmond using Brigantian slaves to dig for lead, suggests that the Romans were mining lead in Arkengarthdale in the 2nd century. The plethora of Viking names, including Fagger Gill, Kitley Hill, Langthwaite and Whaw, indicates that the Vikings were around during the 10th century.

ARMISTEAD
The hermit's place. Its derivation is from the Middle English "(h)ermite", hermit, and "stede", place, but ultimately from the Old French "ermite", and Olde English "stede". The pronunciation of the word "ermite" was "armit", hence the drift to a phonetic spelling.

ARMITAGE BRIDGE
A rare French place name for West Yorkshire. Near Huddersfield it comes from Old French hermitage.

ARMLEY
Part of Leeds. Etymology is Arm or Orm, a proper name, and ley, field. Home to Armley Gaol and Armley Mills, now the superb Leeds Industrial Museum.

ARNCLIFFE
Arncliffe means cliff of the eagles from the Old English earn, eagle, sadly no more in this attractive Littondale village on the River Skirfare. The pub here, the Falcon, is ancient and typical of the early public houses which were essentially a private house in which the beer was brewed in an adjoining beer house out the back and dispensed in a room from cask into a jug and then into your glass. This is still the way it is served to this day. Arncliffe was the setting for the fictional village of Beckindale in the ITV soap opera *Emmerdale Farm* from 1972 until it moved to Esholt in 1976. The Falcon was The Woolpack.

ARRATHORNE
This hamlet six miles south of Richmond was originally called Erg Thorne which means the shieling near the Thorn Tree.

ASKHAM BRYAN

The village has also been called East or Great Askham. Askham comes from Ascam or Ascha meaning "enclosure of ash-tree" as given in the *Domesday Book*. It is derived from the Old English pre-7th century 'aesc', ash (tree), with 'ham', settlement or homestead. Bryan was Bryan Fitzalan, son of Scolland, a 12th century owner. Bryan FitzAlan (d. 1st June 1306) was Lord of the Manor of Bedale in Richmondshire, Askham Bryan in the Ainsty, Bainton, Heworth, in Yorkshire, Bicker and Graby in Lincolnshire, a JP, and High Sheriff of Yorkshire. He was a Guardian of Scotland and brother-in-law to King John of Scotland. The village is six miles south west of York and home to Askham Bryan College of Agriculture.

ASKHAM RICHARD

The Richard at this Askham was probably Richard Duke of Cornwall from the 13th century. It is close to Askham Bryan and is home to Her Majesty's Prison Askham Grange. Richard (1209 –1272) was second son of King John, Count of Poitou (1225-1243), Earl of Cornwall (from 1225) and King of the Romans. He was one of Europe's wealthiest men and was a leading figure in the Barons' Crusade.

ASKRIGG

Askrigg is Old Norse, made up of a combination of askr, ash tree and hryggr, ridge: the ridge where ash trees grew, which tells us that the village was settled by Vikings. The oldest settlement probably dates back to the Iron Age. In 1066 the manor was held by Arnketil. Clock-making and the knitting of hosiery once were the industries here. 'Drunken Barnaby,' whose *Journeyings* were published in 1638, wrote: *'Thence to Askrigg, market noted, But no handsomeness about it. Neither magistrate nor mayor Ever were elected there. Here poor people live by knitting, To their trading, breeding fitting.'*

ASKWITH

Near Burley in Wharfedale; Askwith is a Viking name meaning ash with – the ash woodland.

ATTERMIRE

Audulfr's Marsh (Old Norse personal name). Attermire Scar is near Settle.

AUSTWICK

Means the dairy farm on the east side (Old Norse + Old English). The parish takes in the wonderfully named Wharfe, parts of Keasden, Feizor, Lawkland and Eldroth. Austwick is near Settle. A local folktale has it that when an Austwick man fell into a deep pool his friends could hear the words "T' b-best's at t' b-bottom", so they too jumped into the pool, and were never seen again.

AYRESOME

Ayresome was originally separate from Middlesbrough. Ayresome Park is, of course, famous for once being the home of Middlesbrough Football Club as all 'Boro supporters will know. Ayresome goes back to the Vikings: the name derives from the Old Norse 'ar husum', which translates as the houses near the river. We can assume that Viking settlers built houses here convenient for the Tees where their longships or fishing vessels were unloaded and moored. The place name Aarhus in Denmark has the same derivation and meaning as Ayresome. Ayresome started life as Arushum in 1129, changed to Arsum in the 13th century and appears on Saxton's map of 1577 as Arsham.

AYSGARTH

The name means a gap in the hills where oak trees grew. The village is mentioned in the *Domesday Book* as Echescard. Aysgarth is derived from the Old Norse words eiki, meaning oak, and skarð, meaning open space. The famous Falls are a spectacular triple flight of waterfalls on the Ure over a one-mile stretch. Ruskin, Turner and Wordsworth painted or composed poetry here with the Falls as their subject.

BAGBY
The Viking place which belongs to Baggi, three miles south east of Thirsk. Bagby comes from an Old Norse personal name Baggi plus Old Norse býr, meaning "settlement" or "farmstead". Bagby is in the *Domesday Book* as Bagebi/Baghebi.

BAINBRIDGE
Simply, the bridge over the River Bain near Hawes. Bainbridge, Roman Virosidum, is notable for the remains of a Roman fort which can be found east of Bainbridge on Brough Hill. Nearby is Cam High Road, which follows the line of a Roman road. The Rose and Crown is one of Yorkshire's oldest pubs, serving since 1445. The River Bain is officially a Main River, and is, therefore, at around two and a half miles long, the shortest river in England.

BALDERSBY
The place belonging to a Viking settler called Balderhere, it lies six miles west of Thirsk. The village appears in the *Domesday Book* as Baldrebi and in the early 13th century as Baldeby.

BALK
A neighbour of Bagby, Balk means ridge; the village has given its name to the Balk Beck.

BALKHOLME
Near Howden; in Scotland holm has the meaning flood meadow, other holms are islands this may have once been Balki's island or meadow

BANNER CROSS
Sheffield. From Old Norse baena-cross = prayer cross.

BARDALE
Near Countersett. The beaver valley (Old Norse).

BARDEN
The valley where barley is grown (Old English). Barden is both a civil parish in the Craven district which consists of the hamlet of Drebley, and a village south of Richmond.

BARDEN TRIANGLE
In Lower Wharfedale. It includes mystical places with supernatural characteristics such as Troller's Gill, the conical knoll of Elbolton Hill (the "Hill of the Fairies") and the Dibble's Bridge allegedly built by the Devil. Villages lying within the triangle include Appletreewick, Burnsall, Linton and Grassington.

BARMBY MOOR
Originally a Scandinavian settlement called Barne's farm, it was Barmby in the late 13th century and then Barnby. The suffix 'by Pocklington' was adopted in the 14th century, interchangeable, it seems, with 'in the Moor' or 'upon the Moor'. In 1935 the name we know today was officially adopted.

BARNINGHAM
Barningham is an Anglo-Saxon name meaning 'The homestead of the people of Beorna.' It is nine miles north west of Richmond. Historically it was in the North Riding of Yorkshire but along with the rest of the former Startforth Rural District it was transferred to County Durham in 1974, under the Local Government Act 1972. Here the telephone boxes are green and the 19th century Milbank Arms is Grade II listed and on the Campaign for Real Ale's National Inventory of Historic Pub Interiors: 'it is a tiny pub with no bar – they serve from the cellar'.

BARNSLEY

This means Beorn's Ley, the clearing belonging to Beorn. The first reference to the town is in the *Domesday Book*, in which it is called 'Berneslai' with a population of around 200. Another etymology has it from the Saxon word "Berne", for barn or storehouse, and "Lay", for field. Barnsley had the first bottle bank for glass recycling collection in the United Kingdom – something to do, no doubt, with Barnsley's long lived glass industry.

BARWICK IN ELMET

Barwick-in-Elmet is seven miles east of Leeds and is one of only three places in the area explicitly associated with the ancient Celtic kingdom of Elmet, the others being Scholes-in-Elmet and Sherburn-in-Elmet. The name Barwick is derived from the Old English for "barley wick", and appears in the *Domesday Book* as Bereuuith. Elmet was an independent Brittonic kingdom covering what became roughly the West Riding of Yorkshire in the Early Middle Ages, between the 5th and 7th centuries.

BATTERSBY

Battersby is a corruption of Borthvarr's-by, the Viking farm or village belonging to a man called Borthvarr.

BATTY GREEN

One of the shanty towns built by workers on the Ribblehead Viaduct. Batty Wife Cave was a deep pothole and the place where the Batty marriage came to a tragic end. Mr and Mrs Batty had separated after an argument but later agreed to meet up at the pothole and make up. When Mr Batty failed to show up his wife was so distraught she drowned herself in the hole – hence the name. An alternative version tells how Mr Batty murdered his wife after yet another argument.

BECKERMONDS

At the end of Langstrothdale. It is first recorded in 1241 as Beckermotes, from the Old Norse bekkjar mót, meaning "the meeting of the streams". The 'n' came later under the influence of Old French mont, "hill".

BECK HOLE

The stream in the valley, although the first records show that the village was known as Amerholm in the late 16th century, and mention a single farmstead and a fulling mill. The cottages of Beck Hole are around an old fording point on the Eller Beck, before it meets West Beck to become Murk Esk and eventually the River Esk. Some of these cottages around the green date back to 1728. Algernon Newton RA painted the sign on the Birch Hall Inn here – one of the few inn signs to be painted by a member of the Royal Academy. Beck Hole, off the road between Whitby and Pickering, is part of the Duchy of Lancaster.

BECKWITHSHAW

Just south of Harrogate, the name derives from the Viking words beck and vith meaning stream and wood. The suffix "shaw", first recorded in 1323, is from the Old English *sceaga*, meaning a copse.

BEDALE

From the Anglo Saxon Bedas Halh – a secret corner or retreat belonging to someone called Bede, but not the Venerable Bede. Bedale is seven miles south west of Northallerton. It is listed in the *Domesday Book* as part of Catterick wapentake, also known as Hangshire which gets its name from Hang Bank in Finghall, so called because of the many gallows used to hang marauding Scots.

BEDLAM

This Bedlam is north of Harrogate. Its name comes from Old English Botlum: "at the buildings" or its

Old Norse equivalent; there is no connection with the old Bedlam lunatic asylum (now Bethlem Psychiatric Hospital), from which our word bedlam denoting uproar and confusion comes.

BELLASIZE
Beautiful seat near Howden from the French belle + assis.

BELL BUSK
The bell-shaped bush (Old English + Old Norse). Near Malham.

BENINGBOROUGH
According to the *Domesday Book*, the Anglo-Saxon stronghold belonging to Beonna. It is six miles north west of York and famous for its Georgian Hall. Beningborough Station was the first station out of York on the line to Newcastle. The station opened in 1841 and was closed to passengers in 1958, then to freight in 1965.

BESSACAR
Near Doncaster – Bessies' field (Old Norse akr).

BEVERLEY
An Anglo-Saxon name which means beaver's clearing. It was originally known as Inderawuda and was founded in AD 700 by Saint John (of Beverley) during the time of the Anglian kingdom of Northumbria. From the Vikings it passed to the Cerdic dynasty when it gained religious prominence and became a place of pilgrimage throughout the Middle Ages on account of its founder. Beverley became a leading wool-trading town and was at one time the tenth-largest town in England, as well as one of the most prosperous.

BICKERTON
Bickerton near Wetherby means the beekeeper's farm.

BILSDALE
Bilsdale is the most westerly of the dales of the North York Moors. The name Bilsdale comes from the Old Norse personal name "Bildr" and means "Bildr's valley". The main settlements are the ancient hamlet of Urra, the village of Chop Gate and the hamlet of Fangdale Beck.

BILTON
Bilton is a suburb of Harrogate, and was first recorded as Billeton in the *Domesday Book*; the name is of Old English origin and means "farmstead of a man named Billa"
.

BILTON IN AINSTY
A Bronze Age hoard tells us that there was a prehistoric settlement here. Bilton is an Anglo-Saxon personal name meaning Bilo's or Billa's homestead. Ainsty is the name of the wapentake. The village appears in the *Domesday Book* as Biletone of the Annesti. A Cistercian nunnery was founded near here, at Symingthwaite, in about 1160, by Bertram de Haget. The parish registers for 1644 record the burial of soldiers killed in the Battle of Marston Moor nearby, after which Royalist prisoners were confined in the church. There is another Yorkshire Bilton – Bilton-in-Holderness, a village five miles east of Hull.

BIRDSALL
The piece of land belonging to Brid; the village is about four miles south of Malton.

BIRKBY
The etymology is from the combination of the Old Norse personal name Bretar and the suffix 'by' giving the meaning Bretar's farm. Birkby is six miles north of Northallerton; it is mentioned in the *Domesday Book* as Bergbi in the Allerton hundred.

BIRSTWITH
Possibly from Burg's staith, a landing place on the River Nidd. Birstwith is near Harrogate.

BISHOP BURTON
Fortified place (Old English burh) held by the Archbishop of York.

BISHOPDALE
Biscop's valley (Old English personal name + Old Norse). A dale on the south side of Wensleydale.

BISHOP WILTON
Near Pocklington. Wilton is not the name of a bishop but a description of the area as wild and uncultivated. The 'Bishop' in the village's name derives from the fact that it was once the Archbishop of York's palace, built in around 1220, during the office of Walter de Grey who was Archbishop from 1216 to 1255. Unfortunately, it was not to last long and was in a state of some disrepair by around 1388. Nevertheless, the site of the palace and part of the moat can still be seen in the fields opposite the school.

St. Edith of Wilton Church is part Norman but much of what we see is due to the restoration carried out by Sir Tatton Sykes in 1859. This includes the superb hammer-beamed roof and the magnificent floor designed by J. L. Pearson and Temple Moor. The floor is based on a design by Salviati copied from a floor in the Vatican, itself inspired by the Palace of the Caesars in Rome. It was delivered by train to Fangfoss Station and shipped on to Bishop Wilton by horse and cart.

BLUBBERHOUSES
The word blubber is Old English meaning foaming and boiling and may have been a description of the nearby lake. The many other attempts at the etymology include: from the blueberry according to Ely Hargrove in his *History of Knaresborough*; from the Blue Boar, a former inn there; from "Blueberg", "blue mountain" descriptive of the local terrain; Anglo-Saxon bluberhūs = "the house(s) which is/are at the bubbling stream". Early spellings include "Bluburgh", "Bluborrow", "Bluburhouse", (1172) "Bluberhusum". These suffixes may come from the Anglo-Saxon burh, the word for "fort". The village is on the A59 Harrogate to Skipton road.

BOGGLE HOLE
A pretty inlet south of Robin Hood's Bay. A boggle is a local name for a hobgoblin, the 'little people' who lived in caves along this coast and in the more remote corners of the Moors. More prosaically Boggle Hole was where smugglers used to land their prodigious contraband. See Hob Hole.

BOLTBY
Boltr's village – A Viking name. Boltby is about six miles north east of Thirsk and is in the *Domesday Book* as Boltebi in the Yalestre hundred. After 1066, the land was owned by Hugh, son of Baldric who granted Lordship of the local manor to Gerald of Boltby. Before that the Lord of the manor was Sumarlithi, son of Karli. There is no pub there now but it had four during the building of a reservoir; the last of these was The Johnstone Arms. Boltby possesses a deed giving free water 'in perpetuity' to the buildings in the area. It dates from the late 19th century when the reservoir was being built and water piped through the land of Ravensthorp Manor.

BOOSBECK
This name means the stream near the cow shed. Beck was Viking for a stream. Boosbeck is near Redcar.

BOOZE
Booze is a hamlet in Arkengarthdale which was afflicted by a tragedy during the 18th century when miners underground near Boldershaw blasted into an underground lake. Twenty-four miners and two pit ponies were drowned; eighteen of the dead came from Booze. The seam became known as the Water Blast Vein.

The interesting name of Booze comes from Old English boga and hus, making 'the house by the bend' – a reference either to the bend in the nearby beck or a curve on hillside. It is called Bowehouse in 1473.

BOROUGHBRIDGE
The Bridge near Aldborough. The first mention is in 1155 in the Latin *pontem de Burgo* in a charter of Newburgh Priory in 1145, and then in 1298 as Burghbrig – "the bridge near Burgh or Aldborough". A new town, Boroughbridge, grew up at the bridge and the old town became known as the "Ald-Borough". In 1697, the intrepid Celia Fiennes wrote:

> "...we went to Burrough Bridge a famous place for Salmon, but then we could not meete with any but we had a very large Codfish there, above a yard long and more than half a yard in compass very fresh and good and cost but 8 pence; I saw as big a one bought for 6 pence, and six Crabbs as big as my two hands – the least was bigger than one of my fists – all cost but 3 pence."

According to the local website – http://www.boroughbridge.org.uk

> 'In the busy season two thousand cattle a day were driven across the bridge on their way from Scotland to markets in the south. In its heyday the town boasted 22 inns which served not only the drovers but travellers by road and river; the crews of the river boats with their cargoes of lead, linen, wines, spices, etcetera; the horse traders who came to do business on Horsefair; the gipsies who flocked to the Barnaby Fair … various trades came and went: smiths, farriers, candlemakers, thread and ropemakers, millers, boatbuilders, saddlers, fishermen, farmers and much more'.

BOYTHORPE
Boia's village. The *Domesday Book* gives Buitorp. Near Great Driffield in the parish of Foxholes.

BRACKENBOTTOM
The valley bottom where bracken grows (Old Norse + Old English). Near Horton.

BRADFORD
Just means in Old English the Broad Ford, a reference to a crossing of the Bradford Beck at Church Bank where a settlement grew in Saxon times. The *Domesday Book* has it as "Bradeford".

George Weerth, the German writer friend of Marx and Engels, in between researching the impact of the Industrial Revolution on the relationship between property owners and the workers, worked in Bradford as a representative for a textile firm. In 1846 he described the town in *Neue Rheinische Zeitung* as follows:

> 'Every other factory town in England is a paradise in comparison to this hole. In Manchester the air lies like lead upon you; in Birmingham it is just as if you were sitting with your nose in a stove pipe; in Leeds you have to cough with the dust and the stink as if you had swallowed a pound of Cayenne pepper in one go – but you can put up with all that. In Bradford, however, you think you have been lodged with the devil incarnate. If anyone wants to feel how a poor sinner is tormented in Purgatory, let him travel to Bradford.'

BRAFFERTON
Brafferton derives its name from Old English 'Broad-ford-ton; it is almost contiguous with Helperby and is close to Easingwold. Ralph Rymer was Lord of the Brafferton Manor in 1641; their son, Thomas, became a barrister, translator, critic and poet. To Alexander Pope he was 'one of the best critics we ever had' but to Thomas Macaulay he was 'the worst critic who ever lived'. We might perhaps sympathise with

Macaulay when we learn that Rymer believed that Shakespeare had no genius for tragedy and considered Othello ' a bloody farce without salt or savour'. When Robert Boyle (he of the famous physics Law) died in 1691 his executors were charged with using the proceeds of his estate to spread the Christian word amongst 'infidels'; land was duly bought, including Brafferton Manor, and their rents went towards the construction of the Brafferton Building at the College of William & Mary in Williamsburg, Virginia in 1723 this was for the education of native Indian children under the aegis of the Society for Advancing the Christian Faith amongst the Infidels of the British Colonies in America, later the Society for the Conversion and Religious Instruction and Education of the Negro Slaves in the British West India Islands, and later still with an even less pithy name, too long to record here. Suffice to say that the CFS, as it became known, has left its mark in Brafferton with a plaque outside Brafferton School and the initials CFS engraved on the facades or gable ends of a number of the village's houses.

The First World War claimed 30 villagers' lives including two nurses and the Gallant Band of Five. These were five territorials in the 4th Btn Yorkshire Regiment who were sent up the line near Ypres in April 1915 to reinforce Canadian and Algerian troops who had just endured the first gas attack of the war. The Algerians had fled leaving the line exposed but the Canadians and the Yorkshire recaptured St. Julien in the face of German infantry, artillery and mustard gas attacks. A shell exploded above the trench and killed five Helperby men. Norman M'Neile, known as "the blind vicar" and completely blind from the age of twelve served at St. Peter's here for fifty years.

BRAMLEY
Bramley is in west Leeds. The name derives from bram or bramble, and ley, field. The *Domesday Book* lists it as "Brameleia" and "Bramelie". Ernie Wise was born here.

BRANDSBY
A village belonging to a Viking called Brand. Brandsby was, in the Cold War, the site for the York 37 Royal Observer Corps Post (Brandsby) Nuclear Monitoring Post, between here and Crayke at Zion Hill Farm. It formed part of the York No 20 Group ROC HQ which opened in June 1964 and closed in September 1991. It is now a Grade II Listed building.

BRIDLINGTON
An Anglo-Saxon name meaning Beohrtel's farm. Bridlington makes its debut in the *Domesday Book* as Bretlinton although it also appears as Berlington, Brellington and Britlington. Other personal names for the first part of the name include Bretel, Bridla or Berhtel prefixed on ingtūn, the Saxon name for farm. The Roman maritime station of Gabrantovicorum was near here and in the early 2nd century AD Ptolemy described Bridlington Bay in his *Geography* as 'Gabranticorum Sinus', with many harbours.

From the 1920s, 21 Air Sea Rescue Unit operated from where the Lawrence building is now until 1978. In 1932 T. E. Shaw, or Lawrence of Arabia, stayed here to train the crews of the armoured target boats of RAF 1104 Marine Craft Unit. He stayed at the Bay View Hotel, reputedly sleeping with a dagger on a chair next to the bed. On later visits in 1933, 1934 and 1935, he stayed in the tower room at the Ozone Hotel, now the Royal Yorkshire Yacht Club.

BROADRAKE
The broad sheep-walk (Old English); near Chapel-le-Dale.

BROMPTON
Brompton is a suburb of Northallerton and means the ton or farm where broom grew, in short: gorse farm. The village appears in the *Domesday Book* as Bruntone in the Allerton hundred. Brompton is the location for the site of the Battle of the Standard in 1138, and where militia mustered prior to Edward I's campaign to retake Scotland in 1303.

BROTTON

Derives from Brook Ton, the farm near the stream. It is 2.5 miles south east of Saltburn-by-the-Sea. During World War I Lumpsey ironstone mine had a rail-mounted artillery piece used to defend the mine against Zeppelin attack. Sculptor Charles Robinson Sykes (1875-1950), was born here, famous for designing the Spirit of Ecstasy badge for Rolls-Royce cars.

BROXA

Near Scarborough it means Brock's enclosure (Old English haeg).

BUCKDEN

A picturesque village in upper Wharfedale where the pub, The Buck, shares its name. The etymology derives from the Old English words bucca and denu meaning he-goat, or buck, and valley. Buckden was founded by the Normans as the centre for the hunting forest of Langstrothdale Chase, one of ten hunting forests in the dales controlled until 1534 by the Percy family. It is on the Roman road from Ilkley (Olicana) to the fort at Bainbridge (Virosidum). Buckden Rake follows the path of this road, through Rakes Wood to Cray and over Stake Moss. Lead mining was developed above Buckden in 1697 at the Buckden Gavel mine on Buckden Pike. In 1964, a skeleton was found in Buckden Gavel mine: it was never identified and was nicknamed "Buckden Bill"; coins and a funeral card found amongst the bones suggest that it dates from 1890. The bridge at Buckden is called the "Election bridge" because, when the bridge at Hubberholme was destroyed by flooding in the late 18th century, the prospective local MP promised to give £200 towards the cost of a new bridge if he was elected. On the 30th January 1942 a Wellington bomber with a Polish crew crashed on Buckden Pike in a snowstorm. Only rear gunner Joseph Fusniak survived; he followed the tracks of a fox down from the Pike to safety at the White Lion in Cray. In 1973 he built the memorial to his compatriots on the mountain. The late Denis Healey, Labour Chancellor of the Exchequer (1974–1979), spent his honeymoon in a converted stable next to the Buck Inn. There is another Buckden in Cambridgeshire on the A1 which was originally called Bugden and has a different etymology.

BURLEY LEEDS

Bur a tree and ley, field. 'Burley' first appears in 1195 as "Burteg" and, around 1200, as "Burcheleia". An alternative etymology argues for Old English burh, a 'fortification' and lēah an 'open space' or field.

BURNSALL

Bruni's nook of land in the river bend; Bruni is an Old English personal name.

BURTON AGNES

Burton means the farm on the burgh or fortified manor. Agnes is Agnes de Albermarle who witnessed a deed at Burton Agnes in 1175. The village is between Driffield and Bridlington. 17th September 1947 was the day when a truck carrying German prisoners of war collided with a train at the Burton Agnes level crossing killing two British and ten German soldiers.

BURTON CONSTABLE

Burton Constable is nine miles north east of Hull, east of Swine; like its namesake, Constable Burton, it is famous for a hall. Unlike its namesake, the constable element has nothing to do with the office of constable. Burton Constable was the seat of the Constable family, lords of Holderness. The Burton element was qualified in the *Domesday Book* with the prefix 'Santri' to form 'Santriburtone; in 1190 the name of its previous tenant, Erneburga, was tagged on to differentiate it.

BURTON LEONARD

Near Knaresborough. This is the same as Burton Agnes. Leonard is St. Leonard, to whom the church is also dedicated. One of the two pubs is the Moody Cow. Burton Leonard is seven miles south of Ripon.

BUTTERCRAMBE
A bend in the river with rich pastures. It is eight miles to the north east of York.

BUTTERSETT
Near Hawes. Also goes by the names of Burtersett and Butterside. Sir Edmund Hillary, the first man to climb Everest, is a direct descendant of John and Mary Hillary of Hillary Hall, Burtersett. The village water taps can still be seen; today water is carried from the beck for two old cottages which are still occupied. The old candle mill survives – candles were made by William Metcalfe, who had the nickname 'Candle Willie'. Electricity was finally installed in 1951. 'Bump Knitting', knitting with thick yarn, was done by the women to make stockings, jumpers and jackets.

BUTTERTUBS PASS
Also near Hawes. Possibly named after potholes used by farmers to cool their butter in while resting on the way to market.

CALCUTT
Nothing to do with Calcutta as often thought, but a part of Knaresborough. Calcutt is a contraction of Caldecott, which in one form and another is common as a place name; (Welsh: Col—dow—cwtt, Colcoit, the neck of the wood. Caldecott from Cald–i–scot, the enclosure of the Scot?

CALDBERGH
The cold hill (Old Norse) four miles south of Leyburn.

CALTON
The farm where calves are kept (Old English). In 1851 75 people lived here, of whom 33 were called Shackleton in five households. The village is near Kirkby Malham.

CANKLOW
Rotherham. The burial place of Canka or Kanki – from Old English hlaw = burial ground.

CARGO FLEET
Cargo Fleet owes its name to the cargoes which passed through the port of Middlesbrough. It predated Middlesbrough by hundreds of years and was important in the Middle Ages as a fishing village called Caldcotes or Kaldecotes, meaning 'the cold-shelter cottages' situated at the confluence of the Marton and Ormesby Becks and the Tees. Here fishermen or travellers could shelter from the inclement weather. Over time the name changed into Cawker, then Caudgate Fleet and finally (and, appropriately, given the mercantile activity here) Cargo Fleet was adopted. During the 18th century Cargo Fleet also went by the name of Cleveland Port, the place where large ships off-loaded their cargoes onto fleets of smaller vessels. From here these smaller vessels were able to continue the journey to Stockton, the main port at the time.

CARLIN HOWE
This is a Viking name which means old woman's hill or hill of the witch. It is south of Redcar.

CARLTON IN CLEVELAND
The dilapidated church here, St. Botolph's, was reputedly rebuilt by one of the vicars, the Revd. George Sangar who raised the money and worked on it day and night himself. Completed in 1879 it was destroyed by fire two years later. Sangar was charged with arson but acquitted. The present St. Botolph's is somewhat quirky with the tower half in and half out the nave. Carlton has two fine houses: the mid 1700s Busby Hall, home of the Marwoods, which the ironmaster John Gjers rented in the early 20th century; and the Queen Anne style Manor House, built by Captain Christopher Prissick, the owner of the alum works on Carlton

Bank, in 1707. The Blackwell Ox pub is named after a shorthorn bull bred near Darlington.

CARLTON HUSTHWAITE

Carltons or Carletons are legion in Yorkshire and are found in areas where Vikings settled; they are Viking forms of the original Anglo-Saxon place name Charlton. In non- Viking areas like Northumberland and the south of England the earlier form Charlton is common. 'Ton' is Anglo-Saxon and means 'farm' while Charl and the Viking form Carl mean 'churl' – a freeholding peasant. Carlton is near Stockton-on-Tees while Carlton-in-Cleveland is near Hutton Rudby which is in North Yorkshire and was never in Cleveland County. Carlbury near Piercebridge means the Churl's stronghold and, like Carlton, is mixed Viking and Saxon. The two Carltons near Thirsk are Carlton Miniott and Carlton Husthwaite. Husthwaite is the name of a Viking place near Carlton Husthwaite and means the thwaite or meadow with houses on it. The *Domesday Book* has it as Carleton in the Yarlestre hundred. In 1066 the lord of the manor was Ulf of Carleton; the lands were later granted to the Archbishop of York. Carlton in Coverdale also means the freeman's farmstead (Old Norse).

CARLTON MINIOTT

Minniott was the name of a family who lived at Carlton Miniott in the 14th century. Carlton Miniott is west of Thirsk and was formerly Carlton Islebeck.

CARPERBY

Carper is an Old Irish personal name, Caipere, meaning charioteer. By is the Viking word for a settlement leading us to believe that the founder of this place was of mixed Irish Viking origin. The village is eight miles west of Leyburn. In the 17th century the village was a centre of Quakerism: its largest building today is the classical Friends' Meeting House built in 1864. The name of the Wheatsheaf Hotel betrays important corn growing at some time in the past.

CASTLE HOWARD

One of England's finest stately homes, Castle Howard is fifteen miles north of York. It has also been the private home of the Carlisle branch of the Howard family for more than 300 years. Castle Howard is not a castle, but is called a castle because this is the term used for English country houses built on the site of a former military castle. Castle Howard began life in 1699, taking over 100 years to complete to a design by Sir John Vanbrugh for the 3rd Earl of Carlisle. This was Vanbrugh's first architectural commission – he was much better known as a playwright at the time. The site was on the dilapidated Henderskelfe Castle, which the Howard family inherited in 1566 through the marriage to Lord Dacre's widow of Thomas, 4th Duke of Norfolk. The station at Castle Howard was used by Queen Victoria and Prince Albert when they visited Castle Howard as a guest of Earl of Carlisle in August 1850. Castle Howard shot to fame as "Brideshead" in Granada Television's 1981 adaptation of Evelyn Waugh's *Brideshead Revisited* and then again as the location for the 2008 film.

CASTLETON

Castleton on the North York Moors got its name from the triple-moated 12th century Norman castle built by the de Brus family. The "Hand of Glory" was found in Hawthorn Cottage in the High Street. This was the hand of a criminal who died on the gibbet; it was drained of blood, cured in saltpetre and pepper and dried for two weeks; a candle was then placed in its clutch with a wick made from the hair of the corpse and it was then used by burglars to illuminate the houses they were burgling. The alleged magic properties of the hand ensured that the occupants remained asleep for the duration of the raid; if they did wake they would have been petrified at the sight of the glowing hand. The only way to break the spell was to drench the hand in blood or skimmed milk. Today the hand can be seen in the Pannett Museum at Whitby.

CATCLIFFE

A suburb of Rotherham which means the cliff where the cats live.

CATRIGG FORCE
The waterfall by wild-cat ridge (Old English + Old Norse). A scenic waterfall near Horton-in-Ribblesdale.

CATTERICK
Catterick is derived from the Latin *cataracta*, the word for waterfall, and the name of the Roman fort here, Cataractonium. The Romans may have got the name from the Celtic name Catu-rātis meaning "battle ramparts", as adopted later by Ptomely as Κατουρακτονιον in his map of the world. Catterick gave its name to the Celtic kingdom of Catraeth, in the Tees and Swale valleys. It appears in the *Domesday Book* as Catrice. RAF Catterick is now Marne Barracks, named after two major battles of the First World War. Other barracks include Somme and Vimy. Catterick Garrison is the largest British Army garrison with a population of around 13,000 and extending over 2,400 acres.

CAUTLEY SPOUT
The waterfall in a woodland clearing with a fish-trap (Middle English + Old English). Near Sedbergh and historically in the West Riding, Cautley Spout is England's highest cascade waterfall above ground. Gaping Gill on Ingleborough falls a greater unbroken distance into a pothole, and Hardraw Force has a greater unbroken fall above ground. Cautley cascades 650 feet (198 m) down from a plateau called The Calf in the Howgill Fells; it is one of the few cascade falls in England; most are either tiered or plunge falls.

CAVIL
Near Howden where the jackdaws are.

CAWOOD
This onomatopoeic name means wood of the jackdaw. Cawood also went by the name Carwood and lies between Selby and York. Arthur Mee, with one eye on the castle here, refers to Cawood as "the Windsor of the North". It used to serve as the residence of the Archbishops of York. The nursery rhyme *Humpty Dumpty* describes Cardinal Wolsey's 'great fall' at Cawood when he was arrested here by King Henry VIII's men on his way to York Minster.

What must go down as one of history's most sumptuous (and gluttonous) feasts took place here in 1465 at the enthronement of George Neville as Archbishop of York. The menu, for 2,000 or so guests consumed over a number of days, included:

Wheat – 300 quarters; Pikes & Breams – 608; Porpoises & Seals – 12; Oxen – 104; Muttons – 1,000; Porks – 304; Wild Bulls – 6; Veals – 304; Kids – 204; Swans – 400; Capons – 1,000; Biterns – 204; Pheasants – 200; Woodcocks – 400; Egrittes – 1,000; Quales – 100 doz; Fowls – 200 doz.; Cranes – 204; Pigeons – 4,000; Geese – 2,000; Heronshaws – 400; Partridges 500; Curlews – 100; Plovers – 400; Peacocks – 104; Mallards & Teals – 4,000; Chickens – 2,000; Pygges – 2,000; Stags, Does, Bucks – 500; Venison Pasties -1,500 hot; Venison Pasties -4,000 cold; Dishes of Jellies – 300; Baked Tarts – 4,000; Baked Custards – 3,000; Hot Custards – 2,000; Ale – 300 tuns; Wine – 100 tu (25,000 gallons); Ypocrass – 1 pipe; Coneys – 4000.

Presumably, the Good Lord approved…

CHAPEL ALLERTON
The name comes from alder, a tree, and ton town, and is Alreton in the *Domesday Book*. Chapel Allerton was reduced to Chapeltown in 1427, after which both names co-existed and were interchangeable. Ralph Thoresby, the Leeds historian, writing in 1715, records that Chapel-Town was a common name for the township of Chapel Allerton, describing it as "a delicate Green commonly call'd Chapel-Town Moor". By the end of the 17th century it was populated by wealthy people from Leeds and described in 1767 as the Montpellier of Yorkshire.

CHAPEL LE DALE

Literally, the chapel in the valley (Old French + Old English/Old Norse). It is close to the Ribblehead Viaduct, Great Douk Cave and the source of the River Doe.

CHARLTONS

Near Middlesbrough. Nothing to do with Carl(e)ton. Charlton or 'Charltons' dates from the 1860s and the ironstone mine which opened here. The usual village was built by the mine owner who was called Mr Charlton.

CHOP GATE

Pronounced 'Chop Yat' this village in the North York Moors is at the junction of the Bilsdale and Raisdale roads. Chop Yat means pedler's way; 'Yat' being is old Norse for route or gate. 'Chop" is from the old English word "ceap" meaning to barter, indicating that the village was once a centre for trading and probably had a market. This etymology is shared with Cheapside in London. Chop Gate is within reach of such vividly named moors as Cold Moor and Hasty Bank; Urra Moor to the north east of Bilsdale is the highest moor in the North York Moors at 1,454 ft; the summit is Round Hill. The Face Stone is here, a rock about a metre high carved into the shape of a face.

CLAPDALE

The valley of the noisy stream (Old English).

CLAPHAM

The homestead on the noisy stream (Old English) and former home to the *Dalesman* magazine, now based in Skipton. It is often called Clapham via Lancaster, as if there was a need to distinguish it from Clapham Junction. This Clapham is near to Trow Ghyll where a skeleton was found in August 1947 by two members of the Northern Pennine Club, Leach and Burgess, looking for new pots to explore; they discovered a small hole (named Body Pot afterwards) partly covered by stones into which Leach climbed only to discover a pair of shoes, then, looking round he saw the skull and the rest of the badly decomposed body; next to the body was a phial of white powder. The police were duly summoned and the remains taken to Skipton mortuary while the effects were sent to the forensic laboratory at Wakefield. By pure coincidence, a week later, another skeleton was found close by at Gaping Gill but this was a result of a fall into the cave two to three years previously.

The Body Pot post-mortem examination concluded that death had occurred at least two and no more than six years previously. None of the bones were broken or diseased although some were missing, as was the brain. The phial had contained sodium cyanide, a deadly poison, as did an ampule also found at the scene. There were also two pairs of shoes, a watch, handkerchief, studs, toothbrush, fountain pen, propelling pencil, compass, box of matches, tablets, flashlamp, toiletries and a key. The verdict concluded that there was insufficient evidence of cause of death or to identify the remains. The historian AWB Simpson, who happened to be living in Clapham at the time, reported that the only known users of such ampules were foreign spies operating undercover in enemy countries, who used them to commit suicide if necessary. Simpson suggested that the victim was "plainly connected in some way with the German secret service". He added enigmatically that "Such enquiries as I have made from persons who ought to know have produced evasiveness". According to MI5, Germany had deployed around 115 agents in Britain during the war, most of whom had been identified and caught, with the exception of one, Willem Ter Braak, who had committed suicide before being captured. The identity of the skeleton remains a mystery.

CLEVELAND

Cleveland means the cliff land or hilly region, the word cliff in its old sense referring to rolling hills rather than steep-faced cliffs or escarpments. The cleve element in Cleveland may also be related to cleavage. Historically, Cleveland was a part of north Yorkshire to the south of the River Tees. The earliest record is Viking when Harald Hardrada is reported to have landed in part of Yorkshire called Cliffland.

Guisborough was the ancient capital of Cleveland. Old Cleveland stretched as far south as Whitby.

COATHAM
See Redcar.

COGDEN GILL
Woodcock valley (Old English).

COLD KNUCKLES
South of Darlington – named presumably after the effect of the local weather on your knuckles.

CONEYSTHORPE
Nothing to do with rabbits. The thorpe or farm belonging to the King near Malton and Castle Howard (which owned it from the 19th century). Before the Conquest it was owned by Torchil and then among the lands of the Count of Mortain in 1086. Name variations are as follows: Coningestorp, Counsetorp, 11th century; Cuningestorp, 12th cent.; Cuningesthorp, 11th-17th cent.; Coningesthorpe, 13th-17th cent.; Conysthorpe, from 13th cent; Conyncrosthorp, 16th cent.

CONISBROUGH
The name Conisbrough comes from the Old English Cyningesburh, first recorded c.1000. It means 'king's stronghold' or 'king's fortified place'. The striking castle inspired Walter Scott's 'Coningsburgh Castle' in his *Ivanhoe*.

CONISTONE
Near Grassington; the king's farm (Old Norse + Old English). There is another, more famous, one in the Lake District.

CONSTABLE BURTON
Burton means farm on a stronghold. The constable concerned derives from the constable of the Earl of Richmond around 1100. Constable Burton and its famous Hall and Gardens is three miles east of Leyburn. Not to be confused with Burton Constable (qv).

COPMANTHORPE
Copmanthorpe is just outside York to the south west. In the *Domesday Book* it is Copemantorp, from Old Norse Kaupmannaþorp, meaning traders' village or craftsmen's village. Before 1066 the Lord of Copmanthorpe Manor was an Anglo-Saxon called Gospatrick.

COSH
The hut in the green open pastures (Middle English + Old English) in Littondale. Cosh is the last house in the dale which before 2011 was 'the most remote home in the Dales with no electricity, no gas, no mains water and accessible only by off-road vehicles up a rough mile-and-half-long track'. In the 1950s the owners of Cosh were offered electricity but declined as they didn't want to pay the bills.

COTHERSTONE
An Anglo-Saxon name meaning Cuthere's farm although some like to link the name with St. Cuthbert. Cotherstone is in Teesdale, close to Barnard Castle. The swing bridge in Cotherstone was the scene of a tragic accident in 1929 when football supporters at a game between Mickleton and Cotherstone crowded onto the bridge; twenty-five of them fell the 22 feet into the river, and one, Sally Nattrass, later died. Cotherstone is famous for its cheese: its reputation goes back to 1858 and is based on a non-monastic form of Wensleydale originally made from ewes' milk. Hannah Hauxwell, who achieved fame through a Yorkshire Television documentary, farmed nearby at Low Birk Hatt Farm and moved in to the village itself in 1998.

COTTERDALE

The valley with the huts (kotar) or cottages (Old Norse). It is a small dale and hamlet north of Wensleydale to the west of Great Shunner Fell. East Gill and West Gill and their nine waterfalls join to form Cotterdale Beck, which flows over three more waterfalls, including Cotter Force, into the River Ure.

COTTINGHAM

North of Hull and probably England's biggest village with a population of 17,000 – not including the Hull University students at the Lawns and in Needler Hall. Cottingham derives from both British and Saxon words: "Cot" from Ket, referring to the deity Ceridwen; ing a water meadow; and ham meaning home thus making to "home in the water meadows of ket". The name may also come from a man's name "cotta" plus -inga- (OE belonging to/named after) and ham – making "habitation of cotta's people". Old spellings include Cotingeham (the *Domesday Book*), and Cotingham (Charter, 1156 and John Leland, 1770). The pre-conquest owner was Gamel, the son of Osbert, in the reign of Edward the Confessor in the 11th century. Post-Conquest the land was owned by Hugh FitzBaldrick; in 1089 the manor was given to Robert Front de Boeuf, founder of the de Stuteville family line. Philip Larkin is buried in the village.

COTTINGLEY

A suburb of Bradford it derives its name from the Cota or Cotta family and so means meadows of the sons of Cota, "Ing" being wood, "ley" field. Alternatively, "ting" or "ding" might mean moot or court here. There is another Cottingley in Leeds. Bradford's Cottingley is famous for its fairies: the Cottingley Fairies feature in five photographs taken by Elsie Wright (1900–88) and Frances Griffiths (1907–86), two cousins; Sir Arthur Conan Doyle, a spiritualist, used them to illustrate an article on fairies in the *Strand Magazine* as evidence of psychic phenomena. In the early 1980s Elsie and Frances admitted that four of the photographs were fakes – they had used cardboard cutouts from a children's book but Frances insisted that the fifth photograph was genuine.

COUNTERSETT

Constance's seter (Old French personal name + Old Norse); seter is a summer pasture with barns; this one is near to Semerwater. The word is still used in Norwegian (seter) and Swedish (säter) to denote a mountain pasture used for making milk and cheese, to which a farmer takes his livestock as part of transhumance.

COVERBRIDGE

The hamlet near Leyburn at the confluence of the River Cover and the River Ure; it consists of Clarkson's farm and the Cover Bridge pub.

COVERDALE

Dale of the River Cover, a tributary of the Ure. It extends south west from the eastern end of Wensleydale to the dale head at Park Rash Pass, between Great Whernside to the south and Buckden Pike to the north. Coverdale cheese comes from the valley and is another variant of Wensleydale cheese, produced at the Wensleydale Creamery in Hawes.

COWGILL

The dam in the ravine from a dialect word 'caul' meaning dam or weir and Old Norse. It is near Dent, formerly in Yorkshire.

COWLING

See Ickornshaw

COXWOLD

The origin of Coxwold is Cuhu walda: the wold belonging to someone called Cucha. Cuhu is a personal name and walda is a wood. However, to the Normans it was Cucwald: cuc meaning to crow as cocks do. Shandy Hall in Coxwold was a priest's house in the Middle Ages, later to become home for Laurence Sterne (b. 1713) for the last eight years of his life. Shandy Hall was probably built around 1430 by George Dayville in what was then called Cuckwold. Sterne wrote *A Sentimental Journey Through France and Italy* and *Sermons of Mr Yorick* here as well as seven of the nine volumes of *The Life and Opinions of Tristram Shandy, Gentleman* from 1759. Shandy Hall is now a museum housing, among other things, the world's largest collection of Sterne's manuscripts and first editions.

Sterne died of pleurisy in London in 1768; he was buried in the churchyard in Coxwold but only after a circuitous journey... He was originally interred in St. George's churchyard, Hanover Square, London, but his body was snatched by 'resurrection men' for use in medical dissection at Cambridge University. Once on the table the cadaver was recognised by the Professor of Anatomy who had known Sterne; he fainted and had it hastily reburied. In 1969 the Laurence Sterne Society obtained permission to remove Sterne's remains to Coxwold for further re- burial.

CRACKPOT
Nothing eccentric about this derivation. In 1298 Crackpot in Swaledale was called Crakepot, the name deriving from the Old English 'Kraka', a crow and the Viking word 'Pot' – often a deep hole in a river bed, but in Crackpot's case refers to a rift in the limestone. This meaning of pot also crops up in Potto near Swainby, Sand Pot near Northallerton and in Pot Hall and the Pot Beck near Masham. The word is still used in Swedish today. There is a Crackpot Hall near Keld.

CRACOE
Crow hill (Old Norse). Near Skipton. Nearby are Cracoe Reef Knolls which are geological remnants of an ancient coral reef. Cracoe was the home of the original Calendar Girls: members of the Women's Institute who in order to raise money for leukaemia research produced and starred in their own calendar of traditional WI activities, like knitting or baking, whilst nude.

CRAKEHILL
Crakehill near Dishforth denotes the hill belonging to a Viking man called Craca. Crakethorn near Pickering is named after the thorn bushes frequented by crows, likewise Crathorne near Yarm. Near Newcastle crows were evident at Crawcrook – the crook of land inhabited by crows. Craster on the Northumberland coast was once Crawcestere and refers to an abandoned fort populated by crows.

CRAMBE
From the Anglo-Saxon word 'crumb' meaning a bend in the river, the Derwent in this case. Crambe appears in the *Domesday Book* as "Cranbone" in the Bulford hundred. It is six miles west of Malton.

CRAVEN
The name of this district in the north west of Yorkshire comes from the Welsh word ' craf' denoting the garlic which grows in the region. Other derivations include the Celtic 'krab' – scratched or scraped, and the pre-Celtic word 'cravona', meaning a stony area.

CRAY
Nothing to do with crows, as might be assumed, but the fresh stream – from Old Welsh 'crei'. Cray is a hamlet near Buckden with a fine pub, the 700 year old White Lion, originally a drovers' hostelry, a stopping place for farmers taking their cattle and sheep to market. Wainwright described it as a "tiny oasis". It has recently been renovated to a high standard.

CRAYKE
Derives from the Celtic word kraik meaning a rock and is the same as craig in Celtic place names; some

say it is from the Saxon 'creca'. Crayke is near Easingwold. There is evidence of Roman activity here with the most significant being a large stone building along with roundhouses, metalworking paraphernalia and a kiln. The building includes a portico and may well perhaps have been a British temple. Cuthbert, later Bishop of Lindisfarne (c. 634-687), was granted Crayke and the surrounding land to an extent of three miles by Ecgfrid, the Saxon king of Northumbria; it then served as a resting place for Cuthbert on his journeys between Lindisfarne and York. The timber Bishop's cottage from 1615 was demolished, reputedly on the orders of a Miss Mathews who lived in the Hall, because it spoilt her view down the hill. Crayke can boast two witches: Molly Webster practised her infernal arts mainly on cows whose milk she turned sour; she was also in the habit of stabbing people with her pins; Mabel Thornton was the other.

There were some fascinating place names extant in the manor in 1648: Nyne Penny Piece, Fower Megge Flatte, Heather Intacke,Crooke Inge, Fosse Flatt, Two Sam Peeces, Slee Close, Great and Little Hagg Inge, Weight Land, Bulpitt, Mart Gate Inge, Oxeclose, Sir Richard Close, Overfossette, Claude, Fetherstons and Cow Close. All very descriptive of a rural community dependent on agriculture.

CROOKRISE CRAG
The brushwood by the bend in the valley (Old Norse). Near Embsay Reservoir.

CRUMMACKDALE
The crooked valley (British + Old Norse/Old English). Near Austwick and close to the Norber Erratics and Nappa Scar.

CRUNKLEY GILL
A half mile long gorge carved by glacial melt waters (now the River Esk) near Lealholm.

DANBY
The etymology is the Old Norse words Danir and 'by' meaning the farm of the Danes. Danby Castle, built in the early 1300s, is now a farm and was used for the meetings of the Danby Court Leet and Baron established in 1656. It is reached by crossing the 1836 Duck Bridge and was once the seat of the Latimers; Catharine Parr lived there when she married John Latimer after the death of Henry VIII. Two miles outside Danby in Danby Dale, near to where the original Danish village was, consisting of wooden buildings, St. Hilda's Church has a 15th century tower and an 18th century nave. It was restored in 1903. John Christopher Atkinson (1814-1900) is buried there – ornithologist and author of the famous *Forty Years in a Moorland Parish* which describes the 70,000 miles he is said to have covered walking the moors over 50 years. He was vicar for 53 years and died in 1900 but not before he had married three times and fathered thirteen children.

DANBY WISKE
The suffix Wiske refers to the nearby river. Danby Wiske was mentioned in the *Domesday Book* as Danebi. The lands were the property of Kofse at the time of the Norman Conquest. After 1086 the manor was granted to Landric of Hornby.

DANYDRYMIRE
Andy's Marsh (Old Norse). Dander is an old form of Andrew.

DEE RIVER
The modern name of the River Dent from the Welsh 'dwfr' meaning 'water' which when applied to rivers can mean 'holy' or 'sacred' water.

DELPH
Saddleworth. The name for a quarry. Old English doelf.

DENT
The hill, probably from Old Irish 'dind'. Dentdale – Dent Valley.

DERWENT RIVER
Celtic name meaning oak river. It flows from Fylingdales Moor to its confluence with the River Hertford then through the Vale of Pickering, south through Kirkham Gorge and the Vale of York, meeting the River Ouse at Barmby on the Marsh.

DEWSBURY
Watery 'burgh' or fortified manor. The *Domesday Book* records the name as Deusberie, Deusberia, Deusbereia, or Deubire, literally "dew hill", from Old English dēaw (genitive dēawes), "dew", and beorg, "hill" – Dewsbury is built on a hill. Dēaw may refer to the town's proximity to the River Calder. It may also derive from "Dui's fort" or "God's fort", from the Cornish Duw, "God". Dewsbury, could also mean 'Dewi's fortification', Dewi being David in Welsh, an early form of which was spoken by the people of Elmet.

DIBBLE'S BRIDGE
Old English for the bridge over the River Dibb (The pool). Dibble's Bridge was allegedly built by the Devil and is in the mystical Barden Triangle. The Dibble's Bridge coach crash on 27th May 1975 on the B6265 road, Dibble's Bridge, below Grimwith Reservoir 1.6 miles east of Hebden, is one of the UK's worst road accidents. Thirty-one elderly passengers and the driver were killed, and thirteen others injured when the brakes on the coach, from Thornaby, failed. The owner of the coach company was later fined £75 (£562 in 2015) for operating a motor vehicle with defective brakes.

DIGGLE
Saddleworth. The name is from the Saxon degle, meaning valley.

DIRTCAR
Near Wakefield, it appears as Drytkar in 1284 and is Old Norse from drit – dirt- and kjarr copse.

DODD FELL
The hill with a round summit (Middle English + Old Norse). Dodd Fell is a Marilyn – a hill with over 150 metres (492 feet) prominence from the surrounding terrain, regardless of absolute height. The name derives from a pun on Munro, a Scottish mountain over 3,000 feet (914.4 m), which is homophonous with (Marilyn) Monroe.

DONCASTER
Danum to the Romans – an important fort on the route between Lincoln and York. There is another River Don at Jarrow. Doncaster is the Cair Daun – one of the 28 cities in the 9th century *History of the Britons* by Nennius. It was an Anglo-Saxon burh called Doncaster "Don-" (Old English: Donne) from the Roman settlement and river and "-caster" (-ceaster) from an Old English variation of the Latin castra ("camp").

DORE
A suburb of Sheffield. This means door or pass between two kingdoms. The Limb Brook, River Sheaf, and Meers Brook marked the boundary between the Anglo-Saxon kingdoms of Deira (Northumbria) and Mercia. *The Anglo-Saxon Chronicle* gives the earliest record of Dore, stating that in 829 King Egbert of Wessex led his army to Dore to take the surrender of King Eanred of Northumbria, thereby establishing his control over the whole of Anglo-Saxon Britain.

DORMANSTOWN
The Dorman Long & Co steelworks were built in 1916-1917 after Dorman Long had taken over the old Warrenby Works and introduced new mixers, furnaces and plate mills. At its peak the works employed

over 5,000 men; Redcar's 'Garden City' was built at Dormanstown, originally, Dormantown, for the workers. The village included houses for the elderly – the first in the United Kingdom. A road to a proposed new railway station and footpaths across the marsh to Warrenby and the Redcar Ironworks; a hospital, chapel, library and technical school none of these projects ever got off the ground. Building took place between 1917 and 1920, helped by a light railway from the works to bring in materials.

DOWBIGGIN
Near Sedbergh; it means Dufa's building, or the dove building (Old Norse personal name or Old English + Middle English); alternatives are 'gathering of buildings (biggin) near the dovecote (dow), or 'gathering of buildings near the cave.'

DRAX
Long stretch of river derived from the 1208 spelling Langrak = Old English lang + racu.

DRIFFIELD
Or Great Driffield, and Little Driffield. First reference comes with the *Domesday Book*, and means 'dirty, manured, field'; Anglo-Saxon origin. Pubs include the Original Keys (once the Ferret and Sprout, previously the Cross Keys), the Buck, the Full Measure, the Rose and Crown, Mariner's Arms and the Bell Hotel, an old coaching inn famous for its prodigious selection of whiskies. In the second series of *Monty Python's Flying Circus* Michael Palin announces that "The Silly Party have taken Driffield".

DRINGHOE
Near Skipsea. Made up of dreng – a tenant + Old English hoh = hill. The *Domesday Book* has Dringholme so it could be water meadow.

DRINGHOUSES
Suburb of York which in the 13th century was Drengus and Drenghous from Old Norse drengr meaning a young person and then privileged peasant who held land by Pre-Conquest tenure.

DUNKIRK
There are Dunkirks at Sowerby, Denby and Golcar. Possibly connected to the French port by the 1793 battle of Hondshcoote.

DUTCH RIVER
For centuries Goole was little more than a fishing village, with a population in 1821 of 450. It owes its growth and prosperity as a major port to the Dutch civil engineering expert Cornelius Vermuyden from Zeeland. On instructions from Charles I, in his 1629 Dutch River project, he diverted the Dutch River, or River Don, northwards to join the River Ouse and thereby drain the marshland of Hatfield Chase, a favourite hunting ground of the king. This also had the effect of making the lower Don navigable for small barges, bringing coal to Goole from the South Yorkshire Coalfields for transfer to seagoing vessels.

EARSWICK
The ancient township of Earswick or Edresuuic, as it was known before the Norman Conquest, derives from the Anglo-Saxon meaning "dwelling or farm of a man called Æthelric". Earswick is just north of York.

EASBY
Ese's village – a Viking place name near Richmond, on the Swale. The hamlet is mentioned in the *Domesday Book* as Asebi. There is another Easby two miles south east of Great Ayton.

EASINGWOLD
Long Street here was originally called Low Street because it was the southern end of what could well

be described as two towns – Uppleby being the northern, Danish settlement under the control of the Danish chief Uplleby. Low Street was inhabited by the Angles. The name Easingwold probably derives from ease which means 'rich irrigated land prone to flooding', and wold or 'forest'. Alternatively, it may come from the Saxon family name Esa: the wold belonging to Easa. As well as the Toll Booth and the Shambles there was also a cucking stool in the Market Place which claimed its last victim, Peggy Johnson, in 1763; a row of cottages called the Squad; the town lock-up and pinfold and the inevitable stocks and a whipping post. The Butter Cross is a reconstruction of an original; a bear-baiting ring was at the north end of where the Town Hall is now. The register of burials for any town usually makes interesting, if uncomfortable, reading, and Easingwold's for 1777-1780 is no exception: sixteen children died of smallpox, 21 (mainly adults) of consumption, four (children) of whooping cough, four from dropsy (heart failure); one in childbirth; two from mortification of the bowels and one each from apoplexy (stroke), palsy (paralysis), marasmus (malnutrition), gravel (kidney stones), bladder inflammation and asthma.

EAST WITTON
East Witton means the eastern woodland farm. It is south of Leyburn.

EGTON
West of Whitby, and Egton Bridge nearby: Ecga's farm – an Anglo-Saxon place name. The village was included in the *Survey of English Dialects*, published between 1962 and 1996 because, being an isolated village, the speech of the villagers was very unusual. Egton holds the Gooseberry Run, an annual charity race around the village.

EGYPT
There's one in Gomersal and another in Thornton, and the original in north Africa.

ELBOLTON
Elbolton – the village among the alder trees (Old Norse). The hill here is one of the Cracoe Reef Knolls and is possessed of strange, magical powers. Known as the "Hill of the Fairies", Elbolton is one of several supernatural places in the so-called "Barden Triangle". Potholes on Elbolton include "Navvy Noodle Hole" where prehistoric remains have been excavated.

ELLERKER
West of Hull, means alder tree marsh from Old English alor + Old Norse kjarr.

ELLOUGHTON
Farm with a temple derived from Old Norse helgr = temple + ton. North of Brough.

EMBSAY
Near Skipton. The name means Embe's enclosure or hill (Old English personal name + Old English).

ESHOLT
"Esholt" tells us that the village was established in an area of ash trees. It lies between Shipley and Guiseley. Between 1976 and 1996 Esholt was the setting for the Yorkshire Television soap *Emmerdale Farm*.

ESK RIVER
A Viking river name denoting a pass, or valley. The 28 mile Esk enters the sea at Whitby. There are five other Esk Rivers: four in Scotland and one in the Lake District. Alternatively, the name may well be derived from the Brythonic word *isca* which means "water". The same derivation applies to the Rivers Axe, Exe and Usk with the slight changes attributable to over ten centuries of usage.

The Brittonic, Brythonic or British Celtic languages are one of the two branches of the Insular Celtic language family the other being Goidelic. Brythonic was coined from the Welsh Brython, an indigenous Briton as opposed to an Anglo-Saxon or Gael. Brittonic is derived from *Prettanike*, the word used by the Greek author Pythias for the British Isles, 'literally land of the painted people', in the 4th century BC; in the 1st century BC, Diodorus Siculus mentioned Pretannia. The Brittonic languages are derived from the Common Brittonic language which was spoken throughout Great Britain south of the Firth of Forth in the Iron Age and Roman period.

ESKELETH
A hamlet in Arkengarthdale. This Old Testament-sounding name has an obscure first part but the second is Old Norse/Old English for a slope. It was Exherlede in 1280.

ESTON
A Saxon name meaning the East farm. The Eston hills overlooking Middlesbrough were the site of a beacon to warn of Napoleonic attacks, the remains of which can be seen at Eston Nab.

EVERINGHAM
Everingham near Pocklington has the unusual distinction of having two churches both dedicated to St. Everilda, a 7th century saint who founded a convent in the village and gave the village its name St. Everilda's (Church of England) and Sts. Mary and Everilda, (Roman Catholic). Moreover, the only other church in Britain dedicated to St. Everilda is at Nether Poppleton to the west of York. After the Reformation, Everingham was, in effect, a recusant village, and the Italianate style St. Mary & Everilda was built in the grounds of Everingham Hall within a decade of the Catholic Emancipation Act of 1829. It was designed in Italy by Agostino Giorgioli, inspired by the Maison Dieu at Nîmes. Its construction was supervised by John Harper of York. Tragically, the church is on private land with very limited access – a shame on a number of counts, both religious and secular.

FACEBY
Feitr's place, a Viking name meaning the fat person's village. It is near Stokesley.

FAGGERFILL
The ravine in a sheep enclosure (Old Norse). Appears as Fagardegile in 1280.

FANGFOSS
Near Pocklington. Called Frangefos in the *Domesday Book*, the name possibly means the ditch used for fishing, from the Old English foss and Scandinavian fang for fish. Fangfoss is home to the fascinating Rocking Horse Shop. In October 2011 their Bigger Bertie, the world's biggest rocking horse, was the main attraction at the World Skills competition at London's Excel Centre. It measures over 14 feet high, 5 feet 8 inches wide and more than 28 feet long.

FEIZOR
Fech's upland pastures, Old Irish/Old Norse personal name + Old Norse. Fech was a landowner from the area before 1066. Near Giggleswick.

FELIXKIRK
This village near Thirsk gets its name from the local church, which is dedicated to St. Felix, a Burgundian who travelled with St. Paulinus converting the Saxons in the 7th century to Christianity. There are five other churches dedicated to St. Felix: all of the others are in East Anglia. In the *Domesday Book* Felixkirk appears as Fridebi with the manor lands shared between Gamal, son of Kalri and Ligulf. After 1066 these passed to Hugh, son of Baldric, who made Gerard of Boltby, lord of the manor. Fridebi may share its name with Firby near Snape Castle in Bedale, and means Peaceful Place from the Danish word for peace

which is 'fred'. Alternatively it may just be Freda's or Frithi's dwelling. Felixstowe in Suffolk may also have a connection with St. Felix. Bede extolled Felix for delivering "all the province of East Anglia from long-standing unrighteousness and unhappiness".

FERRENSBY
North of Harrogate. From Old Norse faeryingr meaning men from the Faroe Isles.

FILEY
Filey means the five leys – 'the five meadows or forest clearings'. Filey Brigg, the long ridge of rocks nearby, is steeped in mystery: it was allegedly built by the Devil, who, having lost his hammer in the sea, groped for it with his hand but caught a fish instead. The Devil exclaimed, "Ah! Dick!" (why?), and gave us the name of the fish – haddock; the Brigg now bears the marks of the Devil's grasp. Another legend states that the rocks are the bones of a dragon drowned by the townsfolk when it plunged into the sea to wash parkin from between its teeth.

Charles Dickens visited Filey and recorded these observations in his *Household Words* in 1851:

> 'The sea-side churchyard is a strange witness of the perilous life of the mariner and the fisherman. It is only by a walk in it that we acquire a clear conception of the real nature of that mode of livelihood which such hundreds of thousands, all round these islands, embrace, as a choice or a necessity... Filey, a mere village, well known to thousands of summer tourists for the noble extent of its sands, and the stern magnificence of its so-called bridge, or promontory of savage rocks running far into the sea, on which you may walk, at low-water; but which, with the advancing tide, becomes savagely grand, from the fury with which the ocean breaks over it. In tempestuous weather this bridge is truly a bridge of sighs to mariners, and many a noble ship has been dashed to pieces upon it. One of the first headstones which catches your eye in the little quiet churchyard of Filey bears witness to the terrors of the bridge. "In memory of Richard Richardson, who was unfortunately drowned December 27, 1799, aged forty-eight years"...'

FLAMBOROUGH
Flamborough means Flein's fort, the site of a fort situated on Flamborough Head. According to legend, the village is haunted by the ghost of a suicide called Jenny Gallows. The Old Dog and Duck pub is at Dog and Duck Square.

Flamborough was for many years a shipwreck waiting to happen. The headland juts out into the North Sea by 6 miles, its cliffs are 400 feet high, the scars below are many and razor sharp, and the currents treacherous. Indeed, between 1770 and 1806, 174 ships were wrecked here leading to the construction of a lighthouse in 1806. The 92-foot-high lighthouse was brick built from the inside without the use of any scaffolding. It is still in operation today with a light equivalent to three and half million candle power visible up to 21 miles away. On 10th February 1871 a violent storm hit Bridlington Bay with the loss of over 70 seamen and 30 ships. It was after this disaster that the lifeboat stations at Flamborough were established. Two lifeboat stations were built – one at North Landing, and the other at South Landing. The idea was to ensure that at least one of the lifeboats could be launched into the lee of gale. The local fishermen had been doing this for years, keeping cobles at both landings.

FLASBY
Flasby was first mentioned, as Flatebi, in the *Domesday Book*. The name is of Old Norse origin, meaning "the farmstead of a man called Flat" and may be the same origin as Flaxby near Knaresborough. But see below for an alternative.

FLAXTON
North east of York – a place where flax was grown. Likewise Flaxby.

FLOTMANBY
Near Filey: the place where the Vikings were. Flotman was an Anglo Saxon word for a Viking. Old Norse flot = ship + mathr = sailor.

FOGGATHORPE
Near Goole. Bulmer's 1892 *History and Directory of East Yorkshire* states that the village is called "Fulcathorpe" in the *Domesday Book* and that it was given by William I to his standard-bearer, Gilbert Tison.

FOLLIFOOT
The name Follifoot, near Harrogate, is derived from Old Norse meaning "place where the horses fought"; horse fighting was popular amongst the Vikings, and this was the beginning of a long local association with horse sports. The earliest record is 'Pholifet' from the 12th century. Anglo-Saxon remains have been discovered in and around the village and an Anglian Cross stands at the crossroads. In the 19th century the village was a thriving community with its flax industry, tannery, tailors, joiners, a wheelwright, cordwainer and blacksmiths.

FOSS RIVER
Foss means ditch-like river and derives from the Latin fossa, ditch. The Foss is a tributary of the Ouse, the confluence is in York.

FOULNESS RIVER
A river around Market Weighton. Like the island in Essex, its name is derived from Old English fulga-naess meaning wild birds nest; others maintain that Foulness means dirty river.

FOUNTAINS ABBEY
The original Cistercian monks found springs here.

FOXUP
This means a valley or 'up', inhabited by foxes. Near Litton.

FRIDAYTHORPE
The thorpe or farm belonging to a Viking called Frigdaeg, a personal name derived from Frigg or Freya, the Old Norse god of fertility from whom we get Friday. Fridaythorpe is near Pocklington.

FULFORD
A suburb of York. This means foul or dirty ford. In 1828 it was Fulfords Ambo signifying two villages: Water Fulford due to the River Ouse and Gate Fulford due to the fact that this one was around the bridge carrying the Doncaster to York road over a stream.

FYLINGDALES
The dale of Fylga's people. The 7th century Lilla Cross is on the moor here – one of the oldest Christian monuments in northern England. Lilla was a servant of King Edwin of Deira; he was killed in AD 626 when trying to protect his master from a poisoned dagger attack. The 20th century Ballistic Missile Early Warning Station here was built in 1962; Pevsner described it as "the geometry of the space age at its most alluring and frightening." Each radome weighed 100 tons, was 154ft high and 140ft in diameter; they were made of 1646 laminated glass fibre panels (hexagonal and pentagons). The 84ft diameter radars inside swivelled around and had a range of 300 miles. It cost £54 million and was only ever out of commission

once – for twelve hours; 900 people were employed there in the 1960s; nowadays it's nearer 400. The three radomes have been replaced by the pyramid-shaped Solid State Phased Array Radars (SSPARs); each comprises 2,560 transmit/receive modules; total peak power output is about 2.5MW, with a tracking range of over 3,000 miles.

GAMMERSGILL
Gamel's shieling (hut or high pasture); Old Norse personal name + Old Norse. Near Leyburn.

GARGRAVE
Gara's grove. Or the copse in a triangular plot of land (Old Norse + Old English). Gargrave had its very own witch: Anne Greene, described in this extract from *Witchcraft in Yorkshire* by Patricia Crowther:

> 'Anne Greene of Gargrave was examined by John Asheton and Roger Coats in 1853. John Tatterson testified, and this is how the clerk of the court reported it. Being disabled in body he was troubled with ill spirits. He asked Anne's advice for pain in the ear. She told him that black wool was good for it, whereupon she crossed his left ear three times with her garter and got some hair out of his neck without his consent. When he got home he suffered more pain than before, and returned to her and said " to look to it or he would look to her". Having crossed his ear three times again, she said it would mend, and, with corruptible matter running out, it did. The accused herself explained that she, knowing a charm for curing earache, twice used it on Tatterson by crossing her garter over his ear and saying "Boate help" (this was the name of an old god). For a pain in the head she required the patient's water and a lock of hair, which she boiled together, and threw into the fire. The verdict of the jury of life and death was not guilty'.

GARSDALE
Garth's valley (Old Norse personal name + Old Norse/Old English).

GAUBER HIGH PASTURE
At SD 76507830. Gallows Hill near Ribbledale.

GAWTHROP
Cuckoo farm – Old Norse. Near Dent.

GEARSTONES
The stony triangular plot of land (Old English) – near Ribblehead Viaduct. The earliest reference to the lodge here is "Crossing a ford, Mr. Blakey led me to a public house called Griestones, the seat of misery in a desert" – from the diaries of Lord Torrington in 1792. Not the best of recommendations.

GIGGLESWICK
Appears as Ghigeleswic in the *Domesday Book* meaning 'Dwelling or (dairy) farm of a someone called Gikel or Gichel'. An Old English or Middle English personal name, probably a short form of the biblical name Judichael + wic. The parish church is dedicated to St. Alkelda, an obscure Anglo-Saxon saint associated with Middleham.

GILLING WEST
Near Richmond, the name derives from Getlingas, meaning the Anglian people of Getla possibly after Ingetlingum Bede in his *History of the English Church and People* of 731. The area around was known as Gillingshire ruled by the Earls of Mercia. The *Domesday Book* has it as Ghellinges. Similarly Gilling East near Helmsley.

GLAISDALE

Valley of the River Glas. Glaisdale is eight miles west of Whitby. The Esk is bridged three times at Glaisdale. The best known, Beggar's Bridge, was built by Thomas Ferries in 1619. Before the bridge was built, in order to meet Agnes Richardson the squire's daughter and the love of his life, Thomas had to wade through the river. When he asked for Agnes' hand in marriage the squire refused because he was "no more than a beggar". Understandably disappointed, Thomas went off to Whitby and joined the navy, seeing action against the Spanish. As a pirate under Drake he won a share of a sizable booty from a captured galleon and returned to Glaisdale a wealthy man, eventually becoming Mayor of Hull and Warden of Trinity House in Hull in 1820. The squire relented and Agnes and Thomas were married; Thomas pledged that no man should ever get his feet wet crossing the river and paid for Beggar's Bridge to be built.

GOATHLAND

Goda's land – probably a Viking name. The 1892 Mallyan Spout Hotel is here, named after the waterfall – the tallest in the North York Moors at 70 feet. Goathland was the setting for the village of Aidensfield in the popular serial, *Heartbeat*. The name Aidensfield was arrived at after a visit to St. Mary's Church where members of the crew saw stained glass images of St. Aidan. A Viking fertility dance survives here in the form of the Plough Stots Sword Dance performed annually on the first Saturday after Plow Monday. The dance is intended to banish evil spirits and guarantee a good harvest; latterly it took the form of locals dragging their ploughs around the village collecting beer money – refusal to contribute apparently led to your garden being ploughed up. The headquarters of the Goathland Plough Stots dance team is in the Goathland Hotel where you can still see the "swords" over the fireplace arranged in the Star of Bethlehem formation of the dance.

GOATHLAND STATION

Built in 1865 this quaint halt originally known as Goathland Mill is probably most famous now as Hogsmeade Station, the stop for Hogwarts School of Witchcraft and Wizardry in *Harry Potter and the Philosopher's Stone*; the *Hogwarts Express* stops here on arrival from platform 9¾ at King's Cross. According to J. K. Rowling's instructions, Hogsmeade Station is not in Hogsmeade, but on the opposite side of the lake. The final scene in the film has the train leaving Hogsmeade Station, and thanks to special effects, Hogwarts Castle in the background.

Goathland is also famous in the history of Rowntrees: Joseph Rowntree instituted the work's outing, intended, no doubt, as a bonding exercise. One such was perhaps a little too bonding and something of a disaster. On a trip to Whitby members of the party left their chartered train at Goathland intending to walk the rest of the way and meet the main group for an afternoon stroll along the beach. Rain intervened and diverted the walkers into a local hostelry for 'shelter'; many emerged much the worse for drink and had to be escorted back to the station by the police. Needless to say, there were no more outings for a while.

GOLCAR

Huddersfield. Named after St. Guthlac, who preached thereabouts during the 8th century, its name is in the *Domesday Book* as Goullakarres. – car is from Danish kaer – bog.

GOLDSBOROUGH

The burgh or fortified manor belonging to Golda. In the *Domesday Book* Goldsborough is referred to as "Godenesburg". In the 1920s HRH Princess Mary, the Queen's aunt, came to live at Goldsborough Hall following her marriage to Viscount Lascelles. Goldsborough is near Knaresborough. There is another Goldsborough near Scarborough – a Roman signal station.

GOODMANHAM

The home of Godmund and his people and originally Godmundin Gaham village approximately two miles to the north east of Market Weighton. It was the site of the most important pagan shrine in the

Kingdom of Deira (Southern Northumbria) in pre-Christian times – a great temple of Woden, the father of the gods. St. Bede describes the overthrow of this temple in AD 627 by the high priest Coifi on the conversion of King Edwin of Northumbria (in his *History of the English Church and People* – *Historia ecclesiastica gentis Anglorum*).

GOOLE
Unusually for English place-names, "Goole" is derived from the Middle English word *goule*, meaning 'stream', or 'channel'; some, less flatteringly, say 'open sewer', or 'outlet to a river'. It is first recorded on a map in 1362 as 'Gulle', in 1552 as 'Golflete' and then 'Goule'. Goole is the most inland port in Britain and, because of its quasi-rural setting, took the name 'the Port in Green Fields'. The current station is name-checked in the Flanders and Swan song *Slow Train* about closed lines on the British railway network: 'No one departs, no one arrives, From Selby to Goole, from St. Erth to St. Ives. They've all passed out of our lives On the Slow Train, on the Slow Train.'

GORDALE
The dirty valley or the valley covered with manure (Old Norse + Old Norse/Old English). As in the Scar near Malham. Wordsworth wrote in the sonnet *Gordale*, "let thy feet repair to Gordale chasm, terrific as the lair where the young lions couch"; Turner painted it in 1816; the result now hangs in Tate Britain.

GORMIRE
The reputedly bottomless 10,000-year-old Lake Gormire is below Sutton Bank, complete with the massive boulders on its bed which fell from the cliff above in 1755 – a catastrophic event witnessed and described graphically by John Wesley who attributed it to the power of the Almighty. Some say that a complete village lies at the bottom of the lake, submerged due to the meanness of the inhabitants' when they each (bar one) refused an angel, dressed as a beggar, a cup of water. It is one of only three natural lakes in Yorkshire (the others being Malham Tarn and Semerwater) notable for the fact that no streams flow into or out of it. One of the many legends surrounding the lake says that one day the Devil was walking thereabouts when he trod his hoofed foot in some mud, which formed Lake Gormire. He tripped over and in trying to pull himself out, with one arm flailing around – flattened the surrounding land. The other arm gouged out the hillside, forming Sutton Bank. If you look into the waters of Lake Gormire, guess who you will see looking back at you.

GRANGETOWN
A grange is a farm. It has been overrun by Middlesbrough.

GRASSINGTON
Logically, this name means grazing land farm. Or it could be town of Gersent or Gersendis.

GREASBROUGH
Another suburb of Rotherham. The *Domesday Book* has it as Gersebroc meaning 'grassy brook'.

GREAT AYTON
Derives from Ea-tun the tun or farm on an 'ea' or river. The *Domesday Book* has it as Aytun. Great Ayton was never famous for its wild social life – due to the lack of a market and the influence of the Quakers: in 1890 there were only two inns while in nearby Stokesley which was smaller at the time there were fourteen. In 1896 a Ladies Dance Quartette was permitted to go ahead only because there was 'no exposure of the limbs, as, if held up at an angle of 90 degrees [the dress] is so fully pleated that it does not even expose the underskirt at all'.

GREAT BUSBY
From Buski's by – a farm or village belonging to a Viking called Buski. Near Stokesley.

GREAT FRYUP DALE

As with Little Fryup, the name Fryup derives from the Old English reconstruction Frige-hop: Frige was an Anglo-Saxon goddess equated with the Old Norse Frigg; hop was a small valley. The Fryups are near Danby. An old woman or seer of Fryup was notorious for keeping the ancient practice of Mark's e'en watch (24th April), living as she did alongside a corpse road known as Old Hell Road. This involved keeping vigil between 11pm and 1am to watch for the ghosts of those who would die in the following year.

GREAT SMEATON

From the Anglo-Saxon Smideton – the smith's farm. It lies just off the A1 between Darlington and Northallerton. The Church of St. Eloy's there is the only church in Britain named after St. Eloy, and stands on the site of an 11th century Saxon church. Eloy is patron saint of goldsmiths, metalworkers generally, coin collectors, vets, and the Royal Electrical and Mechanical Engineers (REME).

GREEN HAMMERTON

Green Hammerton, west of York, is famous for three characters: Alleluia Tommy, real name Thomas Segmore, a prominent Methodist, who lived here; Dick Turpin who lodged here on his way to York; and Wishy Watson who habitually slept in a tree at the north end of the green. (H)ambretone, a place-name reflected both in nearby Kirk Hammerton ('Hammerton and the church', from Old Norse kirkja 'church') and in Green Hammerton ('Hammerton on the green', from Middle English grene), appears in the *Domesday Book*. Hammerton derives from the Old English plant-name hamor (hammer-sedge or pellitory of the wall?) + tūn 'settlement, farm, estate'. In 1861 there were four pubs in the village: the Sun, the Railway Tavern, the Rose and Crown Inn and the Victoria.

GREWELTHORPE

Grewelthorpe is north of Ripon. This delightful name derives from Gruel – a family name and thorpe meaning "outlying farmstead". Nearby is Hackfall, a Grade I Garden; the landscape was created by the Aislabies of Studley Royal. As in Victorian times it is a popular attraction offering grottoes, surprise views, waterfalls, a fountain and several follies, including Mowbray Castle, a hill top ruin.

GRIMSTON

Grimston means the farm belonging to Grim. Ton is a Saxon word and Grim is a Viking personal name: mixed Viking and Saxon place names are referred to as 'Grimston hybrids'. There are Grimstons near Withernsea and just outside York, at Grimston Bar.

GRIMWITH

The wood haunted by a ghost or goblin (Old English + Old Norse). Famous for its reservoir, it is near Pateley Bridge.

GRISEDALE

The valley where young pigs were kept (Old Norse + Old Norse/Old English); near Sedbergh.

GROSMONT

A Norman French name meaning large hill. Grosmont was originally built to accommodate railway workers and was originally called Tunnel but the name had changed by 1894 to commemorate the 1204 Benedictine priory founded by Johanna Fossard and monks from Grandimont in Normandy. The Whitby to Pickering line was endorsed by George Stephenson and opened in 1835 carrying 6,000 passengers in the first three months – including Charles Dickens. The complete line opened in 1836 with trees and heather wrapped in sheepskins being used as foundation for the tracks in boggy areas.

GUISBOROUGH

The borough or fort belonging to a Viking called Gigr. John Oxlee was born in Guisborough in 1779 –

one of the world's greatest linguists ever, proficient in an astonishing 123 different languages and dialects; he often had to compile his own grammars and dictionaries, so rare were some of his languages. One of his most celebrated books was *One Hundred and More Vocabularies as from the Stamina of Human Speed Commencing with the Hungarian and Terminating with Yoruba*, published in 1840.

GUNNERFLEET
Gunnar's river (Old Norse personal name + Old Norse). Near Chapel-le-Dale. Gunnerfleet Farm breeds and sells pedigree Gunnerfleet Limousin cattle.

GUNNERSIDE
A Viking name meaning Gunnar's slope. It is near Muker.

HACKNESS
Hook shaped headland. The site near Scarborough of, according to Bede, a double monastery – that is, a separate community of monks and nuns, co-existing in one institution. Bede calls it Hackenos, the headland of Hacce. Sir Thomas Posthumous Hoby (1566–1640) was lord of the manor and possibly the inspiration for Shakespeare's Malvolio in *Twelfth Night*.

HADES
Nothing to do with the Underworld but rather a place behind a hill that is out of sight. There are Hades in Marsden and Holmfirth.

HALIFAX
The first record we have is from 1091 as Halyfax, from the Old English halh-gefeaxe, meaning "area of coarse grass in the nook of land". An alternative is the Old English halig (holy), in hālig feax or holy hair, proposed in the 16th century. This has spawned two legends: the first concerned a maiden murdered by a rapacious priest whose advances she spurned. Another, medieval in origin, maintained that the head of John the Baptist was buried here after his execution; the town coat of arms bears an image of the saint. Yet another derivation is a corruption of the Old English hay and ley, a clearing or meadow, based on Haley Hill, the nearby hamlet of Healey and the frequent occurrence of the surnames Hayley/Haley around Halifax. An erroneous derivation from halig has led to the demonym Haligonian. Demonyms (from the Greek *demos*, people) are used to identify residents of a specific place and are derived from the name of that place.

HALLAM
As in Sheffield; it is either dative plural of the Old Norse hallr, a slope or hill; or of Old English heal, a mansion or hall.

HALTEMPRICE
An area to the west of Hull which became a civil parish in 1858, and in 1935 was expanded by the urban districts of Cottingham, Anlaby, and Sculcoates to form a new urban district which included Anlaby, Cottingham, Hessle, Kirk Ella, Skidby, West Ella and Willerby. Urban districts were abolished 1974. Haltemprice Priory was established as an Augustinian house in the 14th century. The name comes from the French haute emprise, high enterprise.

HALTON EAST
Near Bolton Abbey. The farm in a nook of land (Old English). 'East' is to distinguish this village from West Halton near Long Preston.

HALTON GILL
The farm in a nook of land by a ravine (Old English + Old Norse) + gill, stream. It was Haltongyll in 1457. Halton Gill is in Littondale. The bridleway over the Horse Head Pass to Yockenthwaite in

Langstrothdale was routinely used by the priest from Hubberholme to reach his chapel in Halton Gill. To the west, paths lead to Pen-y-ghent via Plover Hill.

HANGING GRIMSTON
A Wolds village near Painsthorpe, the name of which means Grim's farm on a slope, from Old Norse kengja.

HANLITH
Hagne's hill slope (Old Norse personal name + Old Norse). It was called Hangelif or Hangelief meaning 'King's land' in the *Domesday Book* and is near Malham.

HARBER SCAR
The hillside where oats are grown (Old Norse hafri + Old English beorg/Old Norse berg. In 1297 it was Haverbergh. It is near Horton.

HARDRAW FORCE
The shepherds' row of cottages (Old English) + Old Norse fors, foss; near Hawes. It is also spelt Hardrow; 1606 saw it as Hardrawe. This is England's largest single drop waterfall at 100 foot drop and is in the grounds of the Green Dragon Inn.

HAROME
Harome means rocks/stones, and translates from old English meaning a heap of stones. Near Helmsley.

HARROGATE
From Har-low-Gata meaning Grey-Hill-Road. Harlow still survives in Harrogate at Harlow Carr. An alternative is enclosed corner from Old Norse hagr, hedge + wraa a turn + Old Norse gata, way or road. We have to wait until 1332 before its first historical reference, as part of the roll for Knaresborough Court. The name comes from the Norse 'Here gatte', the road to Harlow, or to Haverah, which in turn means the road to the soldier's hill. Haverah was a royal park dating back to 1100.

To add to the confusion and uncertainty Thorpe's *Early History of Harrogate* published in 1891 tells us that

> Harrogate is derived from the ancient British of Heywray–gate, i.e., Hey a forest, park, or moor–wray, a brook or stream – and gate, a road. Another fixes the derivation as Harw–gate, the road of robbers...The titles with which Harrogate has been credited are so innumerable, as to suggest imperfect orthography as their source. The name may still be found in some old established railway guides as "Harrowgate;" though the w is fast losing its hold upon the heretofore confident railway tabulators. It may not be uninteresting to state that the following, besides the above mentioned, are said to have done duty in turn: "Harloo–cum-Bylton Banks," "Harlowgate," "Harrogat," "Harry-gate," and "Harrowgait."

HARTLINGTON
The farm belonging to Heortla's people; (Old English personal name + Old English). The *Domesday Book* has it as Herlintone. It is near Grassington.

HATFIELD
Hatfield near Doncaster means Heath field and was part of a district known as Meicen or Meigen and the site of its palace – Meicen was a Welsh kingdom resistant to the Anglo-Saxons for a while. Hatfield was also called Heathfield. In AD 633, King Edwin was killed here by Penda, King of Mercia. Penda was supported by the Welsh under Cadwallon ap Cadfan, Welsh (British) King of Gwynedd. Osric, a successor to Edwin, was also killed in the battle. Edwin's son Edfrith also surrendered to Penda. This battle is the origin of Slay Pit Lane in Hatfield where the battle took place and the bodies of soldiers lay nearby.

HAWES

This derives from the old Norse hals – a narrow neck of land (between mountains). Hawes was the home of Kit Calvert (b. 1903), the saviour of Wensleydale cheese.

HAWKSWICK

Hauk's dairy farm – (Old Norse personal name + Old English). Or, Middle English hauk: someone who trained hawks + wick, meaning dairy farm. Hawkswick is in Littondale near Kettlewell. In the *Domesday Book* it is Hochesuuic.

HAWNBY

Originally Halmi's 'by' but corrupted from that. It was the village belonging to a Viking called Halmi. The village, north of Helmsley, is mentioned twice in the *Domesday Book* as Halmebi, in the Allerton hundred. The 17th century Arden Hall, seat of the Earls of Mexborough is here. Mary, Queen of Scots spent a night here just before her execution. John Wesley said of his visit: "I rode through one of the pleasantest parts of England to Hawnby." Nearby lived George Baxter, better known as the Hermit of Rosedale or, as he liked to call himself, Lord Rosedale, Sultan of Zanzibar, Admiral of the French Fleet. George lived in virtual isolation resolutely refusing to pay his bills – attempts to persuade him were often met by a salvo from his double-barrelled shotgun. Even an aptly named PC Tom Shooter failed in his attempt to bring him to book. George died in 1959 and is buried in grave 1926 in Pickering Churchyard. All Saints Church here features a poetry shrine.

HAWORTH

Derived from Old English haga, an enclosure as in Hageuuorde, and weorth a farm.

HAWSKER

South of Whitby. Hawk's enclosure – a personal name rather than the raptor. Hawsker Bell is a ship-warning fog horn nearby.

HAXBY

The earliest references to Haxby, in the 11th century, refers to it as Haxebi ("Hacca's Farm" in Norse). There is evidence of a Roman presence in the form of what was possibly a villa on Haxby Moor, pottery found in Station Road and a silver signet ring. A 9th century Viking settlement is indicated by the discovery of the base of a cross in St. Mary's Churchyard and in 1978 two large fragments of a 10th century Anglo-Scandinavian cross shaft with Celtic markings were found. Up until recently the 2,000 acres of the parish were almost totally devoted to agriculture. 1,100 acres were under cultivation and 800 as pasture at the time of enclosure in 1769. Parish registers from around 1850 show that of the 218 men recorded, 144 were farmers or farm labourers and a further 46 were in trades supporting farming, such as blacksmiths and carpenters. The *1941 Farm Survey* shows there to be no fewer than 38 farms in and around Haxby including many, like the 107 acre Church Farm at what is now 44 The Village, in the centre of the village itself. Haxby is north of York.

HEALAUGH

The clearing in the high forest (Old English from Heah) near Reeth. The village telephone box is unusually well furnished, with a carpet, waste paper bin, ash tray, directories and fresh flowers. Visitors are encouraged to leave a donation. There is another Healaugh near Tadcaster. Here, Healaugh Park Priory is now called Healaugh Manor Farm, founded in 1218 by Jordan de Santa Maria and his wife, Alice, who was the grand-daughter of Betram Haget who had granted the lands for a hermitage to Gilbert, a monk from Marmoutier.

HEBDEN

Near Grassington. The name Hebden may be derived from either heope, Old English for a rose-hip or heopa, Old English for a bramble, and dene, Old English for a valley, or from the Scandinavian Hebban, a ridge forming an elevated site above a small valley. The *Domesday Book* refers to it as Hebedene held by Osbern d'Arques, of Thorpe Arch. In 1066 the land was held by Dreng, a Viking.

HELLIFIELD
Helgi's or Halga's open land (Old Norse personal name + Old English; or holy field from Old English haelig + feld. The *Domesday Book* lists as Helgfeld, Helgeflet and Haelgefeld.; the village may also have been dedicated to the Anglo-Saxon Goddess 'Hel' so that the name derives from the Norse 'The Farm of Helgi'. In the 12th century, Hellifield was "Nether Hellifield" and in the 17th and 18th centuries "Hellifield Pele" and later "Hellifield Cochins". In the Middle Ages, the area was plagued by wolves, so Hellifield men were employed to guide travellers in the vicinity to safety.

HELMSLEY
The name Helmsley derives from the Saxon for Helm's Clearing (Ulmetum in the *Anglo Saxon Chronicle*); then Hamelake and to the Normans it was Elmeslac after the elms that stood there. The Lord of the Manor was Ughtred. William I gave Helmsley land to Robert de Moutain, his half brother, but when he rebelled against William Rufus in 1088 it passed to Walter l'Espec whom Abbot Aelred from Rievaulx described as "having a voice like the sound of a trumpet". Canon's Garth was restored in 1893 when it housed the Sisters of the Holy Rood. Around 1860 the illegitimacy rate in Helmsley was 15%; Canon Gray was warned not to raise the issue with unmarried mothers, and the mother of one threatened to douse him in boiling water if he did. One of the more celebrated and colourful vicars of All Saint's from 1870 to his death in 1913 Gray was staunchly anti-Catholic and anti-Methodist. Amongst his pet grievances he managed to put right were the lack of good sanitation – the town drain contained "enough filth to poison everyone", housing – "utterly unfit for man or beast…no house need be dirty…a woman is worth nothing if she cannot keep her house clean" the over-tight lacing of stays and the abolition of uniforms for children in the poor house so as to make them inconspicuous in the town.

HELWITH BRIDGE
Bridge by the ford made of flat stones (Old Norse)

HELPERBY
A Viking name meaning Hialpar's farm or village. Hialpar was a woman's name and although women's farms were not unknown, they were unusual. Helperby is virtually joined to Brafferton and is near Easingwold. The name Helperby derives from 'help hard by' (or Helper-By) when St. Paulinus, disciple of St. Augustine and first Bishop of York, needed water for baptisms. St. Paulinus, who converted Edwin, the Saxon king of Northumbria, to Christianity used the River Swale here as a place of baptism. Allegedly in 626 at Christmas 10,000 people went into the river to be Christened, with no casualties despite the numbers. Indeed, those with a "feeblenesse and infirmitie" re-emerged "whole and reformed". This, and similar mass baptisms in the region, for example at Catterick, led to the Swale being christened the River Jordan of England. The antique shop here is called Junk & Disorderly.

HESSAY
From Haesal Sae, a lake where hazels grew. Hessay is five miles west of York.

HESSELSKEW
Near Market Weighton, this name means hazel wood from Old English haesel + Old Norse skogr, wood.

HETTON
The farm on the heathland (Old English).

HINDERWELL

Hinderwell is between Whitby and Staithes and was listed in the *Domesday Book* as Hildrewell or Ildrewell becoming in the 12th century Hilderwell and Hylderwell corrupted in the 15th century to Hynderwell or Hinderwell. Hinderwell means Hild's or Hilda's Well named after St. Hild, or Hilda, the abbess of Hartlepool and, later, Whitby. Hinderwell's 18th century church is dedicated to her, but the holy well of Saint Hilda in the churchyard is much older and gave its name to the village. St. Hilda is responsible for the ammonite shells found in abundance along this coast: the ammonites look like curled-up headless snakes because, it is believed, St. Hilda prayed that all the snakes nearby lose their heads and turn to stone. For this reason ammonites are known locally as St. Hilda's Snakes.

HINDRELAC

See Richmond.

HIVE

From Hyth – an Old English word for a landing on a river. Near Howden.

HOB HOLE

'Hob' is a generic name for a goblin, boggle or brownie. Hobs are often described as short, hairy, ugly and bad tempered, malevolent; they sour milk, turn sheep and cattle lame and hide peoples' belongings. Hob Hole is near Runswick Bay and is reputedly inhabited by a Hob with a special gift: locally the hob or boggle was believed to be able to cure whooping cough. The fishermen were too scared to cross the Hob's cave at night so their wives got on with the job by carrying their sick children down to the cave with them to take advantage of the Hob's amazing healing powers.

HOLE OF HORCUM

On the Pickering to Whitby road. It is 400 ft deep and ¾ of a mile across creating a magnificent "Devil's Punchbowl" feature. According to local legend it was created when Wade the Giant scooped up a handful of earth to throw at his wife during a row. SE 853 937.

HOLME ON SPALDING MOOR

Also known as Holme-upon-Spalding-Moor. Pre 1600 it was listed as Holme, Spalding Moor, Yorkshire. The word Holme is Danish in origin and means island. Spalding Moor was a marsh, dominated by a single hill comprising Keuper mar where a small church was built in the 13th century. The village was built on the holme around the church. Through the 17th and 18th centuries, the main industry was growing and dressing hemp giving rise to the village being called "Hemp-Holme".

HORNBY

Once called Horenbodebi. It is a Viking name meaning Hornbo's farm or may be a shortening of the Viking name Hornbothi. Famous for its castle between Bedale and Leyburn. There is another Hornby south of Yarm.

HORNSEA

This is on Hornsea Mere (Yorkshire's largest lake) and means the lake lying on a projecting piece of land, from Old English and Old Norse horn – corner of land, and Old English sae – pool or lake. Hornsea was famous for its pottery factory, Hornsea Pottery, which closed in 2000. Fittingly, the largest display of Hornsea Pottery in the world is in the Hornsea Museum. Opposite it is 'Bettison's Folly', a tower built by a local businessman in the 19th century which contains the only fully operational retractable flagpole in the country.

HORTON IN RIBBLESDALE

The farmstead on muddy soil (Old English horh or horu tin) or, possibly, an area of horse rearing. Ribble comes from Old English ripel – tearing. The *Domesday Book* lists as Hortune; in the 13th century Rybbelsdale. There is also a Horton in Craven. In 1597 Horton in Ribblesdale was struck by a plague with 74 deaths that year (one eighth of the population) compared with seventeen deaths in total during the preceding and succeeding years.

HOWDEN
Howden derives from Hovedene. Early records tell us that King Edgar of England gave Howden Manor to his first wife, Ethelfleda, in 959. Former residents include Roger de Hovedene, friend to both Henry II and Thomas a Beckett; novelist Nevil Shute; and Barnes Wallis, of airship R100 and 'bouncing bomb', 617 Dambuster Squadron fame. Interestingly named places within the parish of Howden include Backenholme with Woodale, Balkholme, Barmby-on-the-Marsh, Belby, Bellasize, Blacktoft, Bubwith, North Cave with Drewton Cheapsides, Cotness, Flaxfleet, Foggathorpe, Gilberdyke, Gribthorpe, Harlthorpe, Holme upon Spalding Moor, Hotham, Kilpin, Loxton, Metham, Newport Wallingfen, Newsham & Brind and Wressle & Loftsome, Portington & Cavil, Saltmarsh, Scalby, Willitoft, Yokefleet.

Shute and Wallis worked together at RNAS Howden from 1916. The role of this airship station was to protect ports and ships from German U-boat attacks. Shute, in his autobiography, *Slide Rule: Autobiography of an Engineer*, (1954) was not very complimentary:

> 'The lads were what one would expect, straight from the plough, but the girls were an eye-opener. They were brutish and uncouth, filthy in appearance and in habits. Things may have changed since then – I hope they have… I can only record the fact that these girls straight off the farms were the lowest types that I have ever seen in England, and incredibly foul-mouthed.'

Nevertheless, the blue plaque marking his former home still decorates the wall at 78 Hailgate.

HOWGILL FELLS
The name Howgill comes from the Old Norse word haugr meaning a hill or barrow, plus gil meaning a narrow valley.

HUBBERHOLME
Hunberg's homestead (Old English personal name + Old English, pronounced 'Hubberham')

HUBY
In earlier times it was known as Hobi. It means the settlement on the 'hoh' or spur of land. There are Hubys near Easingwold and near Otley.

HUDDERSFIELD
The field belonging to a man called Huder. Huddersfield is the eleventh largest town in the UK; rugby league, Harold Wilson, and James Mason were all born here. A Roman fort was excavated in the mid 18th century at Slack near Outlane; Castle Hill was the site of an Iron Age hill fort. Huddersfield is in the *Domesday Book* as Oderesfelt and Odresfeld. Huddersfield Railway Station was once described as 'a stately home with trains in it', and by Pevsner as 'one of the best early railway stations in England'. In 1845 Friedrich Engels described Huddersfield as 'the handsomest by far of all the factory towns in Yorkshire and Lancashire by reason of its situation and modern architecture'. There are over 1,700 listed buildings here, – the *Guardian* called it "the Athens of the north"; only Westminster and Bristol have more listed buildings than Huddersfield.

HULL
See Kingston upon Hull.

HULL POT
The pothole near the hut. Old English + Middle English: hulu + potte.

HULL RIVER
A Celtic river name which has given its name to Kingston upon Hull.

HUMBER RIVER
Another Celtic river name meaning good well river. The root can be traced back to the Sanskrit 'Ambhas' meaning water. The Humber gave its name to the ancient kingdom of Northumbria and subsequently Northumberland, from Anglo-Saxon Norððhymbre (plural) = "the people north of the Humber". Humber is recorded in Anglo-Saxon times as Humbre (Anglo-Saxon) and Humbri (a Vulgar Latin dative) or Umbri (Classical Latin dative). The Humber was also known as the Abus, as in Edmund Spenser's *The Faerie Queene*. The Latin *abus* from Latin verb *abdo* which means to cover with shadows means black or dark river. Later names Humbre/Humbri/Umbri had the same meaning. The Humber is named in Geoffrey of Monmouth's 12th century fictional chronicle *Historia Regum Britanniae*. Geoffrey claims that the Humber was named after "Humber the Hun," who drowned there in an invasion attempt. In 2005 Graham Boanas, a Hull man, became the first man to wade across the Humber since Roman times. He started the feat, for charity, at Brough and arrived four hours later on the south bank at Whitton. Boanas is 6 feet 9 inches tall and took advantage of an exceptionally low tide.

HUMBLE JUMBLE
A stream and bridge at Alverthorpe. Humble may be from Old Norse humli =hop plant; or hummell = barley or humul = boulder. Jumble = a rough uncultivated hollow.

HUNMANBY
Hundsman's village, the village of the dog keeper from Old Norse hundemanna + by. The dogs were used for hunting wolves. Hunmanby, near Scarborough, claims to be the largest village in the UK. The *Domesday Book* lists it as 'Hundemanbi'. A landslip in 1907 exposed a British chariot burial site from the 1st or 2nd century BC, in which a chariot was found buried complete with horse. A tumulus on a local farm revealed an ancient burial site containing fifteen skeletons.

HUNSINGORE
Means the ridge of Hunsige's people. Near Wetherby.

HUNSLET
In Leeds; made up of Hounde, hound, and leet, a meeting. However, an alternative etymology gives 'Hūn's inlet', from an Anglo-Saxon personal name Hūn and the Old English word flēot 'creek, inlet', possibly referring to an inlet from the River Aire.

HURST
An Anglo-Saxon name for a wooded hill. Hurst is north of Richmond; the Romans mined lead here.

HUSTHWAITE
Near Easingwold. The name derives from the Middle English 'hous', from Old English 'hus' meaning a house and thwaite – "a piece of land or land cleared of woods and converted to tillage". The *Domesday Book* has it as Bachesbi. William Peckitt was born here in 1731 – one of England's foremost glass painters and stain glass makers – in fact he is widely regarded as the most prominent and prolific glazier of his day and responsible for keeping the craft alive in the 18th century. The family moved to York around 1750 where William worked in his father's glove making business before setting himself up as a glass painter in Colliergate. He died in 1795 and is buried in St. Martin-cum-Gregory where Mary, his wife, made a memorial window to him in the church next to a memorial to two of his daughters by Peckitt himself.

HUTTON BONVILLE
One of many Yorkshire Huttons; there are eighteen. Hutton is Anglo-Saxon and derives from Hoh-Ton meaning high farm. The Bonville family owned Hutton Bonville during the reign of Henry III (1216-1272). Near Northallerton.

HUTTON BUSCEL
The Bushell family held Hutton Bushell in the 12th and 13th centuries. Near Scarborough.

HUTTON COLSWAIN
See Huttons Ambo.

HUTTON CONYERS
Near Ripon. Hutton Conyers once belonged to the Conyers family. It features in the *Domesday Book* as Hotone in the Hallikeld hundred and was owned by Bishop of Durham, St. Cuthbert.

HUTTON HANG
Hutton Hang is situated near Hang Bank – which means the hanging bank. It is east of Leyburn. Nearby interestingly named villages include Finghall (fing is Old Norse for assembly), Akebar, Thornton Steward and Constable Burton.

HUTTON LE HOLE
Hutton-le-Hole near Pickering is the Hutton near the hollow between two nabs but was formerly known as Heg Hoton – a heg being land enclosed for hunting. Originally called Hotun (as in the *Domesday Book*); then Hege-Hoton, Hotun under Heg, and Hewton in 1579. Hutton signifies the place near the burial mounds. The well-named Boxing Tom (Tom Proud) was landlord in 1870 at the Crown here. John Richardson lived in one of the cottages – a Quaker and good friend of Robert Penn's – he travelled far and wide in America working with native Indians as well as white men. There was a meeting house here and a Quaker burial ground nearby.

HUTTON LOWCROSS
Hutton Lowcross is near Lowcross Farm near Guisborough.

HUTTON MAGNA
Hutton Magna means the great or large Hutton, *magna* being Latin for great.

HUTTON MULGRAVE
Hutton Mulgrave is situated near Mulgrave which is near Whitby. The original Norman castle was a Royalist garrison slighted in 1647. The later castle, a castellated mansion, was built for the Duchess of Buckingham (Lady Catherine Darnley), James II's illegitimate daughter who married the Earl of Mulgrave. The surrounding woodlands were landscaped by William Repton in 1792 and feature an amazing artificial battery called the Quarter Deck which was danced on by Charles Dickens, among many others, in 1844. In 1858 Dalip Singh Sukerchakia, the last Maharajah of the Punjab, stayed here with his elephants for five years; in 1860 he paid for two miles of road to be built leading to the mansion because his elephants were irritated by sand between their toes. Initially it was a toll road: 1d for a horse; ½d for a pig; 9d for a 3-wheeled motorcar; 1/- for a 4-wheeled car.

HUTTON RUDBY
Rudby is Viking and means Rudi's village. It is near Stokesley and has a cholera mound, the grave of 23 local people who died in the cholera outbreak of 1832.

HUTTON SESSAY
Hutton Sessay is situated near Sessay near Thirsk, and means Seg's watery land.

HUTTONS AMBO
Huttons Ambo refers to three settlements called Hutton, all in the same parish near Malton which, therefore, shared the same pulpit or 'ambo' from Medieval Latin, derived from the Greek ambōn – raised rim, pulpit. Surprisingly, it is not from *ambo*, Latin for both. Huttons Ambo itself was once called Bardolf Hoton after a family who owned it in the 12th and 13th centuries. Nearby we find High Hutton and Low Hutton, the latter once known as Hutton Colswain or Colswayn; Colswain was the name of a Viking settler. The villages are listed in the *Domesday Book* as Hotun in the Bulford hundred. After the Norman invasion, the lands were split between the King and Berengar of Tosny. Low Hutton was owned by the King, while the land near Hutton Hill was known as Hutton Mynchon. The land at High Hutton has been known as Hutton Bardolf. These suffixes indicate the names of the landowners.

ICKORNSHAW
Ickorni is Norse for squirrel, shaw Old English for wood, squirrel wood. The village is Saxon and was originally made up of three separate hamlets: namely Ickornshaw, Middleton, Gill and Cowling Hill which is in the *Domesday Book* as 'Collinge'. This name means Coll's people or tribe. Ickornshaw is near Keighley.

IDLE
A suburb of Bradford, and home to 'Idle Working Men's Club' which has has acquired cult status around the world with an official 'Idle Working Men's Pass' much in demand and hghly prestigious. It was established in 1928 by local sewage workers whose shifts and the pub licensing hours left them unable to have a drink after work. The name may derive from the Anglian leader in Northumberland, Ida of Bernica with children named after him as Idas or Ides; their children would have been called Ideson.

INGLEBOROUGH
The fort on the hill (Old English ingel and burh). Ingleborough is the second highest mountain in the Dales, at 723 metres 2,372 feet. It is one of the Three Peaks, the other two being Whernside, 736 metres 2,415 feet, and Pen-y-ghent, 694 metres 2,277 feet. In 1346 it was referred to as Ingelburc. Excavations at the peak have revealed the remains of an old walled enclosure (the fort) along with foundations of Iron Age huts.

INGLEBY ARNCLIFFE
Unusually, there are four elements to this name; Ingle means English from Scandinavian "Englar + by" – by is a Danish word for village, Arn is an eagle and cliffe is a hill from Old English "earn + cliff". So, we then have 'Englishman's village near the eagles hill'. The distinction of an Englishman is accounted for by the ubiquity of Vikings in this area so that the presence of Anglo-Saxons was somewhat unusual. Other Inglebys in the area include Ingleby Cross next door; Ingleby Greenhow, the Englishman's green hill (grene + haugre) and Ingleby Barwick, the Englishman's barley farm; bere is Saxon for barley and wick means farm. They are all near Stokesley.

INGLEBY BARWICK
See Ingleby Arncliffe.

INGLEBY GREENHOW
See Ingleby Arncliffe.

INGLETON
The farmstead by the hill (Old English) near Settle. Arthur Conan Doyle was a regular visitor; he married locally, and his mother lived at nearby Masongill from 1882 to 1917. The Reverend Todd Sherlock was

vicar of Ingleton from 1874 to 1879. His brother, Randall Hopley Sherlock, was killed by lightning at Ingleton Railway Station in 1875; the area below the north end of Ingleton Viaduct is known as Holme Head on the way to Masongill. Who can say if this is where the name Sherlock Holmes came from?

IRTON
Near Scarborough – the farm of the Irishman – from Old Norse Iri which meant a Viking who had lived in Ireland.

IVESCAR
The scar covered in ivy (Old English ifig + Old Norse sker). In 1346 it was Inesker. Near Chapel-le -Dale.

JANET'S FOSS
Foss is the Old Norse word for a waterfall or force while Janet (or Jennet) was the queen of the local fairies who live behind the falls in a cave, Janet's Cave; this was (more historically proven) inhabited by smelters working the copper mines at nearby Pikedaw to the west. The foss is used as a natural sheep dip by local farmers.

JERVAULX ABBEY
Jervaulx in the valley of the River Ure (Norman French) is a reference to the 12th century Cistercian abbey's setting. In 1135 it was Jorvalle. It is near to Ripon.

JINGLING POT
The pothole with a tinkling or rattling noise (North Country Dialect + Middle English). SD698783 near Chapel-le-Dale.

JOLBY
Jolby is near Croft; the name is Old French for Joel's place made up of the name Johel + by.

JUMP
A village near Barsley. Jump = a rough uncultivated hollow like Jumble.

KAIL HILL
The cabbage field (Old Norse).

KALDECOTES
See Cargo Fleet.

KEIGHLEY
The clearing (a ley) belonging to Cyhha; it was mentioned in the *Domesday Book* as "In Cichhelai, Ulchel, and Thole, and Ravensuar, and William had six carucates to be taxed."

KELD
Keld derives from the Viking word Kelda meaning a spring. The place was once called AppletreKelde – the spring near the apple trees. The ruins of Crackpot Hall are a mile east of Keld at grid reference NY906008.

KELFIELD
South of York, the name comes from Old English caelc, chalky field.

KEPWICK
Market place – from Old English ceap. Near Northallerton.

KETTLENESS
See Neasham.

KETTLEWELL
Kettlewell is Anglo Saxon and derives from Chetelewelle – a bubbling spring or stream; Old English cetel + wella. In the 13th century the Thursday market mostly sold corn outside the King's Arms. Later, textiles and lead mining were important to the local economy. The remains of the smelting-mill, which flourished from 1700 to 1880, can still be seen near the confluence of Cam Gill and Dowber Gill Becks half a mile above the village. Kettlewell is upstream from Grassington.

KILBURN
Kilburn is at the southern end of the White Rose Walk, the other end being at Roseberry Topping. It appears as Chilburne in the *Domesday Book* and means a cell by a stream. Today it is world famous for two things: the White Horse and the work of Robert Thompson. Robert Thompson's Craftsmen's Ltd was set up by Robert Thompson; he was born in the Old Hall in 1872 and was inspired by 15th century carvings in Ripon Cathedral to emulate mediaeval craftsmen. Thompson's wood of choice was the oak; he used an adze in preference to a plane – a tool which created a wavy surface and emphasised the grain to beautiful effect – characteristics of Thompson's work – and his chosen style was classic 17th century English. The famous mouse signature came about apparently when he heard one of his carvers, Charlie Barker, say "We are all as poor as church mice" whereupon Robert spontaneously carved a mouse on the church screen he was working on and took it up as a symbol of industry in quiet places, and as his trademark.

With an eye big enough to seat twenty people the famous horse on Roulston Scar is 304 feet long and 228 feet high taking in two acres. 'Delivered' in 1857 by John Hodgson, the village schoolmaster and sometime surveyor with the help of 33 men, the lime needed to paint it weighed six tons. Although the largest of the eleven surviving White Horses in Britain, it is of course an imitation of the White Horse of Uffington in Berkshire. Thomas Taylor, a native of Kilburn and rich from his Yorkshire hams business in London, saw the Uffington horse and determined that Kilburn should have one of its own. It can be seen up to 40 miles away and was covered over in the Second World War so as not to provide a landmark for German planes.

KILDALE
Near Great Ayton. Kildale is a Viking name meaning narrow valley; the Normans had it as Childale. Local Captain James Cook's monument is nearby: it towers 51 feet high 1,000 feet up on Easby Moor; erected in 1827 the inscription reads: "massacred at Owyhee". This, the place where he was murdered on Hawaii, was bought for Britain and has since been maintained by the Royal Navy.

KILNSEY
The marsh by the kiln in Old English – cyln + saege – a reference to the lime burning here. The *Domesday Book* calls it Chileseie. Kilnsey, near Grassington, is famous for Kilnsey Crag, which is around 170 feet high, with an overhang of 40 feet. Heading west towards Malham is Mastiles Lane, a Roman marching road and later drovers' way for Fountains Abbey sheep flocks. The Old Hall was a medieval administrative site for the local wool trade. Most of the present building dates from 1658.

KINGSDALE
The valley where cows were kept (Middle English kyen + Old Norse/Old English dael). In 1695 it ws called Kinesdale. It is between the hills of Whernside to its east and Gragareth to the west. Kingsdale is drained by Kingsdale Beck which becomes the River Twiss before joining the River Doe at Ingleton to become the River Greta.

KINGSTON-UPON-HULL
Often abbreviated to plain old 'Hull', after the river of that name on which the city stands. Trade on

the busy river included the export of wool from Meaux Abbey which owned the fledgling port which was acquired from the abbey by King Edward I, who on 1st April 1299 granted it a royal charter. Hence King's town upon Hull or Kingston upon Hull. Meaux was a Cistercian Abbey founded in 1151 near Beverley. JC Craggs, in his *Guide to Hull* (1817), gives us more detail when he writes that the King and his hunting party were pursuing a hare which "led them along the delightful banks of the River Hull to the hamlet of Wyke … [Edward], charmed with the scene before him, viewed with delight the advantageous situation of this hitherto neglected and obscure corner. He foresaw it might become subservient both to render the kingdom more secure against foreign invasion, and at the same time greatly to enforce its commerce".

The city's official name lives on in Hull Kingston Rovers rugby league club, rivals with Hull FC.

KIPPAX
In Leeds. A corruption of Cyppa's ash, an ash tree belonging to someone called Cyppa. The name Kippax is of Anglo-Saxon origin and is first found as Chipesch in the *Domesday Book*, and as "Kippeys" from the 1090s to the 1270s, and Kypask and Kypax from the 13th century. This is a good example of a locational surname which developed when inhabitants of a place moved somewhere else, usually for work, and were henceforth identified by the name of their birthplace. Kippax as a surname appears from the late 14th century and include: Johannes de Kypax, Johanna Kepas, and Johannes de Kepax, who were all in the Poll Tax Records in 1379.

KIRKBY MALHAM
The farmstead by the church near Malham (Old Norse); it was Kirkeby Malham in 1154. A free grammar school was founded here in 1606, by John Topham for twenty to thirty children to receive an English education; the classics were taught free.

KIRKBY MALZEARD
Near Harrogate. Malzeard is from Old French 'mal assart' meaning poor clearing. It is famous for the creamery which has been making Wensleydale cheese for nearly 100 years, first owned by Mrs Mason, then Kit Calvert of Hawes; recently it was acquired by the Wensleydale Creamery in Hawes.

KIRKBYMOORSIDE
Places with names Kirkby and Kirby are found in those parts of England settled by the Vikings, which is why they are commonly found in Yorkshire, Cumbria and Lincolnshire but not in Northumberland and Durham. They are often given suffixes to help distinguish one from another. So, we have Kirkbymoorside, originally Kirkbymoorshead, the Kirkby at the head of the moor, Kirkby Fleetham situated near a homestead on a stream called a fleet. Yorkshire's Kirkby Misperton, Kirkby Knowle and Kirkby Wiske were respectively the Kirkbys near the Misper tree, near the Knoll hill, and on the River Wiske.

KIRKBY OVERBLOW
Overblow is a reference to the village's smelting history and is a corruption of Oreblow. The village is between Harrogate and Wetherby. Sadly there is little substance in the etymology which ascribes overblow to the lady, who thwarted in love, jumped off Almes Cliff nearby but was saved from certain death by a sudden gust of wind which caused her skirts to billow out and act as a parachute.

KIRBY SIGSTON
This means the church village near Sigston. Sigston is Sigga's farm near Northallerton.

KIRK HAMMERTON
Hammerton features in the *Domesday Book* as, 'Hanbretone' or 'Ambretone' under the lands of Osbern de Arches, which included a mill and a fishery. The church is Saxon from around AD 950 and, unusually for

a Saxon church, is built in stone. For the first 600 years of its life it was dedicated to St. Quentin. It is thought that casualties from the Battle of Marston Moor in 1644 are buried in mass graves in the churchyard, as a number of skeletons were dug up in 1926 and are thought to be from the battle.

KIRKLEATHAM

Kirkleatham near Redcar derives from the Old Norse 'hlith' meaning slope, the plural for which was lithum. Kirkleatham was originally West Lidium or West Leatham to distinguish it from Upleatham nearby, which means the upper slopes. Around 1181 Kirkleatham got its present name as a result of a medieval church or 'kirk' that was here. Today Kirkleatham is famous as the site of the Sir William Turner Hospital and the baroque Turner Mausoleum at St. Cuthbert's Church. Both were connected with the alum mining family of that name. Sir William was Lord Mayor of London in 1669. 17th century Kirkleatham Hall was the seat of this family but was demolished in 1954 and replaced with a school which is now the Kirkleatham Old Hall Museum. Sir William Turner's Hospital was founded in 1676 as almshouses for the poor but was impressively rebuilt in 1742. Kirkleatham has one of the best collections of Georgian-style buildings in England.

KIRKLEVINGTON

This is Kirk Leven Ton – the church on the River Leven with a farm (ton) just south of Yarm. Kirklevington Hall was, from 1881 the home of the Richardsons (as in Richardsons Westgarth) of Hartlepool. During the Second World War it was a secret command centre for the North East.

KNARESBOROUGH

Knar, a stump plus borough or burgh – a fortified place. The Norsemen tended to settle the Dales, while the Danish Vikings, after taking York in 867, populated the Vale of York and the area around Knaresborough. This is reflected in street names such as Kirkgate and Briggate, in traditions such as the Knaresborough sword dance and in the odd custom of Hoketide, when men took off women's shoes on Easter Sunday, to have their hats taken off by women the day after. Knaresborough Castle was rebuilt in 1312 by Edward II; in those days it had twelve towers and a fine keep. *The Chronicle of John de Brompton*, tells us that the four knights who murdered the Archbishop Thomas Becket in Canterbury Cathedral, on 29th December 1170, fled north and took refuge in Knaresborough Castle; their leader, Hugh de Morville, was constable of the castle. The *Chronicle* adds that the castle dogs, taking the moral high ground, declined to eat the scraps which the four murderers threw down from their table. Captured in 1644 by Cromwell in the Civil War it was 'slighted' in 1648. In April 2010 the 800th anniversary celebrations of the first Maundy giving by King John were held there, the very first giving having taken place in Knaresborough in 1210.

LACKENBY

A Viking settlement or 'by' which belonged to someone called Hlackande. In between Redcar and Middlesbrough.

LANGBAURGH

Langbaurgh gets its name from an ancient hill called Langbaurgh near Great Ayton: lang meaning long and beorge meaning hill. Beorge is not the Saxon word burgh meaning fortified place. Langbaurgh was the meeting place of a Viking Wappentake, or administrative district; it was also known as Cleveland.

LANGCLIFFE

The long cliff (Old English) (lang + cliff) near Settle; Langclif in the *Domesday Book*; the lord was Fech. The original settlement was closer to the foot of the scar than it is now, in a field called Pesbers near the lane to Winskill. The move came when Scottish raiders laid waste the village after the Battle of Bannockburn in 1314 and was rebuilt ½ mile away; in 1513 the muster rolls of the Battle of Flodden show that nine men from Langliffe fought the Scots army. Samson's Toe is one mile to the east of Langcliffe, a large glacial erratic boulder which is approximately eight feet high. "*According to legend, [Samson] lost his footing when jumping across from Langcliffe Scar or Ribblesdale, breaking off his toe whilst attempting this*".

"Samson's Toe, Langcliffe, North Yorkshire". *The Journal of Antiques*. Retrieved 24th October 2015.

LANGSTROTHDALE CHASE
The valley with a long stretch of marsh overgrown with brushwood: Old English lang and strod and dael or Old Norse dalr. A chase is a Norman French hunting forest. The original Viking farms here became hunting lodges, and are now either isolated farms or hamlets. The first of these is Cray then Hubberholme, Raisgill, Yockenthwaite, Deepdale, Beckermonds and Oughtershaw.

LANGTHWAITE
A Viking name meaning long meadow. It is a remote village in Arkengarthdale, home to an unusual commissioners' church of 1817, built with government money in an attempt to counteract atheism and free thinking after the French Revolution. Langthwaite also has an hexagonal powder house, built in 1807 to store gunpowder used in the nearby mines.

LANGTOFT
Near Driffield. This means a long toft – topt, the site of a house. Pierre de Langtoft (died c. 1305) the historian and chronicler took his name from the village; Margaret de Langtoft, one of the five nuns who formed the Sisterhood of Rosedale Priory, came from here.

LAZENBY
A Viking name which means the village belonging to a leysingr or freeman. In the *Domesday Book* Lazenby was Leisinchbi. Near Redcar.

LEEDS
Our first record of the name Leeds comes from Bede in his *Historia Ecclesiastica*, (Book II Chapter 14) around AD 731 when he mentions an altar from a church built by Edwin of Northumbria, in 'the region known as Loidis'. That region was a Welsh speaking ancient British area in revolt against the Anglo-Saxons, a subdivision of Elmet, also a Welsh speaking area that was later a part of the Kingdom of Northumbria. Nearby Ledston and Ledsham were also part of Loidis and are reflected in its name, a name which may be the name of a tribe meaning 'people of the flowing river' – the river being the Aire on which Leeds stands and on which it has always depended.

We learn from an 11th century manuscript that in the 10th century, Loidis lay on the boundary between the Viking kingdom of Jorvik and the Welsh speaking Kingdom of Strathclyde – Lancashire, Cumbria and south western Scotland. Pen-y-Ghent, Craven, Hatfield, Aldborough and Stanwick provide more evidence of the Welsh influence.

The name appears again in the *Domesday Book* describing a settlement, in Old English as *Ledes*. An inhabitant of Leeds is still known locally as a *Loiner*, a word which may be derived from *Loidis*. In medieval times Loidis was Leedis from which the modern name of the city derives. Leeds is supposed by Thoresby to be derived from the British 'cair loid coit', a town in the woods; others argue that it is derived from German, as there is a town called Leeds, on the River Dender in Austria Flanders.

LEEMING
Derives from an ancient Celtic river name leamh – elm tree. On the A1 near Northallerton.

LEVEN, RIVER
A Celtic river name related to the Welsh ilyfn meaning 'smooth'. Alternatively it may be from a Brythonic word meaning elm, both the Welsh 'llwyfen' and Gaelic 'leamhain' words for elm sound like Leven. The

Yorkshire Leven is the only one of the five rivers Leven in Britain that doesn't connect a Loch or Lake to the sea.

LEYBURN
Leborne in the *Domesday Book*. The name is derived from 'Ley' or 'Le' (clearing), and 'burn' (stream), meaning clearing by the stream. Leyburn is linked to Middleham, two miles away, by one of the most unusual river bridges in England, built in 1829 as one of the first examples of a suspension bridge. Turner passed through Leyburn in September 1816 during his tour of Yorkshire to make sketches for a series of watercolours to illustrate *A General History of the County of York* by Thomas Dunham Whitaker. Mary Queen of Scots was reputedly recaptured on the Shawl above the village after her escape from Bolton Castle en route to Fotheringay.

LINGDALE
Ling means heather: heather-dale. Lingdale, near Middlesbrough, was built in the 1870s as a village for the ironstone mine workers here. On 24th August 1953, fifteen men were critically injured in a horrific gas explosion after which eight of the men died from shock and from their burns.

LINTON
The farm where flax is grown (Old English), near Grassington. Lipton in the *Domesday Book* then Lynton in 1150. The village has many delightful features including the Falls, a 14th century, packhorse bridge, 'Little Emily's Bridge'; almshouses by Vanbrugh and the famous ancient stepping-stones, below an old (renovated) mill house.

LINTON ON OUSE
As above. The Manor of Linton was originally owned by the Catholic Appleby family and then bequeathed to University College, Oxford by a Dr John Radcliffe, Queen Anne's physician, in 1714. The Radcliffe Infirmary maintains his memory. He stipulated that the rents raised should pay for scholarships for two medical students. By 1977 the farms, houses and other buildings had reverted to private ownership. The village is well known for its RAF station and is today the home of No. 1 Flying Training School. During the Second World War it was a bomber base and Squadrons 408 and 426 of the Royal Canadian Air Force, among others, were stationed here. In 1940, after a raid on Cologne, Flying Officer Leonard Cheshire succeeded in getting his badly damaged Whitley bomber back to Linton, for which he was awarded the first of his three DSOs.

LITHERSKEW
Near Aysgarth. Hillside wood from Old Norse hlith = slope and skogr = wood.

LITTLE BARUGH
Barugh is a barrow like hill near Pickering; see also Langbaurgh. In 1871 Barugh was described as:

> "Barughs Ambo a township in Kirkby-Misperton parish, N. R. Yorkshire; 4 miles SW of Pickering. It consists of the hamlets of Great and Little Barugh. Acres, 1,433. Real property, £2,094. Pop., 318. Houses, 60. There is a well-preserved Roman camp at Great Barugh."

The pub, the Golden Lion, dates back to 1632.

LITTLE SMEATON
Near Selby: the smith's farm. There is a Smeaton near Stockton too. Every village or town had at least one backsmith – hence the popularity of the surname Smith and place names derived from the occupation.

LITTON

Near Kettlewell. The farm on the hill slope (Old Norse + Old English hlith); the *Domesday Book*: Litone. Alternatively, village on a roaring stream.

LITTONDALE

The valley with the farm on a hill slope (Old Norse + Old Norse/Old English). Notable for not being named after its river, the Skirfare. Once Littunedale in the 12th century.

LIVERTON

Takes its name from a muddy stream in the same way as Liverpool means muddy pond. Near Guisborough.

LOFTUS

A Viking name which derives from Loft-Hus, a house with a loft. It was once known as Lofthouse but, appears as "Lcotvsv" in the *Domesday Book*, from Laghthus meaning low houses. There has been excavated evidence of life in Loftus since the 7th century, as well as a house owned by Sigurd the Dane, who appears in *Macbeth* as Siward. There is a disused nuclear bunker nearby, opened in 1962 and closed in 1968.

LONG PRESTON

The priest's farmstead (Old English preost)), 'Long' was added to distinguish this from other 'Prestons', a nod to its linear development. Prestune in the *Domesday Book*. Near Settle.

LONSDALE

Valley of the River Lune (Old Norse/Old English), added in qualification to Burton and Thornton to avoid confusion with other places.

LOW HUTTON

See Huttons Ambo.

LUNDS

The small wood or grove (Old Norse lundr) in Wensleydale. There is a Lund near Beverley and another near Selby.

LUNE RIVER

The healthy or full river, connected with the Welsh 'Ilawn' (full) or the Irish 'slan' (healthy). Other possible etymologies include: Anglo-Saxon Ēa Lōn (ēa = "river") as a phonetic adaptation of a Celtic name referring to a Celtic god Ialonus who was worshipped locally. From lune as the crescent shape of the oxbow in the river. Lune is used for a river with a prominent oxbow.

MALHAM

The hollows: 'malr' means 'shaped like a sack' which probably refers to the cove. Malhamdale is the valley near the coves (Old Norse). The ham part is not an Anglo Sax –ham name which is what you might expect. The Tarn is from Old Norse tjorn (pool); the cove from Old English cofa. It was Malgum in the *Domesday Book*. The dale was Malghedale in 1199.

MALTBY

Malti's Village, a Viking name. The Maltby near Rotherham is close to Roche Abbey founded in 1147 by Cistercian Monks from Newminster near Morpeth. When coal was discovered in the late 19th century the colliery company built a large estate known as the 'Model Village' to accommodate the miners. During the Second World War, a munitions factory, ROF Maltby, was established; an estate, 'Little London', was built to house its workers who had moved from Enfield. There is another Maltby near Stockton.

MALTON

Originally Middleton, but the name has been corrupted by the Vikings. Possible etymologies include Old English m(e)alt – tax, tribute town; or maethel – speech – denoting a local parliament. The Roman fort of Derventio was set up here under Agricola and was garrison to a cavalry unit, the Ala Gallorum Picentiana for a time.

MARKET WEIGHTON

Weighton may be from a personal name such as Wigheah or else derived from the Latin *vicus*, a settlement. The tallest Englishman ever was born in Market Weighton. William Bradley (1787–1820) was one of thirteen children and weighed in at 14lbs at birth. He reached his full height of 7 feet 9 inches aged twenty when his weight was 27 stone. His footprint was 15 inches long and 6 inches wide. A star attraction at fairs throughout England, he charged people a shilling to shake his hand. George III presented him with a gold watch and chain when they met, which Bradley proudly wore for the rest of his life. He is now buried inside All Saints' Church after a re-interment to foil grave robbers, and is celebrated every May on Giant Bradley Day. His house in Northgate, now 89 York Road, was specially adapted for him, with rooms and doorways made large enough to accommodate his exceptional build. A plaque on the wall outside shows his remarkable footprint. A life-sized wooden statue of the Yorkshire Giant was unveiled on Giant Bradley Day, 27 May 2007. It was carved by Malcolm MacLachlan, from a 200-year-old English oak log that was growing in Bradley's lifetime. By amazing coincidence, Edwin Calvert was born in nearby Shiptonthorpe – a man who grew only to the height of 3 feet; he died aged seventeen through excessive alcohol consumption.

MARRICK

A Viking name corrupted from Marr – rigg (mar + hyrggr) meaning horse ridge. Marr is related to the word mare: the equestrian tradition lives on: the famous breeder of racehorses, William Blenkiron was born in Marrick. Marrick and Marrick Priory, a former Benedictine nunnery, are near Richmond.

MARSKE BY THE SEA

Marske-by-the Sea near Redcar and Marske near Richmond are Scandinavian variants of the English word marsh, and denoted settlements near marshy land. The Vikings frequently substituted the English SH sound with the Viking SK; it can be seen in place names like Scarborough, Skelton and Skeeby. The Royal Flying Corps had a landing strip and training schools here; 'Captain' W. E. Johns, the author of the Biggles books, was stationed at Marske during the First World War.

MARTON

A suburb of Middlesbrough. This might mean marshy farm, farm near a maer (a boundary), or farm near a mere, a lake. The explorer James Cook was born to James and Grace Cook in a clay cottage here in 1728.

MASHAM

Anglo Saxon Maessa's Ham, the homestead belonging to Maessa. The parish also included the townships of Burton-on-Yore, Ellingstring, Ellington High and Low, Fearby, Healey with Sutton, Ilton cum Pott and Swinton. There are two thriving breweries here: Black Sheep and Theakstons.

MASONGILL

The ravine frequented by birds of the tit family (Old Norse); Old Norse meisingr + Old Norse gil; Maisinggile in 1200. Mary Doyle, mother of Arthur Conan Doyle, lived in Masongill from 1882 to 1917, and Conan Doyle was a frequent visitor. Dr. Bryan Charles Waller (1853–1932) was squire of Masongill from 1877; from 1879, he was a lecturer in pathology at the University of Edinburgh. He lodged with the Doyle family and persuaded Conan Doyle to train as a doctor, and his mother to live in Masongill.

MASTILES

The marshy track in Old English: mersc +stigel. Specifically refers to the frequently boggy lane from Kilnsey to Malham Tarn. Mastiles Lane was once part of a long distance monastic route linking Fountains Abbey estates in the northern Lake District with the Kilnsey Cistercian grange. It was originally known tautologically as 'Strete Gate' (street road from Old English straet, Roman road + Old Norse gata (road). There are the remains of two medieval monastic crosses once used as waymarkers along the route.

MEANWOOD

Goes back to the 12th century, and is Anglo-Saxon meaning the Meene wude – the boundary wood of the Manor of Alreton, the woods to the east of Meanwood Beck. A skirmish, between Royalist and Parliamentarian forces, took place in Meanwood, during the Civil War. The "beck ran red", with the blood of the fallen, hence, "Stainbeck".

MELSONBY

Melsonby was Melsan's Farm or village. Melsan is a mixed Viking-Irish name. It is near Richmond. Nearby Gatherley Moor once had quite a reputation as a racecourse, foreshadowing Catterick Bridge: William Page in his *A History of the County of York North Riding: Volume 1* tells us '*In no part of England, perhaps,*' says Canon Raine '*was horse-racing carried on with more spirit than in Richmondshire during the present and succeeding [15th and 16th] centuries. Gatherley Moor, the most celebrated course in the north of England...and almost the highest ambition of the North-country gentleman was to bear away the bell on that famous field.*' George III is said to have exclaimed on his deathbed, '*Oh for a gasp of Gatherley air!*' the moor being on his usual route to or from Scotland.

MENWITH HILL

The name means stoney hill. A Royal Air Force station providing communications and intelligence services to the UK and the USA. The site, codename MOONPENNY, contains an extensive satellite ground station and is a communications intercept and missile warning site; it is probably the largest electronic monitoring station in the world. Until 2014 support services were provided by the USAF, 421st Air Base Group. Of the 1,800 employees in 2012, 400 were British and 1,200 were American employees of the NSA, the National Security Agency – US government intelligence organisation, responsible for global monitoring, collection, and processing of information and data for foreign intelligence and counterintelligence purposes. It is a ground station for a number of satellites operated by the US National Reconnaissance Office on behalf of the US National Security Agency, with antennae housed in large white radomes; it is alleged to be an element of the ECHELON system –' a signals intelligence (SIGINT) collection and analysis network operated on behalf of the five signatory nations to the UKUSA Security Agreement — Australia, Canada, New Zealand, the United Kingdom, and the United States' ('Five-Eyes').

In the 1990s British journalist Duncan Campbell and New Zealand journalist Nicky Hager alleged in *Somebody's Listening* that the US was exploiting ECHELON traffic for industrial espionage, as well as for military and diplomatic purposes.

MEXBOROUGH

Mexborough combines the Old English suffix burh meaning a fortified place with an Old English or Old Norse personal name, which could be any one of Meke, Muik, Meoc, or Mjukr. We first hear of the place in the *Domesday Book* as Mechesburg, which tells us that before the Conquest the area was controlled by the Saxon lords Wulfheah and Ulfkil and afterwards the area fell under Norman Baron Roger de Busli.

MICKLEBY

Mickleby, near Scarborough, means the large Old English mycel) farm or village. Compare Micklegate in York and Mickleton near Middleton in Teesdale. Mycel also appears in *every mickle makes a muckle*. The well-known phrase is, however, a misquote, mickle and muckle mean the same thing, it was once 'many a little maks a muckle'.

MIDDLEHAM

An Anglo-Saxon name meaning middle village. It was recorded in the *Domesday Book* as "Medelai". Building of Middleham Castle begain in 1119; it was later known as the "Windsor of the North". Richard, Duke of Gloucester (the future Richard III) came here to learn how to be a knight in 1462. Edward IV and Henry VI were held prisoner here during the Wars of the Roses. Richard, Duke of Gloucester became master of the castle in 1471 and used the castle as his political base as he administered the North for his brother Edward IV (Council of the North). Richard married Anne Neville, in 1472; their son Edward was born here (*c.* 1473) and here is where he died in April 1484. Richard III died in August 1485 in the Battle of Bosworth – the last reigning monarch to die on the battlefield.

MIDDLESBROUGH

Middlesbrough's origins are deeply religious: they go as far back as 686 BC when St. Hilda instructed St. Cuthbert to set up a monastic cell on the site of the future town. In 1119 Robert Bruce, 1st Lord of Cleveland, granted the church of St. Hilda of Middleburg to Whitby; the church later became known as Middlesbrough Priory. The Saxon name Mydilsburgh is the first recorded form of Middlesbrough's name we have; 'Mydil' could be the name of an Anglo-Saxon chieftain, or a reference to the town's location, midway between the Christian meccas of Durham and Whitby. Middlesbrough was rapidly transformed from the rural farm and its four or five families with twenty or so agricultural inhabitants in 1800 to the mighty iron and steel town – Ironopolis.

MIDDLETON QUERNHOW

See Ainderby Quernhow.

MIDDLETON TYAS

The first part of the name is Anglo-Saxon and means middle farm. Tyas is a Norman French name but there is no evidence to connect the place with anyone of that name.

MINSKIP

Minskip is in the *Domesday Book* as Minescip, a name derived from the Old English gemaenscipe: a community or communal holding. Minskip is near Boroughbridge.

MOORSHOLM

This seems to mean a holm or island on or near the moor, formed by an island or meander, but early forms are Mooresum and may mean the moor houses. It is Morehusum in the *Domesday Book*. Near Guisborough.

MOSSDALE CAVERNS

The boggy valley (Old Norse), and the site of Britain's worst potholing disaster when six potholers died in the extremely challenging cave system in 1967. The bodies were left *in situ*. The coroner had the cave sealed and concrete was poured down the entrance. In 1971 this was re-opened, with the agreement of the families, and the bodies were reburied by their colleagues in "Mud Caverns", a chamber at the far end of the system. The caverns are north of Grassington.

MOUGHTON

Moughton near Settle appears as Mortuna in the *Domesday Book*. The name means "The farm by the salmon lake" from the Olde English "mort", meaning salmon and "-ton" – a farm or settlement.

MUKER

From the Viking mjor-aker (acre) meaning a small piece of land. In 1274 it was Meuhaker.

MYTON ON SWALE

Myton, on the confluence of the Swale and Ure (thus forming the Ouse), near Boroughbridge is famous for three things: the White Battle or Battle of Myton Meadows in 1319, cast-iron Myton Bridge, built in 1868 and Sir Miles Stapylton, one of the original Knights of the Garter. In the 14th century Sir Miles slew a Saracen chief in front of the Kings of England and France, and took the Saracen's head for a crest. You can still see this depicted on some of the houses in the village. In 1319, 12,000 Scots under the Earl of Moray headed for York, devastating everything in their path. They were finally confronted by a motley force of 10–20,000 clerics and villagers who were massacred or drowned in the rivers. Over 4,000 died – many of whom were ecclesiastics dressed in white robes, thus leading to the conflict taking the name, the 'White Battle'. Myton is in the *Domesday Book* as Mitune, later as Mitona, Miton, or Mitton up to the 15th century.

NAFFERTON

Near Driffield – Natfari's place, an Old Norse nickname which meant night traveller.

NAPPA

Nappa, west of Skipton, is first mentioned in the *Domesday Book* as Napars, and probably derives from the Old English hnæpp ġehæġ, meaning "enclosure in a bowl-shaped hollow". It is Nappay in 1251.

NAPPA HALL

Nappa Hall was a rare fortified farm or manor house east of Askrigg and described by English Heritage as "probably the finest and least-spoilt fortified manor house in the north of England". For etymology see Nappa. Hall is from Old English haeg. Mary, Queen of Scots may have stayed there for two nights while under house arrest at Bolton Castle; James I visited the house.

NESS POINT

See North Cheek.

NEWBIGGIN

The new building or outhouse (Old English + Middle English) in Bishopdale. In 1228 it was known as the very Germanic-sounding Neubigging. There is another Newbiggin just seven miles away near Askrigg.

NEWBY HEAD PASS

The highest part of the land in the manor of Newby (Old English + Old Norse). Newby Head is a mountain pass between Hawes and Ingleton, named after a drovers' inn, Newby Head Inn, which was the fourth highest inn in England. In January 1843 an inquest was held at the inn by the Skipton coroner with regard to Isaac Mason who had been found dead in bed. According to the landlord and the person who was in the bed with him, the latter went downstairs to get a candle. When he returned he found Isaac Mason dead. The verdict was died by the 'visitation of God'. Newby Head Pass is 1,439 feet (439 m) above sea level.

NEWBY WISKE

Newby means new village on the River Wiske.

NEW EARSWICK

A model garden village north of York and named after Earswick (qv). One of the greatest of Joseph Rowntree's social reforms lay in the garden village that was New Earswick or 'The New Estate' completed in 1904. The simple aim of the village was to provide the average worker with a new type of house that was 'artistic in appearance', clean, sanitary, and ergonomically designed in an environmentally friendly village with social, religious and educational amenities. In other words, a decent place to live which was not the usual slum. At least 10% of the village would be parks or recreation areas, houses would only take up 25% of the land and there would be strips of grass between the roads and footpaths.

Rowntree's deep concern for the welfare of his workers, the research findings and solutions proposed by his son, Seebohm Rowntree, into local poverty and the plight of the urban poor published in Seebohm's ground-breaking *Poverty: A Study of Town Life*, his own Quaker beliefs, Cadbury's achievements at Bournville and the pioneering work on garden cities by Ebenezer Howard which manifested in Letchworth in 1903, Saltaire – Titus Salt's 1851 model village, James Reckitt's Quaker garden village in Hull in 1908, and later aspects of William Lever's Port Sunlight – all of these would have conspired in Rowntree's mind to inspire the establishment of New Earswick on a site just minutes away from the Rowntree factory between York and Haxby. By 1924 the population of New Earswick was about 2,000; 850 (42%) of whom worked for Rowntree.

NEWTON UNDER ROSEBERRY
Newton means the new settlement. See Roseberry Topping.

Bizarrely there is a reference to Newton under Roseberry in American band America's "Hat Trick" from the *Hat Trick* album: '*Newton-Under-Roseberry-Topping And it's cold and it's wet And you feel like you're part of all time*'.

NIDD RIVER
A Celtic river name thought to mean 'brilliant'.

NORBER
The hill to the north of Austwick (Old English/Old Norse). Norber is well known for its glacial erratic boulders, one of the finest groups in Britain.

NORMANBY
This might well be either the village belonging to a Norman Frenchman or a village belonging to someone called Norman. It is neither, but it is a Viking name and means the village of the Northman, the Norseman. Near Middlesbrough.

NORTH CHEEK
The promontory that is North Cheek, near Robin Hood's Bay, is also called Ness Point and is close to South Cheek or The Old Peak.

NORTH ORMESBY
A new town now part of Middlesbrough created in 1860 by James Pennyman. Stanley Hollis is from North Ormesby, the only serviceman to be awarded a VC for valour on D-day. See Ormesby.

NORTH YORKSHIRE
Yorkshire is the county or 'shire' of the City of York and has been known in earlier years as Eoferwicscir, the County of York and Le Counte d' Everwyck. North Yorkshire is the biggest county in England, formed partly from the old North Riding of Yorkshire.

NORTHALLERTON
The original name for Northallerton was the Saxon Alfhere's tun, or Alfred's farm – indicating an essentially agricultural character. The *Domesday Book* has Northallerton variously as Alvertune, Aelfereton, Aluertune and Alreton and had featured prominently in William I's shocking harrying of the north – scorched earth devastation from Ouse to Tyne in reprisal for the murder of the Earl of Northumberland. Langdale tells us that the sky went black when William's armies arrived – a manifestation of the saint who protected the town

and who meted out severe punishment on anyone offering even "the smallest injury." William, though, was having none of it and "laid waste the country on all sides" – hence the description in the *Domesday Book* as "modo wastum est." *The Gentleman's Magazine* for February 1844 describes events thus:

> "for 60 miles between York and Durham he did not leave a house standing; reducing the whole district by fire and sword to a horrible desert, smoking with blood, and in ashes."

By the 14th century the place was called Northallerton, perhaps to distinguish it from another Allerton near York. Romanby, to the south of the town is a further indication of Viking settlement, taking its name from a Viking called Hromund. Allerton's Viking wappentake later became Allertonshire and later still the Liberty of Allerton, reflecting this town's important status.

NORTH DUFFIELD
And South Duffield – the field where the doves are. Old English dufe.

NORTON CONYERS
Norton means Northern farm; this particular one was perhaps later associated with the Norman French Conyers family. Whatever, it was once the seat of the Nortons: Richard Norton was Chief Justice of England around 1400. His descendants included Richard Norton who, with his sons, were embroiled in the short-lived religious rebellion of the Earls of Northumberland and Westmoreland against Queen Elizabeth in 1569. Norton, and his sons, with many others, were executed, and the estate handed to the Musgraves.

Norton Conyers House north of Ripon is said to have inspired Charlotte Brontë when she wrote Jane Eyre: the legend surrounding a mad woman in the attic reputedly gave her the idea for the mad Mrs. Rochester, and the house's interior provided source material for Mr. Rochester's 'Thornfield Hall'. The 2004 discovery of a blocked-up staircase connecting the first floor to the attics as mentioned in Jane Eyre did nothing to dampen worldwide interest in the alleged connection with the book. House and garden have belonged to the Graham family since 1624 apart from in a few years. SE3198976245.

NOSTERFIELD
Near Ripon, from Old English eowerstrefelda = the ewes' or sheep fold.

NUN MONKTON
On the confluence of the Ouse and Nidd, Nun Monkton was an estate village until 1934 when the estate houses were sold off. The village green is to this day grazed by cattle and is one of the last working greens in Yorkshire. The Alice Hawthorn public house (*q.v.*), originally the 1787 Blue Bell Inn, is named after the 1840s winner of the Doncaster Cup and Queen's Vase. The Monkton part of the name may well be due to a small monastery from the pre-Viking period, complemented in 1172 by a Benedictine nunnery set up by Ivetta of the Arches, the Anglo-Norman owner of the village. The nunnery lasted until the Dissolution, despite pleas from Anne Boleyn that it be spared. Until the mid-19th century (when it was stopped because the then vicar considered it to be pagan) Nun Monkton traditionally performed the annual ceremony of digging up, parading, and reburying a statue of St. Peter, the village's patron saint. The ferry was closed in the mid-20th century.

NUNTHORPE
Originally just called Thorpe meaning 'a farm'. There was a Cistercian nunnery here in the 12th century, hence the name. It is near Middlesbrough. Around 1912 Sir Arthur Dorman, the owner of the world famous Dorman Long steel company, built a new suburb of 60 or so houses around the railway station for his workers. There were provisos: no shops or public houses; the houses had to have slate roofs and were not allowed house numbers. The development featured tree-lined roads, with spacious houses, each with a garden – all built in terraces.

OLD COTE

The cottage frequented by owls: Old English ule +cot; in the 12th century it was Ulecotes. Near Kettlewell.

ORMESBY

Ormesby is near Middlesbrough. In the old north east dragons were known as worms, the most famous being the Lambton Worm which is said to have slithered around Chester le Street. In Viking mythology dragons were called `Orms'

Ormesby is a Viking place name and means Worms Village, but the Orm of Ormesby was a Viking named after a dragon. Orm appears in other English place names like Ormskirk and Ormside (Worms Hill) in Cumbria.

OSBALDWICK

The farm belonging to Osbald. A suburb of York. It gets three mentions in the *Domesday Book* as Osboldewic. Osbald was an earl in the kingdom of Northumbria. The nun Mary Ward is buried there. She founded the Institute of the Blessed Virgin Mary opening schools in Flanders before the order was suppressed by the Pope. After imprisonment in Munich for heresy she returned to England and re-established the Institute in Heworth in 1644. The fifty pictures on the Bar Convent staircase in York depict her life; they are reproduced from 17th century paintings from the house of the Institute of Augsburg.

OSGODBY

There is one north of Selby and one near Scarborough. Both come from the Old Norse name Asgautr and mean Asgaut's farm.

OSGOODBY

The village belonging to a Viking called Osgood. Near Thirsk.

OSMOTHERLEY

Originally Osmunderly from the Old Norse meaning Osmund's Ley and Asmundrelac – Asmund's clearing. An alternative derivation comes from the legend whereby a soothsayer foretold the death by drowning of King Oswald's son, Oswy. To prevent this his distraught mother took him up Roseberry Topping but she fell asleep and Oswy fell into a pool watered by a spring and drowned. She buried him at a place called Teviotdale which took the name Os-by-his-mother-lay when she died and was buried next to him. Osmotherley had a linen industry in the 18th, 19th and early 20th centuries, producing sailcloth and later coverings for aeroplane wings. The youth hostel was a flax mill in the 1800s. There have been a number of variations in the spelling of the name over the centuries including Asmundrelac, Osmundeslay, Osemunderl, Osmonderlay and Osmthrly.

OSWALDKIRK

This means the church of Oswald. Oswald was a Northumbrian martyr, and the Anglo-Saxon King of Northumbria who was slain by the pagan, Penda in 642. The earliest reference is in the *Domesday Book* where it was referred to as "Oswaldecherca" or "Oswaldecherce". Oswaldkirk means to the south of a steep hill, known as "Oswaldkirk Hagg"; near Helmsely.

OTTERBURN

The otter stream (Old English: oter + burna). The *Domesday Book* calls it Otreburne. It is near Skipton.

OUBROUGH

A village near Ellerby which means owl-haunted fortress from Old English ule.

OUGHTERSHAW
Uhtred's copse (Old English personal name + Old English sceaga). In 1241 it was called Huctredescale. Near Hawes.

OUSE RIVER
A Celtic river name.

OWLANDS
Wolf Grove from Old Norse ulfr + lundr. In the 13th century it was Ulvelundes. Near Richmond.

OXENBER
The hill where oxen – oxa in Old English – graze. Near Austwick.

OXNOP
Valley of the oxen. Oxa + hop in Old English. Oxenhope in 1301. Near Muker.

PANNAL
From pan hal or pan haugh – a rounded pan shaped valley or piece of land. With origins going back to the Bronze Age, Pannal had become a thriving market village with weekly markets and an annual four day fair by the early 14th century. The parish of Pannal covered a large area, including Beckwith, Beckwithshaw, Brackenthwaite and Low Harrogate. In 1894 Low Harrogate became part of Harrogate, and in 1937 the village of Pannal was also added to Harrogate. This left the village outside the civil parish of Pannal, a confusing situation, the like of which only local councillors could contrive. The bungling prevailed until 2010 when the civil parish was renamed Beckwithshaw.

PATELEY BRIDGE
Path – ley – bridge: the path with a clearing near a bridge, as it erroneously remains today. "Pately Bridge", in the Nidd Valley, is known locally as "Pately Brig" – brig being Norse for a large rock outcrop – no sign of any bridge. The error is probably the result of southern cartographers getting it wrong when they labelled the place, believing the etymology to be brycg, Old English for bridge. Pateley is Old English pæþ ('path') + paða + lēah ('open ground, clearing in a forest'); paða lēah then means "woodland clearing of the paths", namely, the paths up Nidderdale and from Ripon to Craven, which met here. In the early middle ages Pateley was owned by the Archbishop of York, and part of Bishopside. In the 12th century the main settlement was at Wilsill, rather than Pateley. Pateley is first known to us in 1175 as Patleiagate, and then in the 14th century as Patheleybrig(ge). There is no evidence to support the local story that the name comes from 'pate', an old Yorkshire dialect word for 'badger'.

Pateley Bridge is home to the Oldest Sweet Shop in England, opened in 1827 and housed in a building dating from the 1660s. Other places in the parish include part of Wath, Glasshouses, Wilsill, Blazefield and Fellbeck.

PAULL
Paull is on the north bank of the Humber seven miles south east of Hull and is the only riverside village downstream of the city. Paull has been in existence since at least the 11th century and most probably much longer. A settlement nearby is recorded in the *Domesday Book* as "Pagula," Latin for a stake marking a landing-place. "Pagula" appears on old maps in various spellings and was soon contracted to "Pagul" and then "Pagil" or "Paghil" and finaly "Paul" and "Paull." The variant Paghill is still in use today, in the area of Paull known as Paghill.

PENNINES
Given that these hills and mountains form the most significant area of upland region in England, the mystery that surrounds the etymology of the name is quite astonishing. The Pennines first appear in an 18th century

chronicle made by the medieval monk Richard of Cirencester, but this is a forgery. Various etymologies have been posited, mainly suggesting that "Pennine" is a Brittonic name related to pen- ("head"). However, it almost certainly derives from 18th century comparisons with the Apennine Mountains.

PEN-Y-GHENT
Pen-y-Ghent is 2,273 feet high and shares its name with Pen-y-Fan Pen y Gadair, Pen y Gaer, Pen y Parc, Pen y Rhwbyn and many others, in Wales. Pen-y-Ghent is an echo of the times when most of the country we now know now as England spoke a language similar to Welsh. Pen usually means hill and y is the definite article 'the', so its name means the *something* hill; the meaning of ghent remains unknown for sure. It may mean 'edge' or 'border', making it 'Hill on the border'; or, it could mean 'wind' or 'winds' – transliterating from the Welsh, gwynt ('wind') thus making it 'Head of the Winds'. SD838733. Compare Penshaw Hill near Sunderland and Pendle Hill in Lancashire.

PIKEDAW
The pointed hilltop (Old English + Old Norse). Pykethow in 1269. Near Malham and famous for the Calamine Caverns.

PICKERING
Pickering means the people of Picer or Picere and may be a personal name for an Anglo-Saxon, or a tribal name that could mean the dwellers at the edge of the 'pic' or hill. As a rough parallel, Dickering, in east Yorkshire, means dwellers at the edge of the dyke. The first owner of Pickering as a surname was Reginald de Pickering in 1165.

A much less banal and much more romantic derivation has it that the town was founded and named by King Peredurus around 270 BC; one day he lost his ring and accused a young maiden of stealing it. Happily, later that day, the ring was found in the stomach of a pike caught in the River Costa for the king's dinner. The king was so delighted that he married the now vindicated maiden and Pickering got the early name Pike-ring.

POCKLINGTON
Pocklington is derived from the Old English "Poclintun" from the Anglian settlement of Pocel's (or Pocela's) people and the Old English word "tun" meaning farm or settlement. Pocklington appears on the 14th century *Gough Map*, Britain's oldest road map. When the *Domesday Book* was published in 1086 Pocklington was the second largest settlement in Yorkshire after York.

Burnby Hall Gardens are home to the National Collection of Hardy Water Lilies – the biggest collection in a natural setting in Europe. Pocklington Canal Head is one of the top ten places to see aquatic wildlife in Britain. In October every year Munich's Oktoberfest comes to Pocklington in the guise the famous Pocktoberfest – an orgy of beer and sausage. Another annual event in May is the Flying Man Festival, to celebrate the showman Thomas Pelling, the "Flying Man of Pocklington", who donned a pair of homemade wings and attempted to walk a rope from the steeple of All Saint's Church to the Star Inn, meeting his end when he fell and smashed into one of the church's buttresses. He is buried precisely where he died, in 1733. He should have read his Greek myths, especially the one about Icarus.

Joseph Terry was born in Pocklington and went on to found one of the world's most successful chocolate companies in York; Thomas Cooke was born in Allerthorpe and went on to build the world's finest (and largest) telescopes with York company Cooke, Troughton & Simms; William Wilberforce, a Pocklington School old boy, was, of course, one of the main driving forces behind the abolition of the slave trade. The first Victoria Cross of the Second World War was awarded to Pocklington School old boy 2nd-Lt Richard Annand.

PONTEFRACT

The name means broken bridge and is part French (pont), part Latin (fractus from frango, I break). In the late 11th century, Pontefract consisted of two separate places known as Tanshelf and Kirkby. As in York, many of the streets are –gate; for example, Baileygate. The contemporary historian, Orderic Vitalis, recorded that, in 1069, William the Conqueror arrived here to quell an Anglo-Saxon uprising – only to find the bridge broken – hence the name. Pontefract was Pontefracto in 1090. Shakespeare mentions it twice as Pomfret – *in Richard III*:

> Pomfret, Pomfret! O thou bloody prison, Fatal and ominous to noble peers! Within the guilty closure of thy walls Richard the second here was hack'd to death; And, for more slander to thy dismal seat, We give thee up our guiltless blood to drink.

and *Richard II* (V, 1, 52).

Pontefract is also famous for its liquorice and Robin Hood.

POSFORTH GILL

The ravine at Posi's ford (Old Norse personal name + Old English + Old Norse). A destructive storm in the 1826 left it with the biblical-sounding and highly descriptive name, the Valley of Desolation. Called Poseford in the 12th century. It is near Bolton Abbey.

POTTO

The village of Potto, near Swainby, is famous for three things. Anyone who has ever driven on Britain's roads and motorways will be familiar with the ubiquitous haulage vehicles of Preston's of Potto discreetly based here. Secondly, the Lyke Wake Walk: named after the Cleveland Lyke Wake Dirge sang over the coffins of those to be transported the forty-two miles over the moors to Ravenscar (lyke means corpse, wake, watch). It was believed that the soul had to cross the moors to reach Paradise. Bill Cowley lived in Potto at Potto Hill Farm and established the walk, making the first crossing in October 1955. In 1966, aged ten, Heather, his daughter, was the youngest person ever to complete the Walk over the moors from Osmotherley to Ravenscar. In the late 1950s Potto became notorious as the village with "the pub that never opened". If you wanted a pint at the Dog and Gun, the owner, a Mr Heslop, would peer through the window to see if he liked the look of you before letting you in.

Potto is from Viking 'pot' – usually a deep hole often in the bed of a river; pot also occurs in Sand Pot near Northallerton and in Pot Hall and the Pot Beck near Masham. The word is still used in Swedish dialects today.

PURSTON JAGLIN

Purston is a corruption of Preston meaning the priest's settlement. Jaglin is a corruption of Jakelin, perhaps a one-time owner. Robin Hood is reputed to have quaffed ale in the Travellers' Rest here. An area of Featherstone.

RAISGILL

The ravine with a cairn or pile of stones from Old Norse hreysi + gil. It was called Risegil in 1241.

RASH

The rush bed, from a local dialect. It was Rashe in 1592. Park Rash is one of the hardest climbs for cyclists in Yorkshire; it is near Kettlewell.

RASKELF

From the Viking raskalf meaning the headland (or sloping piece of land from Old English skjalf) frequented by roe deer. Near Easingwold. The *Domesday Book* has it as Raschel – as it is still often pronounced today. The village has two particularly fascinating features, the first of which is the 12th century St. Mary's 15th century timber tower – one of only two in England, the other being St. Andrew's at Greenstead-juxta-Ongar. Captain Augustus Frederick Cavendish Webb of the 17th Lancers is commemorated in the north chapel, after dying of wounds sustained at the Charge of the Light Brigade at Balaclava in 1854. The second feature is the Old Pinfold, or pound; pinfolds were built to hold animals that had strayed from their owner's land or were found grazing on common land without common rights. They were released after a fine or mulct had been paid to the pinder. Breaking into a pinfold to release animals was punishable by a fine or imprisonment.

RATHMELL
Near Giggleswick. The red sandbank (Old Norse: rauthr + melr). The *Domesday Book* listed it as Rodemele. There is a Rauthamelr in Iceland.

RAVENSCAR
The rock or scar inhabited by ravens. Up until the early 20th century it was known as The Peak. It is near Scarborough. Ravenscar is the resort that never was. At the beginning of the 20th century, plans were drawn up to turn the village into a resort to rival Scarborough. Roads were laid down and sewers were dug. What the developers failed to take into account, however, was the long trek to its rocky beach: Ravenscar never caught on, and the development was abandoned – a ghost town with sewers and streets but no houses.

RAVENSER ODD
Once near Kilnsea. Ravenser Odd also appears as Ravensrodd; it was a port in the Middle Ages, built on the sandbanks at the mouth of the Humber estuary. The name Ravenser derives from the Old Norse Hrafn's Eyr or "Raven's tongue": the lost sandbank promontory which is now known as Spurn Point. The port was founded by the Count of Aumale in the mid-13th century, and had in excess of 100 houses and a buzzing market by 1299, when it was granted a borough charter and was a more important port than Hull, represented even in the Model Parliament of 1295. However, storms in 1356–57 completely flooded the town which was then abandoned and left to be totally destroyed and submerged by the Grote Mandrenke storm of January 1362.

RAVENSWORTH
A village close to the A66 between Barnard Castle and Scotch Corner; early recorded forms are Rafneswad, Ravenswat and Ravenswath meaning the wath belonging to Hraefn. Wath was Viking for a ford. There is also the Viking place name Ravensthorpe meaning Hraefn's Farm in West Yorkshire and Northamptonshire; some place names beginning in 'Raven' refer to the bird, as Ravenscar above. Other ravens include Ravenseat in Swaledale, the hill of the raven, and Ravenglass in Cumbria from the Celtic rann glas meaning the part share of land belonging to someone called Glas.

RAWCLIFFE
The name reflects the reddish colour of the Ouse river bank there.

RAYDALE
Roebuck valley (Old English/Old Norse) – dael + ra. Radale in 1307. Near Bainbridge with Countersett, Marsett and Stalling Busk nearby.

REDCAR
The second part of the name derives from the Viking word kjar meaning marshland. Redcar, called Redker in 1165, Ridkere in 1407 and Readcar in 1653 means either the red coloured marshland from the local red stone, or reedy marsh. In 1510 Redcar was described as a 'Poore Fishing Toune' and was for many centuries overshadowed by its neighbour Coatham, home to a market and fair from 1257.

Coatham's name derives from Cot -Ham and means the shelter homestead where fishing boats took shelter from the seas.

Redcar's Gertrude Bell (1868 –1926) was a writer, traveller, archaeologist, linguist, Alpine mountaineer and spy who had a great influence on British foreign policy-making in what was Greater Syria, Mesopotamia, Asia Minor, and Arabia. Along with T. E. Lawrence, Lawrence of Arabia, Bell helped establish the Hashemite dynasties in what is today Jordan and Iraq. She established the National Museum of Baghdad and reached places never visited by a western woman. Bell has been described as 'one of the few representatives of His Majesty's Government remembered by the Arabs with anything resembling affection'. To them she was a great sheik; many Arabs attended her funeral; one asking in tribute, 'If this is a woman, what must the men be like?'

From the age of two she lived at Red Barns House in Kirkleatham Street, Coatham until she went up to Oxford to read history, winning a first after only two years – the first woman ever to win a history first. Her father, Sir Thomas Hugh Bell, was a director of Bell's Steelworks at Middlesbrough and a director of the North Eastern Railway. Her brother said: "She had a love for Redcar, and all her life had a feeling that Redcar was her home."

A drummer boy routinely alerted the Redcar lifeboat crew with the rhythm 'Come Along, Brave Boys, Come Along'. The nearby Teesmouth lifeboat crew responded to calls on the last leg to the boathouse on a sail driven bogey running through the dunes on railway lines to South Gare, which still can be seen today. During the 1950s and early 1960s the crew met at Redcar Bus Station and boarded a special emergency bus for the Gare, sometimes causing considerable inconvenience to the townspeople.

REDMIRE
The pool covered with reeds (Old English hreod + mere). Ridemare in the *Domesday Book*. Near Leyburn.

REETH
From an Anglo Saxon word meaning at the stream. At one time it was a centre for hand-knitting and the local lead in upper Swaledale. During the Second World War the old school building was used to billet troops attending the six week Battle Training Camp at Catterick. Recent restoration work uncovered tins of boot polish and anti-gas ointment along with packets of Navy Cut and Woodbine cigarettes under the floorboards.

RHOS
A hamlet north of Withernsea whose name is derived from the Old English rhos = moor or heath. The *Domesday Book* has it as Rosse.

RICCALL
This means rye calf (Old English cealf), calf being a small island near a larger one; rye is the River Rye. A Viking army landed here in 1066 under Harald Hardråda who set up camp at Riccall before the victory in the Battle of Fulford. Riccall is near Selby.

RICHMOND
Richmond was originally called Hindrelac, an Anglo-Viking name which reflects a woodland clearing frequented by a hind deer. The present name is Old French and derives from Riche-Monte – strong hill. In 1499 Henry VII, the Earl of Richmond, built a palace at Sheen in Surrey. Sheen was renamed Richmond and is now Richmond -upon-Thames. *The Rough Guide* describes Yorkshire's Richmond as '*an absolute gem*', '*without any doubt Richmond is the most romantic place in the whole of the North East*'. The Georgian Theatre Royal here, built in 1788, is the UK's most complete 18th century theatre we have left. Lewis Carroll went to Richmond School; he lived in nearby Croft-on-Tees.

RIEVAULX

A Cistercian abbey founded in 1132 by twelve monks from Clairvaux Abbey. This means Rye Valley. See also Jervaulx.

RILLINGTON

On the York to Scarborough road. Redlington and Relinton in the *Domesday Book* but Rillington by 1391. It may have once been Hredle + ton = the headquarters of Hredle. It resonates more today with 10 Rillington Place.

RIPLEY

Ripley is famous for Ripley Castle. However, the village itself is not without interest. A 19th century member of the incumbent Ingilby family tore down the old village and rebuilt it modeled after an Alsatian village with an "hôtel de ville" style town hall. The castle and the parish church were unaffected by the 'reconstruction'.

King Edward III stayed several times nearby in Knaresborough Castle, most notably in January 1328 after his marriage to Queen Philippa in York. In 1355 he was attacked by a boar he had wounded, and was thrown from his horse. His life was saved by Thomas Ingilby of Ripley Castle, who killed the animal; Ingilby later received a knighthood, and a boar's head was henceforth included in the Ingilby arms. See Ripon.

RIPON

Ripon possesses a 'folk name' which means it is a name of tribal origin, referring to the people in the area. This is common for counties and regions but rare for the names of villages, towns and cities. Variations over time include Hrypis and Hripis in 715 AD, Inhrypam in 730, Onripum in 890, Rypum in 1030 and Ripun in the *Domesday Book*. Nearby Ripley certainly means the woodland of the Hyrppes. Repton in Derbyshire derives from 'Hyrpa dun' meaning the hill of the Hyrpe tribe.

The Curfew Horn, unique to Ripon, has been blown each night by the Wakeman since the 13th century to 'set the watch'. The ceremony still takes place at the four corners of the obelisk and at the mayor's house. It was originally blown at the mayor's house and then the town hall, but reversed in 1913 so that spectators might catch the 9.29 to Harrogate. The Wakeman also hired constables to help keep order in the city. The office of Bellman dates from 1367, and ever since he can be found ringing his bell at eleven o'clock every Thursday morning in Market Square to open the now defunct corn market. He was empowered to levy a toll on each sack sold (the Market Sweepings), to start the Quarter Sessions and inflict whippings on law-breakers. All householders had to contribute to the cost of this service – twopence for each outer door of their house per annum. Ripon is Britain's oldest city, having been granted a charter by King Alfred the Great in 886 and presented with a horn as a symbol of the charter.

Nanny Appleby, with her hairy warts, bad teeth and bulging eyes, was regarded as a witch but was more of a quack. She was attending a sick boy one day, harassed and heckled as usual by the abusive Tom Moss. Nanny Appleby opened the boy's mouth only to see a grinning demon, which had taken refuge in the boy's stomach: it flew out when she poured holy water down his throat and flew straight into Tom Moss's mouth and into his stomach where it tormented him so badly that he resorted to the lunatic asylum and then the River Ure in which he drowned.

RISE

South of Hornsea, its name comes from Old English *hris* and means among the brushwood, maybe a place where faggots were gathered.

ROBIN HOOD'S BAY

Nothing to do with Robin Hood, it is also known as Bay Town. The tenuous connection comes from a ballad which has Robin Hood coming up against French pirates intent on pillaging the fishermen's boats; the pirates surrendered and Robin Hood returned the booty to its rightful owners. "Robin Hoode Baye" is mentioned by Leland in 1536: "A fischer tounlet of 20 bootes with Dok or Bosom of a mile yn length".

3rd February 1843 was a bad day in Robin Hood's Bay. The lifeboat capsized en route to a brig in distress and four crew members died. The coastguard boat was then launched, only to capsize with the loss of two further lives out of the five-man crew. In January 1881 the brig *Visitor* foundered off the bay during a blizzard; the crew took to their boat, but were forced to remain outside the harbour. It was impossible to launch the Whitby Lifeboat at Whitby and so eighteen horses and around 200 men from Whitby and Robin Hood's Bay hauled the Whitby boat, the *Robert Whitworth*, six miles from Whitby to the bay, in snow drifts seven feet deep in places. At the end of the two-hour trek the men lowered the lifeboat down the steep street towards the seas with ropes. The first launch had to be aborted – the oars were smashed by a wave. At this point John Skelton, a local man with local knowledge of the bay, waded in and swam towards the *Visitor*'s crew, plotting a safe route for the lifeboat, now with eighteen crew on board, to follow.

ROMANBY
This village near Northallerton belonged to a Viking called Romund. It has nothing to do with the Romans or gipsies. See Northallerton.

ROSEBERRY TOPPING
Roseberry Topping is sometimes known as The Cleveland Matterhorn because it looks a bit like it – although hugely smaller. Topping comes from toppen, an Old Danish word for a hill. Roseberry derives from the nearby settlement of Newton-under-Roseberry, then called Newton-under-Ouseberry. The original Old Norse name for Roseberry Topping was Odins-Beorg meaning Odins Hill – Hill from Old Norse bjarg ('rock');. Over time, Odinsberg changed to Othensberg, Ohenseberg, Ounsberry and Ouesberry. The first element is an Old Norse personal name, Auðunn or Óðinn, giving 'Auðunn's/Óðinn's rock'. If the latter, Roseberry Topping is one of only a handful of known pagan names in England,

Despite claims, at 1,049 feet Roseberry Topping is not the highest hill on the North York Moors; nearby Urra Moor is higher, at 1,490 feet. Chris Rea dedicated the song *Chisel Hill* from the album *Shamrock Diaries* to Roseberry Topping.

ROTHERHAM
Formed from Old English hām 'homestead, estate', so 'homestead on the River Rother'. The river name comes from the Celtic words meaning main river. Rotherham-born Archbishop of York, Thomas Rotherham, was responsible in the 1480s for the building of a College of Jesus or Jesus College in Rotherham to rival the colleges of the same name in Cambridge and Oxford. It was the first brick building in the region. Theology, religious chant and hymns, grammar and writing were taught there.

RUNSWICK BAY
This may mean Reagan's creek from Old English Raegan or Old Norse Hreinn + Old Norse vik. In March 1940 it was the local women who went to assist the *Buizerd of Groningen*; the six crew were saved. This was not the first time women had helped. On 12th April 1901 most of the able-bodied men were at sea in their cobles when the lifeboat, *Jonathan Stott*, was needed to offer assistance. Only boys and old men remained onshore at the time so the ladies decided that the men and boys would man the vessel and they would launch it. All the cobles returned to shore safely.

RUSWARP
Ruswarp is near Whitby on the River Esk. Early forms include Risewarp and Rysewarp in the 12th century, Riswarp in the 14th century and Ruswarpe in the 17th century. The first part comes from the

Anglo-Saxon word 'Hris', brushwood. Local dialect is responsible for the change from Hris to Rus. Warp derives from the Old Norse word varpa meaning to throw, possibly a reference to silt thrown up by the River Esk. This also occurs in the Norwegian place name Varpet. 'Warp' in Yorkshire dialect specifically refers to sediment formed by a river, or to mud which obstructs the flow of a river. Ruswarp's name then, (the w is silent) refers to silty land overgrown with brushwood.

RYLESTONE
Farmstead by the stream (Old English rynel + tun). Rilestune in the *Domesday Book*. Near Grassington. Rylstone and District Women's Institute was the inspiration for the 2003 film *Calendar Girls*, although local scenes for the film were shot at nearby Kettlewell. Rylstone is the subject of Wordsworth's *The White Doe of Rylstone*.

SALTAIRE
Saltaire was established in 1851 and is the creation of Sir Titus Salt (1803-1876), a prominent industrialist in the woollen industry. Saltaire is a conflation of 'Salt' and 'Aire', the river on which the town stands. Salt moved his existing mills from Bradford, consolidating it all on this site so as to be close to the Leeds and Liverpool Canal and the Midland Railway. He believed that his commercial success was entirely God-given. At six storeys high and 180 yards long and with a floor space of over eleven acres, the ergonomic mill was the biggest and most modern in Europe. Output exceeded 30,000 yards of cloth per day; the weaving shed housed an incredible 1,200 power looms. Noise, and industrial injuries, were reduced by locating much of the machinery underground. Large flues removed smoke, dust and dirt from the atmosphere and from the factory floor. Fire safety equipment was state of the art. The heavily subsidized canteen was supplemented with facilities for workers to bring in their own food and cook on site. The impressive campanile must be one of the most aesthetic chimneys ever to be built and is based on the campanile on the Basilica Santamaria Gloriosa in Dei Frari in Venice.

SALTBURN BY THE SEA
Saltburn goes back to at least AD 369 when the Romans built a watchtower at nearby Huntcliff. After the Romans had withdrawn in around 410 the Romanised Britons left to defend the coast were murdered and their bodies dumped in a well, where they were finally discovered in 1923. The skeletons of fourteen men, women and children were found. The Anglo-Saxons settled here and named a local stream 'Sealt-Burna' – the salty stream, either from its salty water or because of the salt-like alum found in the vicinity. When the Vikings came they changed the names of all the burns to becks; Salt Burn retained its name, but the stream became the Skelton Beck.

The fishing village of Saltburn gradually grew under the prominent Cat Nab. Innkeeper John Andrew, 'king of the smugglers', operated from his Ship Inn here. The superb 1869 Saltburn Cliff Lift is one of the world's oldest water-powered funiculars—the oldest is the Bom Jesus funicular in Braga, Portugal. Teddy's Nook was built in 1862; Lillie Langtry stayed there between 1877 and 1880 and was visited frequently by Edward Prince of Wales (later Edward VII) who kept a suite of rooms at the Zetland Hotel. Saltburn's first public house independent of an existing hotel was The Victoria, which opened in December 1982.

SCAGGLETHORPE
The *Domesday Book* has it as as "Scachetorp". Scagglethorpe is from the Viking word "Schachetorp", meaning hamlet of a man called Skakull or Ska(k)li. Near Malton.

SCALEBER FOSS
The hill (berg)with the shieling (skali) hut or high pasture (Old Norse + Old English/Old Norse). Skarlebergh in 1651. Near Settle.

SCARBOROUGH

The Viking Sagas make mention of Scarborough: in the *Kormakssaga*, Flateyjarbo Scarborough is Skarthborg and in the *Orkneyingasaga* it is Skarthabork. The Kormakssaga tells how two Viking brothers, Thorgils and Kormak, established a stronghold in AD 966 called Scarborough. Thorgils was known by his nickname 'Hare Lip', or in Norse, 'Skarthi'. 'Hare-Lip' gave his name to Scarborough: Skarthi's Burgh, or Skarthi's Stronghold. In 1000 Christians built a chapel but in 1066 Hardrada, (Harald III, King of Norway) and Tostig Godwinson sacked the town and destroyed the chapel. They did such a good job that there was nothing left for the *Domesday Book* to report.

Scarborough was to be one of four north east coastal towns bombarded by the German fleet on the morning of 16 December 1914. In the space of 40 minutes about 1,000 shells were unleashed on Hartlepool and West Hartlepool from three German heavy cruisers *Blucher*, *Seydlitz* and *Moltke*, killing 63 civilians and nine soldiers in Hartlepool and 56 civilians in West Hartlepool; 400 or so civilians were injured and much housing stock was damaged or destroyed. The raid on Hartlepool was followed by similar assaults on Scarborough and Whitby, in which eighteen and three people were killed respectively. Off Scarborough the *Derfllinger* and *von der Tann* opened fire on the coastguard station and the barracks before shelling the castle and the Grand Hotel, believing it to be a gun battery. As they passed Whitby they fired 50 rounds at the signal station, town and abbey. The attack on the east coast caused outrage in Britain – partly because the Royal Navy failed to intercept the Germans, but also because Whitby and Scarborough, unlike Hartlepool, were undefended, open towns.

SCHOLES

Derives from the Viking word Skali: a shieling. Near Leeds. It is sometimes called Scholes-in-Elmet to distinguish it from the Scholes, Holme Valley and Scholes, Cleckheaton in West Yorkshire.

SCORTON ON SWALE

Scorton dates from Anglo-Saxon times and is thought to mean 'Short Tun'; the nearby village of Langton means 'Long Tun'. The main feature of the village is its raised green, one of only two in England. During the summer it is the venue for local cricket matches and the annual feast which goes back to 1257. The Ancient Scorton Silver Arrow is an archery tournament which was first held here in 1673: 22 archers competed for the prize of a silver arrow; the Society of Archers was formed to organise the event annually. The 2008 event was the 300th meeting and claims to be the oldest sporting event still running.

SCOSTHROP

Skott's outlying farmstead (Old Norse personal name + Old Norse). Scotorp in the *Domesday Book*. Near Settle.

SCOTCHERGILL

'Skott's ravine where flat stones are found'; Old Norse personal name + Old Norse: hella +gill. Scotshelgill in 1676. Near Dent.

SCRIVEN

This name drives from the Anglo-Saxon word scraef, a cave. Originally it was Scriven-with-Tentergate – the place where cloth was stretched for drying. Scriven is near Knaresborough.

SEDBERGH

A hill with a flat or seat-shaped top from Old Norse. Sedbergh is one Britain's book towns (along with Hay-on-Wye and Wigtown) with independent bookshops and dealers working out of the Dales and Lakes Book Centre here.

SEDBUSK

Old Norse for the bush near the shieling: saetr + buskr. In 1280 it was Setebuskste. Near Hawes.

SELBY

Suggestions for the origin of the name include 'Abode of the Seal', indicating seals in the area; 'lucky town'; and 'settlement in a willow copse'. Selby started life called Seletun and is mentioned in the *Anglo-Saxon Chronicle* of 779. Henry I, fourth son of William the Conqueror, was born here in 1068 which explains William and his wife Matilda's unique joint charter of Selby Abbey, founded for Benedict of Auxerre in 1069 when he saw three swans on a lake in Selby as a sign of the Father, Son and Holy Ghost. The official crest of Selby Abbey is three swans; there is still a Three Swans pub.

SELSIDE

Selside is in Ribblesdale near Horton and appears as Selesat in the *Domesday Book*. The name is derived from the Old Norse selja "willow" and sætr "mountain pasture" or "shieling".

SEMER WATER

The lake pool. Semer Water is an example of a pleonastic place name – where more than one word denotes the same thing, but unnecessarily so for the meaning to be clear. The name, first seen in 1153, derives from the Old English elements sæ 'lake', mere 'lake' and water. If you call it "Lake Semerwater", as some do, this introduces a fourth synonym.

Legend has it that Semer Water was the site of a bustling city in which one night an old man (or an angel in disguise) came down to the city, looking for food and drink. He went from door to door but was always turned away until he reached the humble cottage of a poor couple on the edge of town who took him in and fed him. On leaving the stranger cursed the city: "*Semerwater rise, and Semerwater sink, And swallow the town all save this house, Where they gave me food and drink.*" At that, the waters of the lake flooded the city, drowning all the inhabitants except the poor couple.

SETTLE

Appropriately, a dwelling place (Old Norse). Setel in the *Domesday Book*. The Naked Man here is the oldest cafe in the country; there is the annual Settle Storytelling Festival; The Gallery on the Green is the smallest art gallery in the world: drawings, paintings, photographs and installations works are all on display housed in a former BT telephone kiosk. Fossils yielded up in nearby Victoria Cave include a 130,000 years old mammoth, straight-tusked elephant, cave bear, hippopotamus, rhinoceros and spotted hyenas.

SETTRINGTON

A village near Malton derived from Old English saetere meaning robber. Place of the robber gangs then.

SHEFFIELD

The name Sheffield is Old English and is made up of a compound of [the River] Sheaf, which is a corruption of shed or sheth, meaning to divide or split. Field is simply a generic suffix deriving from the Old English feld, meaning a forest clearing. So, we can conclude that the name Sheffield is an Anglo-Saxon settlement in a clearing beside the confluence of the rivers Sheaf and Don between the the 6th century and the early 9th century.

Many localities within Sheffield from the same time have names ending in ley, which is, again, a clearing in the forest, or ton, which is an enclosed farmstead. These include Heeley, Longley, Norton, Owlerton, Southey, Tinsley, Totley, Wadsley, and Walkley.

The Wednesday part of Sheffield Wednesday FC has nothing at all to do with football. The club was initially a cricket club called The Wednesday Cricket Club after the day of the week on which they played their matches. As often, the footballing side of the club was established to maintain the team, team spirit and fitness during winter. Sheffield Wednesday's nickname, The Owls, has nothing to do with owls; it was coined because Hillsborough Stadium is in the Owlerton district of the city.

SHERIFF HUTTON

Once owned by Bertram Bulmer, the Sheriff of York who died in 1166. The village, north of York, features twice in the *Domesday Book* as Hotun in the Bulford hundred. Before the Normans came the manor was divided between several land owners who included Ligulf, Northmann, Thorkil, Thorsten and Thorulf. The name stems from the Old English words hoh and tun, meaning settlement on a projecting piece of land. The prefix of Sheriff is due to Sheriff Bertram. In 1484 Richard III used the castle here to accommodate his nephew Edward, Earl of Warwick and his niece, Elizabeth of York. That same year he established the Council of the North, with its headquarters at Sheriff Hutton. See Hutton Rudby.

SHIPLEY

'Shipley' comes from the Northumbrian dialect form of the Old English scīp ('sheep') and 'ly' the suffix meaning 'open ground, such as meadow or arable land'. It therefore means 'sheep-clearing' or 'sheep-pasture'. Shipley was first settled in the late Bronze Age and features in the *Domesday Book* as *Scipelei(a)*.

SHIPTON

See Skipton.

(GREAT) SHUNNER FELL

The look-out hill or Sjon's hill (Old Norse personal name (sjon) + Old Norse fjal). Between Hawes and Keld at SD848972.

SILPHO

Sylve's hill near Scarborough. Sylve + Old Norse haugr = hill.

SIMON'S SEAT

Simon's Seat is a rocky outcrop 485m above sea level. Legend has it that the name refers to Druids who followed Simon Magus, an ancient magician who claimed to be one of the Three Wise Men. Another possibility comes from Frederic Montagu in 1838, who says that

> "It was upon the top of this mountain that an infant was found by a shepherd, who took it to his home, and after feeding and clothing it, he had the child named Simon; being himself but a poor man, he was unable to maintain the foundling, when it was ultimately agreed to by the shepherds, that the child should be kept "amang 'em." The child was called Simon Amangham and the descendants of this child are now living in Wharfedale."

Gleanings in Craven, Simpkin Marshall: London 1838.
Skyreholme, Bolton Abbey – SE 078 598. The Lord's Seat is immediately to the east of Simon's.

SIMONSTONE

Sigemund's rock (Old English personal name + steinn Old Norse or stan Old English). In 1301 it was recorded as Simoundstane. A hamlet near Hawes, there is another Simonstone nearby in Lancashire.

SKEEBY

The village or farm belonging to a Viking called Skithi. Skeeby was Schirebi in the *Domesday Book* – it is known as Schireby in the 11th century, Scythebi and Scideby in the 12th century, Schideby, Skitteby and Skytheby in the 13th and 14th centuries and finally Skeitby and Skeby in the 16th century. North of Northallerton.

SKELTON

The farm on a shelf (scelf) of land. See Marske by the Sea. There are six Skeltons in Yorkshire or in what was Yorkshire: Skelton, near Howden; Skelton, near Marske in Swaledale, Skelton-on-Ure, near Boroughbridge; Skelton, north of York; Skelton-in-Cleveland, near Redcar and nearby North Skelton.

SKEWSBY

A corruption of Skog's by. A village near a scrog or wood. There is a turf maze at Bonnygate Lane called The City of Troy – the smallest turf maze in Europe. SE625718.

SKIDBY

The means dwelling (-bý) of someone called Skítr, ("Skyti's farm"). An alternative etymology gives 'firewood place' (from ski? and by), or a derivation from the personal name ski?i. Other alternatives are 'dirty place', from the old English scite. 'Skidby' is first recorded by Oswald, Archbishop of York in the 10th century, as Scyteby. In the *Domesday Book* it is Schitebi; Skipbie and Skitby were common in the 16th century it is 'Skitby' in the 19th century, and the current form is Skidby.

Skidby is famous for its corn mill of 1821 and the Half Moon Inn. North of Cottingham.

SKINNINGROVE

Means skinners' grove or pit in Old Norse. It is home to the Cleveland Ironstone Mining Museum, near Redcar. The Auxiliary coastguards here, as elsewhere, were made up of men too old for active service or miners and others in reserved occupations; their role was to man the observation posts looking out for U-boats, enemy aircraft dropping mines and drifting mines. They used the local Gas Board wagon to get their equipment to the cliff top.

SKIPSEA

Lake where a ship can sail from: Old Norse skip + saer = lake or sea.

SKIPTON

Shipton (Viking) and Skipton (Saxon); both mean sheep (sceap) farm.

Claire Whitaker's began as a grocery and drapery shop in Crosshills run by John and Rebecca Whitaker around 1889. Their daughter Ida, a trained baker, persuaded her father to specialise as a bakers and confectioners. He did, and produce was made in a room behind the shop, sold in the front while the family lived above. They moved in 1926 to the High Street, Skipton, and opened a restaurant above the shop. Claire, after whom the shop is today named, was the mother of John Whitaker, who is still chairman today and grandmother of William, the current managing director. Among their bestsellers are Mint Wafer, Mint Cremes and Mint Crisp made with an old family recipe; these are currently the world's best selling after dinner mint chocolates and are to be found in hotels (usually on your pillow), in restaurants, on airplanes and in supermarkets as own brands as well as in the usual sweetshops. In 1999 Chocolate Neapolitan was successfully launched: half a million of these are made every day out of an average daily production total of 1,500,000 chocolates.

SKYREHOLME

The bright water-meadow in Old Norse. Near Appletreewick.

SKYTHORNS

The bright thorn bushes (Old Norse skirr + thorn). In 1567 it was Skytrethorns. Near Skipton.

SLAPE WATH

A combination of the Anglo Saxon word slaep – mud, or marshy and the Viking wath, a ford. So, muddy or marshy ford. The Slapewath Mine was started by Thomas Charlton in 1864 close to the village (Charltons) named after him. The shafts date from 1880 when the mine was being operated by Samuelson & Co. The downcast shaft now surrounded by a high wall is 286 feet deep. Apart from the mine Slapewath is famous for its mineral springs, discovered in 1822 by the Revd James Wilcock, Head of the Grammar School. The spa enjoyed some popularity until the mid 1800s. Near Guisborough.

SLEIGHTS

From the Viking sletta, a flat field (near water?). Presumably, an old location as the modern village is built on hillsides on either side of the River Esk. Related to the common Danish place name Sletten. Sir Walter Scott set a scene from his *Marmion* at the chapel near here. Nearby there is a memorial to the first German aeroplane shot down in the Second World War on the main Whitby to Guisborough road (A171). It was picked up by the radar at RAF Danby Beacon and shot up by Peter Townsend, who went on to have an affair with Princess Margaret. as Group Captain Peter Townsend.

SLINGSBY

A Viking name meaning Slengr's village (near Malton). It is listed in the *Domesday Book* as "Selungesbi" in the "Maneshou hundred". It was part of Hovingham manor, but some land was owned by Orm, son of Gamul when the Normans invaded.

SMEARSETT SCAR

The butter pasture (Old Norse smjor +saetr). Smjor is a common Norwegian name. Near Settle.

SNAPE

An Anglo-Saxon name which might mean pasture, or it could be Old Norse for a boggy tract of uncultivated land. Snape is near Bedale. Catherine Parr lived at Snape Castle before she became the sixth wife of King Henry VIII. It also had an involvement in the Pilgrimage of Grace in 1536, when Parr and her step-children were held prisoner at the castle. There is another Snape near Ampleforth.

SNAYGILL

The snake-infested (snaca) nook of land (Old Norse + Old English halh). Snachehale in the *Domesday Book*. Near Skipton.

SOUTH CAVE

And North Cave. Nothing to do with caves, rather from Old English caf, describing the nearby stream.

SOUTHERSCALES

Sutari's shielings (huts or high pastures); Sutari is an Old Norse occupational name, meaning 'shoemaker'. Suterscales in 1202. Southerscales Nature Reserve is on the slopes of Ingleborough, famous for its extensive limestone pavement and rare wild plant life.

SOWERBY

This derives from Norse Saur-by – meaning muddy village and gives us our word sewer. Traces of a Roman road can still be seen nearby; it was known as The Saxty Way. The village turns up twice in the *Domesday Book* as Sorebi in the Yarlestre hundred. One time owners, the Lascelles family built a terrace of houses in the north of the village, still known today as Blue or Bribery Terrace, since tenants were obliged to vote for the Tory candidate. Pudding Pie Hill – an artificial mound – can be found on the east bank of the Cod Beck; excavations in 1855 unearthed the remains of a Saxon warrior and two other skeletons. Sowerby is a suburb of Thirsk to the south of the centre.

SPACEY HOUSES

The delightful name of Spacey is derived from the Spacey family who lived in the farm house here. The baptismal register for Kirkby Overblow in the 1470s features the christening of Roger, son of George and Isobel Spacey. As it happened, the farm was also an inn thought to have been used by monks travelling to and from Fountains Abbey. Blind Jack was a patron during his time here surveying and building the road.

SPENNITHORNE

A spen (Anglo Saxon) or spenni was a type of hedge and features in High Spen and Spennymoor in

County Durham as well as in Spennithorne. We hear of foxes jumping twice over 'a spenne' leading to the belief that a spen was a hedge or something like a hedge. There may also be a link to the Anglo-Saxon 'spannan' meaning to fasten or the Old High German spanan meaning to entice. Spennithorne near Leyburn was recorded in the *Domesday Book* as Speningetorp and later as Spenithorn in 1150, Spennigthorn in 1289 and Spenythorne in 1285. The – thorne in Spennithorne, probably denotes a thorn tree although the early spelling 'torp' could be 'thorpe', the Danish word for a small farm. The Spen Valley in west Yorkshire is another place containing the name spen.

SPOFFORTH
Spofod in the *Domesday Book* – ford of Spot.

SPURN POINT
Or Spurn Head Spit. In the Middle Ages, Spurn Head was home to the port of Ravenspurn (also Ravenspur or Ravensburgh), where Henry of Bolingbroke landed in 1399 to dethrone Richard II. An earlier doomed village was Ravenser Odd. As with other villages on the Holderness coast, Ravenspurn and Ravenser Odd were lost to the sea. The lifeboat station was built in 1810 and is now one of only a very few in the UK which has full-time paid staff (the others all being on the River Thames in London). On a stormy night here In 1883, however, when the lifeboat men prepared to return to their boat after all night on watch, they found that it had gone. It was later discovered drifting off the island of Texel, off the north coast of the Netherlands. Her boarding boat suffered a similar fate in 1888 when it was washed away and ended up, damaged beyond repair, at Great Yarmouth.

STACKHOUSE
The houses for stacking hay (Old Norse stakkr + Old English/Old Norse hus). Stacuse in the *Domesday Book*. Near Settle.

STAINFORTH
The stony ford (Old Norse + Old English – stein +ford). Stainforth and its neighbour Little Stainforth are near Settle; Stainforth was once owned by Sawley Abbey. It has also had the names Friar Stainforth and Stainforth-under-Bargh (Old English beorgh, hill). Little Stainforth was called Knight Stainforth after the knights of the Tempest family. The *Domesday Book* had it as Stainforde. There is another Stainforth near Doncaster.

STAINSACRE
An area of land or an acre belonging to a Viking called Stein. Near Scarborough.

STAINSBY
A village or 'by' belonging to a Viking called Stein. It is described as a deserted medieval village between Thornaby and Acklam, on the outskirts of Middlesbrough, although it lived on in the name of a school, the girls at which were immortalised by Chris Rea in his *Stainsby Girls*. In 1969 the archaeological site was the first in Britain to have the proposed route of a major road (the A19) diverted to preserve it.

STAITHES
In a deep coastal creek formed by the Roxby Beck, the delightful fishing village of Staithes seems lost in time and has a Viking name meaning landing place. In the north east staithes was the word for wooden piers from which ships were loaded with coal on the Rivers Tyne, Wear and Tees.

STALLING BUSK
The stallion's bush – from Old French estalon + Old Norse buskr. It was Salunesbusc in 1218. On Semerwater.

STAMFORD BRIDGE

In the early autumn of 1066, Harold Godwinson's English throne was under serious military threat on two fronts: from Harald Hardrada (with Harold's disaffected and exiled brother, Tostig Godwinson) in the north and from William of Normandy in the south. York capitulated to the Vikings and left Harold in a quandary: to meet Hardrada in battle and then go on to deal with William or to head south immediately. In the event Harold came north and joined battle with Harald here at Stamford Bridge winning a total and militarily impressive victory. The Normans called the town Pons Belli – Latin for 'Bridge of the Battle'.

STANABER

The rocky hill – stein + berg. In the 13th century it was Staniber and Stainber; Stanabarside, Stanabarclose in 1652 and Stanabarclosses 1679. In Horton.

STANGHOW

Derives from the Viking Stong-how meaning pole hill. How or Howe, comes from the Old Norse word haugr meaning a hill. Near Redcar.

STANWICK ST JOHN

Near Richmond. The name 'Stanwick' is derived from the Old Norse word 'steinvegges', meaning stone ways. Archaeological evidence may suggest that the site was the residence of Cartimandua, Queen of the Brigantes. Rigodonum, a Brigantian fort mentioned by Tacitus, has been proposed by Mortimer Wheeler as a possible candidate for Stanwick. In 1225, Stanwick was known as 'Steinweg'; we have a contemporary document describing a dispute over church revenue, which led to the church being attacked and the vicar barricading himself inside: 'murder, fire and sacrilege within the church at Steinweg'.

STARBOTTON

The valley bottom where stakes are cut (Old Norse stafn + botn). The *Domesday Book* had it as Stamphotne. Alternatively, it may derive from "Stauerboten" – 12th century – Old English "stæfer" replacing the Norse "stafn". Starbotton boasts a Quaker burial ground. The Smelt Flue remains, leading up to the Smelt Chimney above Cam Gill – remnants of the Smeltmill. You can still crawl through parts of the flue – the old job for children at the mill to collect white lead oxide from the sides of the flue which explains the high number of young people buried in the churchyard at Kettlewell in the 18th and 19th centuries. In between Kettlewell and Buckden.

STILLINGTON

Dwelling of Styfella's people.

STOCKHOLM

Near Thorngumbald, nowhere near Sweden. It, like the Swedish capital, means island cleared of trees from Old Norse stokker = tree stump + holmr = small island.

STOCKTON-ON-TEES

Historically, part of Stockton fell into North Yorkshire while part was in Durham. Stockton is an Anglo-Saxon name with the typical suffix 'ton' meaning farm, or homestead. Stocc means log, tree trunk or wooden post so 'Stockton' could denote a farm built of logs. A light came on in Stockton in 1827 when local chemist John Walker invented the friction match in his shop at 59 High Street. Walker was born in Stockton in 1781 and was apprenticed to Watson Alcock, the town's principal surgeon. Walker, however, could not stomach the surgery and changed to chemistry. After studying at Durham and York, he returned to Stockton and set up as a chemist and druggist around 1818. The discovery of the match was all rather serendipitous: Walker had been routinely selling concoctions of combustible materials in powder form to smokers and to a gunsmith; in 1826 he was experimenting with these combustibles when, by chance, he scraped the mixing stick against his hearth: the stick caught fire. Samples were distributed locally while Walker perfected his invention: sulphur, tipped with a mixture of sulphide of antimony, chlorate of potash, and gum, on the end of a stick, were sold as friction matches and supplied with a piece of folded sandpaper as the scraping agent. Price was 1 shilling plus 2d extra for the tin containing 50 of the matches; the sandpaper was free. He called the matches 'Congreves' in homage to the rocket pioneer, Sir William Congreve. His first sale and the first customer to strike a light was a Mr. Hixon, a solicitor. His daybook initially described the phenomenon as 'Sulphurata Hyper-Oxygenata Fric' which, no doubt for sound marketing reasons, he renamed as `Friction Lights'. His first matches were made of paste board, later replaced with three inch wood splints cut by elderly people hired by the chemist. In 1830 an intrigued Michael Faraday came to visit urging Walker to apply for a patent. The reasonably well off Walker did nothing and inevitably a man called Samuel Jones took out a patent for 'Friction Matches', branding the matches as 'Lucifers'. The devil, as ever, is in the detail…. Walker died in 1859 aged 78 and is buried in St. Mary's Church in Norton.

STOCKTON-ON-THE-FOREST
Stockaded enclosure from Old English stocc = tree stump; the forest is Galtres. Note the 'on' rather than the usual 'in'. North of York.

STOKESLEY
Called Stocheslage in the 11th century, Stokesley comes from stoke (wood) and ley (meadow). Stokesley Town Hall was built in 1853 in the Italian style by Colonel R. Hildyard to replace an earlier town hall and "ancient and unsightly" tollbooth where court sessions and market business took place. It also housed a reading room, Mechanics' Institution library and the Langbaurgh West Savings' Bank (£30,023 deposited there by 911 depositors in 1856). A market cross, destroyed in 1783 when a bonfire built to celebrate a naval victory got out of hand, stood in the small square behind. This was originally The Shambles, or butcher's market which comprised 24 butchers' shops; nearby was a fish market and a police station and lock-up where the police station now stands. The area in front of the town hall is known as The Plain; there was a butter market near here at one time. Stokesley has been plagued by floods over many years, notably in 1929 and 1976. In 1939 the Ministry of Defence commissioned Burness Ship Building Company to provide flat-bottomed tugboats for use in transferring troops across shallow waters. Flooding at Stokesley provided just the right conditions and so the town was chosen as the test centre in 1939. Residents were astonished to see HMS *Prima Prilius* cruising up and down the High Street one morning for over an hour; the cameras of enterprising photographers were confiscated.

The first white woman to settle in Victoria, Australia in 1836, Jane Pace (born 1817), was from Stokesley; in 1934 trees were planted on South Levenside in her memory. But more famous is John Wrightson, wise man or witch doctor, who was sentenced to gaol at Northallerton for his alleged crimes. The *Malton Messenger* of 5th September 1863 reported: "*He was taken away in a horse-drawn Black Maria and poisoned himself as it passed through Hovingham.*" Wrightson habitually wore flowing robes and a wizard's pointed hat adorned with astrological signs; it seems that he was nothing more than a harmless quack administering to the minor ailments of men and animals.

STORITHS
The plantations on Beamsley from the Old Norse. In 1190 it was Storthes de Bethmesleia. At Bolton Abbey.

STORTHWAITE
South east of York, meaning bullock field from Old English styric and Old Norse thveit.

STRENSALL
Strensall in the *Domesday Book* is Streonaeshalch, after Streona, a personal name, and halch, a corner of land. The name has changed over the years from Strenshale in the 11th century, to Stranessale in the 14th

century and to Strencile or Strencham alias Trencham in the 17th century. Strensall's association with the British Army began in 1876 when parts of Common and Lord's Moor were bought for military training for £300,000. Initially it was a camp for about 8,000 men living under canvas until the present permanent buildings were erected in 1880. A number of soldiers died from bronchitis and pneumonia as a result of the cold and damp conditions. The commandant in 1890 was Major General N. Stevenson. Today 160-170,000 troops pass through the barracks and the adjacent firing ranges every year on various training activites. The IRA detonated a bomb under a barrack hut here in the 1970s; fortunately it was unoccupied at the time and succeeded in only blowing up the instruments of the army band. North of York.

STRID, THE
The striding place (Old English). At Bolton Abbey, The Strid (SE064565) is a series of waterfalls and rapids at a deep underwater channel caused by the narrowing of the River Wharfe from 30 ft wide to the width of a long stride within 100 yards. It has been the scene of a number of fatalities in recent years.

STUDLEY ROGER
Near Ripon. From Old English/Old Norse stod = horse breeding place. It was held by Roger de Mowbray in 1288.

STUDLEY ROYAL
See above.

SULBER
The sunny hill (Old Norse sol +berg) – still a common name in Scandinavia. Near Settle this is a remote expanse of limestone pavement.

SUTTON ON THE FOREST
The southern farm on the forest. The Blackwell Ox pub here was originally a private residence built around 1823 for a Mary Shepherd. The name derives from a shorthorn Teeswater ox registered under the name of the Blackwell Ox, which was bred and raised by Christopher Hill. The ox was six feet tall and weighed 2278 lbs; when it was slaughtered and butchered in 1779 the meat fetched £109 11s 6d. Laurence Sterne was vicar here (1713–1768) but moved on to Coxwold when his parsonage burnt down. During his stay he published the first two books of *The Life and Opinions of Tristram Shandy, Gentleman*, possibly basing it on the village and its characters. The novel was published over ten years from 1759–1769.

SUTTON-UNDER-WHITESTONECLIFFE
The southern farm near the white stone cliff. It claims to be the longest place name in England with its 27 letters. The village is three miles east of Thirsk at the foot of Sutton Bank and named after nearby Whitestone Cliff. The crab wheel there is in fact a four-foot burrstone or millstone, mounted over a grinding pedestal. It was, according to Edmund Bogg in his *Richmondshire and the Vale of Mowbray* (Leeds, 1906), '*where was made from crab apples the vinegar known as verjuice, an obsolete industry*'. The manufacture of such stones is the origin of the saying that you can tell a hard-working man by his hands, which 'show his steel' – namely, the splinters of steel embedded in the stone-dresser's hands from the sparks. Verjuice is a very acidic condiment or sauce widely used in the Middle Ages and still used today in Iran and Australia. Sutton-under-Whitestone-Cliff is the village at the foot of the bank whose 1:4 incline still continues to cause problems for winter traffic today. It is said that in the early days of the motoring some drivers had to reverse up the bank. It takes the road from 120 metres above sea level to 300 metres in one mile. Above is where the Yorkshire Gliding Club operates: their altitude record is 30,200 feet.

Incidentally, the longest place name in the UK is, of course, Llanfair-pwllgwyn-gyllgo-gerychwyrn-drobwll-llanty-silio-gogogoch (58 letters), which means "Saint Mary's Church in the hollow of white hazel near a rapid whirlpool and the Church of Saint Tysilio near the red cave." The world's longest place name is in Porangahau on New Zealand's South Island: Tetaumata-whakatangihanga-koaua-o-tamatea-urehaeaturipuka-pihimaunga-horo-nuku-pokaiwhenuaa-kitana-rahu (92 letters). It means "The place where Tamatea, the man with the big knees, who slid, climbed, and swallowed mountains, known as land eater, played his flute to his loved one".

SWAINBY
Near Stokesley. Swainby is named after the swains who worked on the estate farms of West Laithes and West Leeths and who lived here. Roman coins found in the river suggest Roman activity of some sort. Swainby first appears in records in 1368 and its settlement may be due to the Black Death driving the ten surviving inhabitants down the hill from Whorlton in 1428. Ironstone and jet mining in the mid 1800s led to some local prosperity and a surge in population. Some of the cottages here go back as far as 1718. Nearby Scugdale was the birthplace of Elizabeth Harland who died in 1812 age 105 and of Henry Cooper a giant who grew to 8ft 6ins. The contemporary 1890 *North Riding Directory* tells us "this remarkable sample of humanity grew 13 inches in the space of 5 months." He went to London and joined Barnum & Bailey's circus touring the USA with them. He returned to England sporting the name Sir Henry Alexander Cooper but died aged thirty-two.

SWALE RIVER
The rushing river (Old English)

SWASTIKA STONE, THE
The Swastika Stone is a fascinating piece of rock art on the northern edge of Ilkley Moor, unique in British rock art. It is identical to some of the Camunian rose motifs found in Val Camonica, northern Italy and it seems likely that the Lingones troops who worshipped Verbeia may have come across the Camunian rose when they migrated across the Alps, and adopted the symbol, carving it on Ilkley Moor when two cohorts were stationed there in the 2nd and 3rd centuries. There is also a possible link between Verbeia and the goddesses Brigid and Brigantia. Brigid's cross is a common swastika-like image in Ireland, suggesting there may be an association here between Verbeia, imported Gaulish cults, and the swastika image.

SWINACOTE
Old English swin + Old Norse vath + Old English cot. The cottage by the ford where the swine cross.

SWINE
Old English swine. Near Hull.

SWINITHWAITE
The clearing made by burning – Old Norse switha + thveit. Near Aysgarth.

SWINTON
Pig farm near Malton. There is another near Masham.

TADCASTER
This may mean Tada's Caster, the land belonging to Tada on the site of a caster or Roman fort. In 1066 it was known as Tada. Tadcaster features in the Anglo-Saxon Chronicle as the place where King Harold assembled his army and fleet before entering York and then proceeding to the Battle of Stamford Bridge in 1066. Bede describes it as Kaelcacestir, civitatem Calcariam. The name Tata comes into play sometime in between Bede and the *Domesday Book*. The Calcaria pub in Westgate is named after the Roman name for Tadcaster and means place of the lime burners indicating the local importance of quarrying going as far back as Roman times, at the very least. The pub was originally called the Fleece.

Think of Tadcaster and you think of breweries and beer. The town has been brewing since 1341 but it really came into its own when domestic production was industrialised by the Smith family and others at the end of the 19th century leaving a legacy in the shape of Samuel Smith and John Smith, complemented today by a third, Molson Coors Brewing Company. Harry Speight, writing soon after Jackson, attests that beer was in the air: "*In our walks about Tadcaster certain odoriferous breezes make us conscious of the presence of these famous breweries... Tadcaster air is surcharged with the extract of malt.*"

TEES, RIVER
The name of the Tees originated from the time of the Celtic speaking Ancient Britons and related to the ancient Welsh 'Tes', meaning 'sunshine and heat' and means 'the seething, surging water'. 'Seething ' may describe the waterfalls and rapids common in upper Teesdale.

THICKET
Near Wheldrake on the Derwent; from Old English thicce thick + heafod = river headland with thick vegetation.

THIMBLEBY
The place belonging to a Viking called Thimmel. Near Osmotherley.

THIRKLEBY
A Viking name meaning Thurgill's village. Thirkleby High and Low with Osgodby is a civil parish consisting of the villages of Great Thirkleby, Little Thirkleby and Osgodby. The *Domesday Book* lists Thirkleby as Turchilebi in the Yarlestre hundred and belonging to the Coxwold manor.

THIRSK
Thirsk is Viking and derives from Thraesk meaning lake or fen. The cobbled area in the market place is the old thirty-foot bullring where all bulls and bullocks had, by law until 1754, to be baited by dogs before they were slaughtered. The Quaker Bartholomew Smith & Son was reputedly the first draper's to be established in Britain in 1580 – now demolished. Hall's Fleece Hotel is now the Golden Fleece. Hall was William Hall who took over the inn at the age of 21 in 1839. At the time, it was one of sixteen public houses in the Market Place. *Bulmer's 1890 Directory* lists five inns here: the Pheasant, the Rising Sun, the Wheat Sheaf, the Dolphin & Anchor and the Lord Nelson. Nelson is the sole survivor.

THIXENDALE
The *Domesday Book* has it as Sixtedale, Sixtendale and Xistendale. All mean Sixteen Dales and that is precisely where the village gets its name: from the sixteen dales that converge here. They are: Blubberdale, Broadholmedale, Buckdale, Bowdale, Breckondale, Courtdale, Fairydale, Fotherdale, Honeydale, Longdale, Middledale, Millamdale, Pluckamdale, Warrendale; Waterdale and Williedale. Thixendale is near Pocklington.

THOLTHORPE
Tholthorpe has Viking origins and is recorded in the *Domesday Book* as Turolfestorp and Turoluestorp. It is perhaps best known for its Second World War RAF station and, in particular, for the Canadian squadrons that flew Halifaxes and Lancasters from here from June 1943. Altogether, 119 Halifax bombers were lost from Tholthorpe. By way of commemoration there is a monument made from Canadian granite and an avenue of oaks and maples, which led from the village green to the airfield in honour of the fallen airmen. Near Easingwold.

THORALBY
Thorold's farm (Old Norse personal name Thoraldr + Old Norse). Toresbi in the *Domesday Book*. Near Aysgarth.

THORLBY

As above. Thorold's farm (Old Norse personal name + Old Norse). Torederbi in the *Domesday Book*. Properly Stirton with Thorlby. Near Skipton.

THORMANBY

Between Easingwold and Thirsk. Thormanby comes from the Old Norse personal name of Thormothr /þórmóðr (Tormod in modern Norwegian) and the suffix bi giving "Thormothr's farm". The name Thormothr means "Thor's gift" – "mind" and "courage"). The village features twice in the *Domesday Book* as "Tormozbi" in the Yarlestre Hundred.

THORNABY ON TEES

Thornaby was named after a Viking called Thormad or Thormoth. There has been a number of variant spellings including Turmozbi, Thormozbi and Tormozbia in the 11th century, followed by Thormodby, Thormodebi, Thormotebi, Thormotheby and Thormotby. Thornaby first appears in 1665; the town was eventually swallowed up by Stockton. When Robert de Thormodbi was wounded in the Crusades at Acre, he swore to raise a shrine to the Virgin Mary if he survived his wounds. He did survive, and placed a shrine to the Virgin Mary, lit by five sanctuary lamps, in St. Peter's Church here.

THORNTON LE BEANS

Thornton means a farm on a small hill with thorn bushes where beans were grown. In 1534 it was called Thornton-in-Fabis, Latin for Thornton-le-Beans. Bill Bryson said in his *Notes From a Small Island* that he wants to be buried in Thornton-le-Beans. Near Northallerton.

THORNTON (LE) DALE

One of Yorkshire's premier picture postcard villages near Pickering in a dale near the North Yorkshire Moors.

THORNTON RUST

Gets the second part of the name from St. Restitutus, the patron saint of the mediaeval chapel here, of which nothing now remains. The first part is derived from the combination of the Old English words of þorn and tūn, Thorn tree farm. Near Aysgarth. Torenton in the *Domesday Book* and Thorneton Ruske in 1153.

THORNTON STEWARD

In the 12th century Thornton Steward belonged to Wymar, the steward to the Earl of Richmond. Near Leyburn.

THORNTON WATLASS

Near Masham. Watlass means water less – or water meadow as there is little sign of a water shortage here.

THORP ARCH

Thorp Arch is mentioned in the *Domesday Book* as a mill used by brewers in Roman times. In 1744 John Shires discovered magnesian, limestone and sulphur springs and so made Boston a spa town known then as Thorp Spaw. It declined about the same time as Harrogate's fame was increasing.

During the Second World War Thorp Arch was the home of a Royal Ordnance Factory ammunition filling factory. It produced light, medium and heavy gun ammunition, landmines and trench mortar ammunition for the Army; medium and large bombs for the RAF; and 20mm and other small arms ammunition for all three services. Some of these were produced in millions and hundreds of millions of units. It finally closed in 1958 after the Korean War.

Part of the site now houses the Northern Reading Room, Northern Listening Service and Document

Supply Collection of the British Library. Over 100km of shelving is devoted to interlibrary loans. The rest of the site is occupied by Thorp Arch Trading Estate and two prisons, now combined with Wealstun Prison.

THORPE

The outlying farmstead (Old Norse thorp). Yorkshire has the following Thorpes: Thorpe, near Leconfield; Thorpe le Street, near Pocklington; Thorpe on the Hill, Leeds; Thorpe, near Grassington; Thorpe Willoughby, near Selby – in 1276 it was Thorp Wyleby from the Willeby family who lived here in the 13th century; Thorpe in Balne, near Doncaster; Thorpe Hesley, near Rotherham – famous for its mines and the manufacture of nails.

THREAPLAND

The land over which there is an ownership in dispute (Old Norse threap). Threpplandes in the 13th century. At Cracoe.

THRESHFIELD

Open land where threshing takes place (Old English thresc). Freschefelt in the *Domesday Book*. Near Grassington.

THURSGILL

The giant's or demon's ravine (Old Norse thurs + gil) Thursgile in 1220. Near Sedbergh.

THWAITE

A Viking name for meadow – thveit. In 1301 it was personalised to Arkeltwayt and became Arkle's wood. Near Muker.

TOCKWITH

This is Tocca's Vithr, the wood belonging to Tocca west of York. The *Domesday Book* has it as Tocvi. Tockwith is famous as a staging post for Oliver Cromwell before the Battle of Marston Moor in 1644. He referred to it as follows in his diaries: "*If heaven should be half as blessed as the fields of Tockwith, all those who should pass St. Peter's Gate shall be met with joys unequalled*".

TOLLERTON

Tollerton is near Easingwold. The name probably comes from the village's position at one of the toll entrances to the Forest of Galtres, where, according to Verstegan, travellers were given an armed guide to escort them as they travelled on to Bootham Bar, York. Gill, in his *Vallis Eboracensis*, adds, 'it [the forest] was the lurking place of large hordes of banditti, who dwelt in caves and lived upon rapine and plunder'. In the 17th century, the village was famous for horse racing on land close to the Great North Road. Drunken Barnaby, a celebrated road writer, tells us:

> 'Thence to Towlerton, where those stagers Or horses courses run for wagers; Near to the highway the course is, Where they ride and run their horses; But still on our journey went we, First or last did like content me.'

TOWTHORPE

One near Malton, another in between Haxby and Strensall. It simply means Tove's village.

TOWTON

Notorious for The Battle of Towton which took place on 29th March 1461 (Palm Sunday). It was a decisive victory for the Yorkists in the Wars of the Roses. Towton is the largest battle ever fought in Britain: between 50,000 and 80,000 soldiers took part including 28 lords– almost half the country's peerage. It was also the bloodiest battle ever fought in England with up to 28,000 casualties: roughly 1%

of the population of England at the time. More probably died in the aftermath than in the battle itself because neither side gave quarter and nearby bridges collapsed under the weight of the armed men. The worst slaughter was at Bloody Meadow, where fugitives are said to have crossed the River Cock using the bodies of the fallen as a bridge.

In August 1996 workmen uncovered a portion of a mass grave during building work at the Towton battlefield. A team of osteoarchaeologists and archaeologists from Bradford University and the West Yorkshire Archaeology Service recovered the more or less complete remains of 43 tightly packed casualties. Most had sustained multiple injuries from projectiles and hand-held weapons exceeding what is necessary to cause disability and death. The distribution of cuts and chops indicate that blows were largely concentrated in the craniofacial area, in some cases bisecting the face and cranial vault or detaching bone; in other cases the nose and ears had been sliced off. The injuries were apparently intended to sufficiently mutilate the bodies as to make them unidentifiable.

TRENCAR
This village near Kilburn gets its name from the cranes which flocked around the marsh here: Old Norse cran + Old Norse kjar, marshland.

TROLLERS GILL
The troll's arse ravine. Old Norse + Old English + Old Norse: troll + ears + gill. The Yorkshire Dales website http://www.yorkshire-dales.com/trollers-gill.html describes it best:

> Troller's Gill is a sinister little ravine at the head of Trollerdale near… Appletreewick… Legend has it that this narrow limestone gorge is the haunt of the "Barquest" or "Barguest" – the terrifying spectral hound of Craven (which is said to have "eyes as big as saucers", and which may have even given part of the inspiration for Sir Arthur Conan Doyle's Sherlock Holmes story *The Hound of the Baskervilles*). The nooks, caves and crannies of Troller's Gill are also said to be the home of Scandinavian trolls, evil bloodsucking gnomes, flesh-eating boggarts, hideous gargoyle-like rock sprites, deranged goblins, predatory pixies and maliciously twisted imps – and perhaps even other sorts of similarly diabolical and fiendishly unpleasant beings lying in wait for the unsuspecting rambler… The trolls in particular are said to hurl rocks down on passers-by walking through the ravine… Near the head of the gill there are a series of disused mine workings as well as natural caves and potholes – including the ominously named "Hell Hole". Troller's Gill is not a place to be visited alone.

The barquest can turn you to stone with just one look.
TROW GILL
The tree or troll's ravine (Old English + Old Norse). Near Clapham.

TUNNEL
See Grosmont.

TURF MOOR HUSH
The hush (a gouged out ravine made by miners) on the moor where turf (for fuel) was dug (Old English). At Langthwaite, in Arkengarthdale it is essentially the remains of a lead mining hush and shaft mounds dating from the 17th to early 19th century. NY992021.

TWISTLETON
The farmstead in a wedge of land formed by a river-fork (Old English twisla + ton). Twisilton in the *Domesday Book*. On Ingleborough.

UCKERBY
The home of a Ukkr – a restless Viking, Úkyrri or *Útkári. Uckerby is first recorded as Ukerby, in 1198. Near Northallerton.

UGGLEBARNBY
Owl beard's farm from uglubatthbi + by. Near Whitby.

ULDALE
The valley frequented by wolves (Old Norse ulfr + Old Norse/Old English).

ULFKIL CROSS
Ulkil's boundary stone arking the northern limit of Malham Moor; erected by monks from Fountains Abbey.

ULLESKELF
Ulleskelf, derived from the Scandinavian, refers to Ulfr's shelf of land. In the *Domesday Book* Ulleskelf was known as Oleschel and was part of the Archbishop of York's land. In 1066 at the Battle of Fulford Earl Edwin of Mercia moored his boats at Ulleskelf to prevent the invading army reaching York. November 1906 saw a collision between two trains in which the driver and firemen were both killed. In 1981 the 13.50 York to Liverpool train left the track at 70 mph here and careered down the embankment. Twenty-two passengers required hospital treatment. An incident on 4th October 2010 involved a 'bovine incursion' (cows on the line to you and me) when two cows were killed. Ulleskelf is near Tadcaster.

UNCLEBY
Hunkel's farm. Near Pocklington.

UNTHANK
The name comes from the Anglo-Saxon Unthances, and refers to a farm once occupied by squatters. This village near Constable Burton no longer exists.

UPLEATHAM
This name means the upper slopes. Upleatham is most famous for the minute 12th century church of St. Andrew which is reportedly the smallest church in England. Not so: Bremilham Church in Wiltshire is 4 metres by 3.6 metres. Upleatham is about 6 metres by 4 metres. Near Redcar.

UPPER POPPLETON
Poppleton means the pebbly farm. There is a Nether Poppleton nearby. The name is derived from popel (pebble) and tun (hamlet, farm) and means "Pebble Farm" denoting the gravel bed upon which the village was built. Upper Poppleton has been called "Land Poppleton" and Nether Poppleton as "Water Poppleton" indicating their position in relation to the River Ouse. Near York. The village features in the 972 *Anglo-Saxon Chronicles* as Popeltun and in the *Domesday Book* as Popeltune. A mayor of York was murdered here during the reign of Richard II. In 1644 the Earl of Manchester's 25,000-strong Parliamentary army built a bridge of boats at Poppleton, later taken by Prince Rupert and his Royalist Forces.

UPSALL
A Viking name from Up-Salir meaning high dwellings. It has the same meaning as the university city of Uppsala in Sweden. Near Thirsk.

URE, RIVER
An old Celtic name related to the Gaulish river name Isura. The holy river, or the strong river from the Celtic river-name, Isura, which means 'power', be it physical or spiritual. Yure is an early form of

Yoredale, an alternative name for Wensleydale.

URRA MOOR
Urra Moor is the highest moor in the North York Moors at 1,454 ft. NZ594015.

WAKEFIELD
The field belonging to Wacca. Alternatively, it could derive from the Old English wacu, meaning "a watch or wake", and feld, an open field in which a wake or festival was held. In the *Domesday Book*, it is given as Wachefeld and Wachefelt.

Wakefield was known as the "Merrie City" in the Middle Ages and in 1538 John Leland described it as, *"a very quick market town and meately large; well served of fish and flesh both from sea and by rivers... so that all vitaile is very good and chepe there. A right honest man shall fare well for 2d. a meal.... There be plenti of se coal in the quarters about Wakefield".*

The Hepworth in Wakefield, named in honour of local sculptor Barbara Hepworth opened in May 2011 and has added about £10 million to the local economy by attracting 500,000 visitors in its first year. Nursery rhymes associated with Wakefield are *Here We Go Round the Mulberry Bush* sung by women inmates at Wakefield Prison and *The Grand Old Duke of York* which may allude to the Battle of Wakefield in 1460 and Richard Plantagenet, the 3rd Duke of York. The lyrics of *Onward Christian Soldiers* were written at St. Peter's Church in nearby Horbury. Wakefield is the capital of the Rhubarb Triangle.

WALBURN
A Swaledale village whose name means where the foreigners (Welshman) live by the stream. From Old English weala + burna.

WALSHFORD
A Nidderdale village whose name means ford of the Welshmen.

WARLABY
From Wareloga's by: the village of the traitor. Near Northallerton.

WARRENTOWN
Iron and steel came to Redcar in 1873 when Downey & Co built the Coatham Iron works one mile from Coatham; Walker, Maynard & Co then built four furnaces at the Redcar Works employing about 200 men. In 1873 Robson had replaced Walker and built Warrentown, a new village of 200 or so good houses in terraces of seven with small gardens and a fence. Allotments were also laid out for the cultivation of potatoes and the keeping of pigs. Streets were Tod Point Road, Downey and Coney Streets. The name was changed to Warrenby to make it more in keeping with the Danish antecedents and the villages around which shared the suffix 'by'. The Dorman Long & Co steelworks were built in 1916-1917 after Dorman Long had taken over the old Warrenby Works and introduced new mixers, furnaces and plate mills. At its peak the works employed over 5,000 men; Redcar's 'Garden City' was built at Dormanstown for the workers.

The horrific thirteen boiler explosion at Walker, Maynard & Co's Redcar Ironworks in Warrenby occurred on June 14th 1895 when eleven workers died and eleven others were seriously injured. The disaster led to concerted charitable efforts to compensate those affected and made good the inadequate assistance provided by friendly societies, the only insurance available to most at the time. After a series of fund-raising events the fund was able to pay widows 2s 6d, 1s 6d to orphans under ten years and 2s to orphans over ten and under fourteen. The injured were similarly compensated.

WARTER

Near Pocklington. The village retains its original cast-iron street lights. Pevsner, in his York and the East Riding volume says, '*Warter is a curious village, perversely attractive... a very pretty row of thatched cottages... for the rest it has fiercely Victorian houses... always accompanied by bulging topiary*'. David Hockney's *Bigger Trees Near Warter*, or, to give it its alternative title, *Peinture en Plein Air pour l'age Post-Photographique* is Hockney's largest painting at 15 feet by 40 feet; it was painted between February and March 2007 and made this picturesque village world famous. Its subject is a copse of trees bursting into life in spring. The title refers to Hockney's technique: painting outside and in front of the subject (sur le motif), incorporating digital photography. In 2008, Hockney donated the work to the Tate Modern.

WARTHILL

Near York – beacon hill from Old English vartha +Old English hill.

WASS

This derives from an Anglo-Saxon word meaning swamp. Officially, Byland with Wass. Near Helmsley.

WATH UPON DEARNE

Wath is listed in the *Domesday Book* as Wad. The origin of its name lies in the Latin vadum or the Old Norse vath meaning ford or wading place. Near Rotherham.

WEEL

Near Beverley, gets its name from Old English wael: deep place on the river. Weel is on the River Hull.

WENSLEY

Once called Wodensley, it means the ley or clearing dedicated to Woden. Near Leyburn on the River Ure. Wendreslaga in the *Domesday Book*.

WENSLEYDALE

The valley with Waendel's woodland clearing (Old English personal name + Old English + Old Norse). Unusually named after a village and not the river. Sometimes called Yoredale.

WESTON

The farm west of Otley. The Redcar lifeboat, the *Emma Dawson* features, unusually, in a window in All Saints' Church in Weston. It was commissioned by the National United Order of Free Gardeners to honour Emma Dawson of Weston Hall after she died in 1880. The Redcar lifeboat crew at the time reciprocated by erecting a wall tablet in gratitude for her support. The death of her husband had made Emma Dawson a wealthy widow and a benefactor of some repute. Every Whit Monday she would go to Redcar where she was well known for her generosity and public spiritedness, particularly towards Redcar's fishermen and their families. In 1858 the existing lifeboat, the *Zetland*, was consigned to the scrapheap by the RNLI although, after much local protest, they relented and allowed the townspeople to make repairs and keep her in service. The problem would not go away, however, and the RNLI persisted in their efforts to replace the *Zetland*. Despite this, the Free Gardeners intervened in 1875 to raise money for a new boat, designed along the lines of the *Zetland*, much to the annoyance of the RNLI who had their own designs. A £600 non-RNLI specification boat and a £700 boathouse, with a fishermens' clubhouse above, were duly built with substantial donations from Emma Dawson and Lord Zetland. The launch took place in 1877 before nearly 20,000 people.

WEST TANFIELD

R. Murray Gilchrist, in his Ripon and Harrogate volume of *Beautiful England* says of this village, '*Of all the places of interest near Ripon none exceeds in loveliness the village of Tanfield. The view from the bridge over the Ure is one of the most charming in England...a wonderful harmony of rich colour.'* The name comes from the Old English tāna feld, meaning "open land where young shoots grow", or possibly "open land of a man called Tana". The village is in the *Domesday Book* as Tanefeld.

WEST WITTON

West Witton means the western woodland farm. The name comes from the Anglo-Saxon Widu-Ton. The village is famous for "Burning of Bartle" ceremony held in August each year. A giant effigy of 'Bartle' is paraded around the village, complete with flaming eyes. Bartle stops at various places to recite the doggerel, before finally being burnt at Grassgill End to much merriment. The doggerel runs:

> On Penhill Crags he tore his rags; Hunter's Thorn he blew his horn; Capplebank Stee happened a misfortune and brak' his knee; Grisgill Beck he brak' his neck; Wadham's End he couldn't fend; Grassgill End we'll mak' his end. Shout, lads, shout.

East Witton is in nearby Coverdale.

WETHERBY

A farm or village where wethers (castrated rams) were kept; alternatively, "settlement on the bend of a river". Wetherby is in the *Domesday Book* as Wedrebi. During the First World War Wharfedale Brewery here was requisitioned to billet troops, and then taken over by Oxleys mineral water company. In 1943 it used to make Coca Cola for the many American troops in the area. As an important staging post on the London to Edinburgh route (it is 198 miles equidistant from London to Edinburgh) Wetherby had its fair share of inns, coaching and post houses. The Angel Inn was one of nine listed in the 1776 census in the High Street with a further three in Market Place and three others in the town. The Angel could boast a smithy and shoeing shop. Between the Angel and the Swan and Talbot there were 25 servants employed.

WETWANG

Wetwang is east of York. The meaning of its name is disputed: one theory is that at first it means 'the Wet field' deriving from the Viking word vangr and the Old English word 'wet'. Wetwangha, Wetwanghe, Wetwange and Wetwong are early forms. Others claim that the name derives from the Viking vaettvangrr meaning the field of summons for the trial of an action. Five miles to the east of Wetwang is Driffield, a name which means a dry field although some prefer dirty field or stubbly field. The village is renowned for its Iron Age chariot burial cemetery at Wetwang Slack and its black swans. The village is recorded in the *Domesday Book* as Wetuuangha.

WHAM

The marshy hollow, nook or valley from Old English hwamm or Old Norse hvammer. A 13th century reference gives Quane. Near Giggleswick.

WHARFE

A corner of land, bend, (Old Norse) and nothing to do with the River Wharfe. It is near Austwick and is the only settlement in Crummackdale, the upper valley of Austwick Beck which runs through Wharfe into the River Wenning which in turn joins the River Lune. Moughton Fell looms behind the hamlet at a height of 1,400 ft.

WHARFE RIVER

The winding river (Old English 'weorf', British uerb, or Old Norse 'hverfr'). Called Weorfe in 963.

WHARFEDALE

The valley of the winding River Wharfe – the winding river. In the 12th century it was Hwerverdale.

WHARRAM LE STREET

A village near Malton. The name means at the bends from Old Norse hvarfum, bends. The affix "le-Street" tells us that the village is on the course of a former Roman road. St. Mary's Church has a Saxon tower; the rest of the church is Norman. Just up the road is…

WHARRAM PERCY

Our best preserved and researched of Britain's 3,000 or so known deserted medieval villages. The *Domesday Book* records it as Warran or Warron.

Wharram Percy was continuously occupied for about 600 years. It was founded in the 9th or 10th century and flourished between the 12th and early 14th centuries when members of the Percy family lived in the village. By the early 16th century it was almost deserted due to gradual abandonment and evictions.

WHAW

A hamlet in Arkengarthdale meaning the enclosure near the sheep fold from Old Norse kvi + hagi. In 1280 it was Kiwawe.

WHENBY

North of York; Quennebi in the *Domesday Book*. From Old Norse kvenna = of women and another example of women giving their name to villages.

WHERNSIDE

The hillside where querns or millstones were found (Old English cweorn + side).

WHITBY

The name Whitby is Viking and could mean White village, but is more probably Hvitabyr -the village belonging to a Viking settler called Hviti. Early variations of the name include Witebi, Witeby and Wytebia as well as Quiteby and Qwyteby, indicative of different pronunciations. Before the Vikings Whitby was called Streanaeshalch, a Saxon or Celtic name of unknown meaning. Streanaeshalch was the site of an Anglo-Saxon monastery founded by St. Hilda, who came here from Hartlepool in 650 AD. St. Hilda's monastery was the home of Caedmon, the Anglo-Saxon poet who has been described as the man "who laid the first great temple of English poetry". In 664 AD Streanaeshalch was the venue for the Synod of Whitby, a meeting held by Oswy, the King of Northumbria, to decide whether his kingdom should adhere to Celtic or Roman teachings of Christianity. The meeting was attended by the king along with St. Cuthbert, St. Wilfrid and St. Colman of Lindisfarne. St. Wilfrid, siding with Roman cause persuaded Oswy to abandon the Celtic Christianity in favour of new Roman ways. For centuries after Roman Catholocism remained the religion of northern England, despite the best efforts of the rapacious Vikings who attacked the monastery at Streanaeshalch and other Christian centres in 870 AD. Places nearby include Murk Head – dark hill from Old Norse myrkr and Ling Hill, heather hill from Old Norse lyng, heather.

WHITE MARE CRAG

Like nearby Lake Gormire, White Mare Crag near Sutton Bank is surrounded in mystery and is the subject of many mysterious tales. One tale involves a witch who was fleeing across the moor. When she reached White Mare Crag she took a running jump and landed in Gormire Lake, which is bottomless and conceals a lost village. The witch was swept along in an underwater current and eventually emerged from a well over nine miles away. There is a similar tale concerning a goose that was dropped into the lake from the cliffs. It too was caught in an underwater stream and emerged in Kirkbymoorside, twelve miles east of Gormire, had been stripped of all its feathers during its journey.

The cliff gets its name from the final two stanzas of the rather prolix poem by Edmund Bogg in *From Eden Vale to the plains of York or A Thousand Miles in the Valleys of the Nidd and Yore* published around 1894.

"And the waters of Gormire, once sparkling and bright, To the blackness of ink were changed in that night; But whether because of the abbot or Nightwind, Tho' I've searched all the records I never could quite find. But the cliff where the white mare met such disaster Was bleached suddenly white as the lawn of her master. And still the good folks of the valley below, When the mist like a curtain hangs from the brow Of the white steep, declare That a terrified mare Will leap from the cliff, and melt into air."

WHORLTON
The *Domesday Book* tells us that Whorlton was a place of some importance; it was originally Whorl Hill or Worm Hill named after the giant worm that lived there terrorising the locals until a baron from the castle slew it. The motte and bailey in the original wooden castle was built by Robert de Meynell on the site of a Brigantian fortification and a later Roman fort. By 1343 it was "ruinous" and rebuilt in stone later in the century by John Darcy. By the late 1500s it was dilapidated again. The plot to marry Mary, Queen of Scots to Lord Darnley was hatched here. A hoard of 4th century AD silver Roman coins and other artefacts was discovered in 1810. In 1956 Len Willison rented Whorlton Castle for £2 per year and used it to keep free range chickens. Up the hill from Swainby.

WIDDALE
The wooded valley (Old Norse vithr +dalr. Withdale in 1213. Widdale is a tributary valley feeding into Wensleydale above Hawes.

WIGGLESWORTH
Wincel's enclosure (Old English personal name + Old English). The *Domesday Book* had it as Winchelesuuorde. Near Settle.

WILLITOFT
North of Howden, it means home near the willows, Old English willig.

WINSKILL
The windy (vindr) shieling in Old Norse. A 1414 reference gives it as Wyndescale. Near Settle, Winskill Stones is a seventy-four acre area of limestone grassland and limestone pavement.

WINTERBURN
The stream which flows only in the winter months. Old English winter + burna. Near Grassington.

WOODALE
The valley where wolves (wulf) live (Old English + Old Norse). Wulvedale in 1203. A hamlet in Coverdale not be confused with Woodale in the parish of Stonebeck Up in upper Nidderdale a mere four miles away.

WORTON
The herb or vegetable garden (Old English wyrt-tun). Werton in the *Domesday Book*y. Near Bainbridge.

WOMBLETON
Originally called Wimbleton, it means Wynbald's farm. Near Pickering.

WYCLIFFE
Derives from the Withclif. 'With' was an old word for a bend, so cliffe or hill on a bend in the River Tees. Near Barnard Castle.

WYKEHAM

Near Scarborough this means small settlement near a Roman outpost, from Old English wicham.

YAFFORTH

Yafforth derives from Ea-ford. Ea is an ancient word for river – so River Ford. The river in this case is the Wiske. Near Northallerton.

YARM

Yarm, on the south bank of the Tees, was once the premier port on the river. Here industries included ropemaking, brewing, tanning and shipbuilding. In the 17th century Yarm's role as a port was superceeded by Stockton and later Middlesbrough. For many centuries Yarm was called Yarum, a name deriving from the Anglo Saxon gear, pronounced yair, a pool for catching fish. The um on the end of the original name Yarum forms an Anglo-Saxon plural, so Yarm means fish pools. According to a humorous song, the Tees winds around Yarum, to keep out County Durham. The river may have served a defensive purpose in historic times but it has also caused problems, inundating the town on several occasions.. A marker on Yarm Town Hall shows the seven feet height of the 1771 flood. *Ord's History of Cleveland* (1846) describes Yarms problematic setting – *Yonder Fair Yarm, extended in the vale, along the Tees as in a circle lies, ill fated spot, by inundation torn.*

The town played a starring role in the birth of the railway in Britain. On February 12th 1821, a meeting was held at the George & Dragon Inn successfully calling for a Bill to grant permission to build the Stockton & Darlington Railway. The grand 2,280 feet (nearly half a mile) long railway viaduct was built between 1849 and 1851 for the Leeds Northern Railway Company. It took seven million bricks and has 43 arches – the two spanning the river are skewed. It was built to extend the Leeds and Thirsk railway from Northallerton to Stockton and Hartlepool. In 1855, three years after the opening, a train overshot the platform on a very stormy and dark night: an unsuspecting passenger got out of his carriage and stepped over the parapet, falling the 74 feet to his death. The inquest recommended that 'some fencing be erected'.

YEARBY

Near Redcar, derives from the Viking Efri + by meaning upper village.

YOCKENTHWAITE

The thwaite or meadow belonging to an Irish Viking called Eogan. Near Buckden.

YORK

The root of the early name was an Ancient British personal name suggesting that the site was founded by someone called Eburos. An alternative theory is that the name is based on the Ancient British word Eburos meaning yew, a sacred Celtic tree from which the personal name Eburos derives. During the Roman occupation there was a Gaulish tribe called the Eburorovices – the 'Warriors of the Yew Tree'. When the Anglo-Saxons replaced the Romans in the 6th century they made Eboracum the capital of Deira, a Northumbrian sub-kingdom. Eboracum was corrupted by Anglo-Saxon speech into Eoforwic meaning 'wild boar settlement'. In 876 Halfdene the Dane made Eoforwic the capital of the Viking Kingdom of York. The Vikings interpreted Eoforwic, the Anglo-Saxon name for York as Jorvik. In the late Viking period the name Jorvik was shortened to something like York, although 'Yerk' is also known.

The Street Names of York

York has some delightful, and fascinating street and snickelway names. It is a city where gates are streets and bars are gates.

Names such Munecagate, Walbegate, and Fiscergate (Monkgate, Walmgate, Fishergate) first appear in a document of about 1080, so most names in York were probably established by that date. Typical Scandinavian names are Stonegate (12th century, 'Steingate' from *steinn gata*, stone-paved street), Skeldergate (shield-makers' street from *skjaldari*), Coppergate (joiners' street, *koppari*), Blossom Street (13th century 'Ploxwangate' *plógr* sveinn, ploughswain) and Blake Street (*bleikr*, white). The medieval 'Ketmangergate' comes from the Scandinavian *kjotmangari*, fleshmonger. Bootham is usually linked with *búdum*, the dative plural of *búd* and derives from something like *farmanna búdum* – 'merchants' booths' – after 1089 when St. Mary's Abbey was founded and the abbey's weekly market grew up there. A word of caution, though, *búd* is widely used for any kind of dwelling or building and has no linguistic exclusivity to merchants' booths. Nevertheless, York's place- and street-names are clearly more Scandinavian than those of any other major town in Britain.

Here is a random selection and their, sometimes putative, derivations and histories:

Aldwark	old works, walls;
Bedern	named after the chapel – a place of bidding;
Blake Street	either from bleke, white paved road, or from the Norse bleg, indicating the Viking leather trade and bleaching;
Blossom Street, formerly Ploxamgate, Ployhsuaingate and Ploxswaingate	street of the ploughmen;
Bootham	street of the market stall holders. This elegant street was originally called Galman. No. 49 was owned by Joseph Rowntree – Lady Johnstone's Mansion – it cost £4, 500 and included six acres of land; it was later taken over by Bootham School. WH Auden's house was opposite.
Brettegate	the 12th-century 'Brettegate' (later Jubbergate) derives from Old Norse Bretar (Britons) and refers to the Cumbrian Britons who accompanied the Irish Vikings.
Brownie Dyke (on the Foss close to Castle Mills)	brun eau dyke – brown water dyke;
Buckingham Street	named after George Villiers, Duke of Buckingham.
Carr's Lane	after architect John Carr;
Church Street	originally Girdlergate – girdle-makers' street;
Coffee Yard	took this name (after Langton Lane) when the coffee houses started to spring up;
College Street	formerly Little Alice Lane and then Vicar Lane – the vicars speak for themselves, not so little Alice; she was possibly an old lady who ran an alehouse there in the 1730s.
Collier Street	after the charcoal burners;
Coney Street	King Street but also Cunny Street in 1622;
Coppergate	nothing to do with copper or cooper, but rather street of the joiners or turners;
Cromwell Road	after Oliver; previously Gaol Lane, after the jail in Bitchdaughter Tower;
Davygate	named after David le Lardiner – clerk of the royal kitchen;

Elbow Lane	describes its crookedness;
Fairfax Street	named after Thomas, Lord Fairfax, the Parliamentarian general whose house was in Skeldergate
Feasegate	Norse for cow house street;
Fetter Lane	Feltergayle, felt workers' street;
Fishergate Postern	previously the Talkan Tower – posternam iuxta Skarletpit – dates from 1502 and is York's only surviving example;
Footless Lane	possibly a reference to the disabilities of some of the patients at nearby St. Leonard's Hospital; later Museum Street (qv); see also Fotlousgeyle
Goodramgate	(12th century: 'Gutherungata') is Gutherun's street;
Grape Lane	the place for a grope;
Hornpot Lane	where the horn and comb breakers worked;
Hungate	originally Hundegat in Mersch = Dog Street in the Bog, formerly Dunnyngdykes = Dung Dump;
Jewbury	or Jew's burh, where the Jews lived;
Jubbergate	Brettegate in the 12th century after the Bretons who lived here (see also Navigation Road); Joubrettgate in 1280 when the Jews moved in; see Brettegate.
King's Court	appears in the 13th century as 'Kuningesgard', a name connected with the *Konungs-gardr* of *Egil's Saga*, referring to the residence of Eric Bloodaxe in York;
King Street	once Kergate, meaning muddy street;
Lady Peckett's Yard	after Lady Mayoress Alice Peckett; formerly Bacusgail or Back House Lane, and Trichourgail, street of the tricksters;
Layerthorpe	hamlet where the deer congregate; a reference to the Forest of Galtres on the edge of the city;
Lendal	formerly Aldeconyngstrete or Old Coney Street. Lendal is a contraction of Landing Hill – a reference to St. Leonard's Landing, a staithe or landing on the Ouse used to import stone for the building of the Minster;
Lord Mayor's Walk	formerly Goose Lane; opened in 1718 in a grand ceremony to mark its elegance;
Mad Alice Lane	named after Alice Smith, a resident hanged for the crime of being insane in 1825.
Micklegate	Great Street; originally Myglagata;
Minster Gates	formerly Bookland Lane and Book-binders Lane in the 16th century;
Mucky Peg Lane	named after a resident of ill repute; other etymologies derive from Pig rather than Peg;
Museum Street	in the 13th century Ffotelsgate or Footless Lane (qv); then Finkle Street and in the 17th century Back Lendal and Little Lendal in 1782;
Navigation Road	after the Foss Navigation; in the 13th century it was Little Brettgate – another street of the Bretons, French traders;
North Street	Nordstreta, one of the few streets to have retained the Anglo Saxon strete rather than adopting the Norse gata or gayle;
Nunnery Lane	after the convent, once Beggargate;

Ogleforth	simply Ugel's place;
Parliament Street	after the Act of Parliament of 1833 which allowed for the market here
Pavement	The *Domesday Book* has it as Marketshyre; Pavement is called thus because around 1329 it was the only clear piece of paved land in the centre of the city. Paving was unusual then. Before that it was called Marketshire and was the site of markets, proclamations and public punishments in days when the punishment was made, and seen, to fit the crime: for example, drunks were made to stand on barrels with pint pots on their heads and goose thieves were put in the stocks with goose wings draped unceremoniously around their necks. Catholic Thomas Percy, Earl of Northumberland, was executed here in 1572 for his opposition to Elizabeth I. The superb Market Cross was demolished in 1813 to make room for more market stalls.
Peasholme Green	place where peas were grown; later the site of the wool market;
Piccadilly	created in 1840 and named after Piccadilly in London;
Pope's Head Alley	a reference to a papal effigy here?
Shambles	originally 'in Macello' – the first of many names; Shambles = street of the butchers
Silver Street	after the fish in the fish market;
Skeldergate	from the Norse skjaldari, Shield Makers Street;
Spen Lane	once Ispyn Lane and Isping Giel, referring to the aspens growing here;
Spurriergate	street of the spur makers;
St. George's Fields	York's ducking stool was here – for scoundrels and women who sold short measures or bad beer, and '*scolds and flyters*'. The gallows nearby attracted large crowds, some coming by special train excursions as late as 1862.
St. Maurice's Road	once Barker Hill – street of tanners and parchment makers – both used bark to make tannin; in 1340 the ramparts here were called Herlot Hill after the local beggars. By the eighteenth century it was Love Lane or Harlot Hill denoting it as a denizen of prostitutes;
St. Saviourgate	formerly Ketmongergate or flesh seller street;
Stonebow	stone arch, possibly Roman; once Whitefriar Lane after the Carmelite friary here;
Stonegate	By common consent one of the finest streets in England, if not Europe, and York's first 'foot-street'; it was pedestrianised in 1971, paving the way for many more. You can still see the gallows sign of the Olde Starre Inne stretching across the street. Stonegate was once famous for its coffee shops (hence Coffee Yard). The old Roman stone paving – hence the name - survives under the cobbles complete with the central gulley for the chariots' skid wheels. It was the Roman *Via Praetoria*. Queen Mary, wife of George V, when living at Goldsborough Hall near Knaresborough, was a frequent shopper here in the 1920s and 30s: unfortunately for the shop owners she was a devotee of 'honouring' – the practice whereby patronage alone was considered sufficient payment for the goods she left the shops with.
Swinegate	originally Patrick Pool then Swyngaill after the pig houses and the 1605 pig market;
Tanner Row and **Tanner's Moat**	signified the tanneries located around here
Thief Lane	the road along which convicted robbers were led to the scaffold at Garrow Hill

Thursday Market	The square was the venue for the Thursday hardware market and boasted a fine market cross until its pointless demolition in 1705. Plays were staged here on the upper floor. It was described by CB Knight in his *A History of the City of York* (1944) *"In 1429 a new stone cross had been erected in Thursday Market…This Cross was described by a writer in 1683 as "a fair Cross of stone, built upon the ascent of five steps, and hath neatly cut in stone a turret or battlement eight square, upon which is placed a round pillar with a four-square stone upon the top, which hath a sundial placed upon every square, and a vane above. The Cross hath a penthouse round about it, covered over with tile, to shelter the market people in rainy weather, and is supported upon eight posts, upon one of which, on the south side, is fixed an iron yard-wand, the standard measure of the market." In 1705 the ancient Market Cross…was pulled down."*
Tower Street	originally Castlegate Postern Lane after Castlegate Postern since demolished; site of the ducking stool;
Victor Street	after Victoria Bar in 1838; once St. Mary's Road after the church and Lounelithgate: hidden gateway.
Water Lane	Duke 'Butcher' Cumberland on his victorious return from bloody Culloden left a number of prisoners here to show his gratitude for the city's hospitality: the Sheriff's chaplain read out the message: *'And the Lord said unto Moses "Take all the heads of the people and hang them up before the sun"'*. Twenty-three were duly left to hang for ten minutes, stripped and quartered, their heads stuck on Micklegate Bar. Water Lane was renamed Cumberland Street after the butcher Duke.
Whipmawhopmagate	what is quite remarkable is the mix of languages represented: Latin, Anglo Saxon, Norse, Early English, Early German, Norman French – all tracking the city's history over time. Some say it was the place where dogs called whappets were whipped on St. Lukes Day.

Some Lost Streets of York

Beggergate	the bag maker's street – now called Nunnery Lane.
Bookbinders' Court	after the bookshops and publishers in the area – now Minster Gates.
Cargate	former name of King Street running from Coney Street to King's Staith; it means the marshy street.
Divlinstones	a lane that led from North Street to the Ouse comes from Scandinavian *Dyflinn* (Dublin), and was coined by Vikings from Ireland;
Fotlousgeyle (i.e. 'Footless Lane')	the place where the Master of St. Leonard's Hospital kept the crippled poor from about 1100;
Galmanhowe	Galman's high ground near St. Mary's Abbey;
Glover Lane	a street near Petergate where glove makers worked;
Girdlegate	now Church Street; the girdle makers' street;
Golmanlythe	Golman's gate in Bootham;
Graypecuntlane	nothing to do with grapes; now Grape Lane though.
Hartergate	(12th century 'Hertergate'; 16th century 'Hatterlane'; now Friargate), which derives from either *hjartar* ('hart's street') or from the personal name *Hojrtr*, the street belonging to a Viking called Hjartar.

Haymongergate	part of the Shambles: the hay merchant's street.
Ketmongergate	now St. Saviourgate, a Viking street: the flesh-sellers street.
Langton Lane	after Johannis de Langton; now Coffee Yard.
Lop Lane or **Flea Alley**	demolished around 1864 to create Duncombe Place. It was named after Dean Augustus Duncombe who himself subscribed £1,000 to help finance the project. St. Wilfrid's Church was completed in 1864.
Lund's Court	once Mad Alice Lane – after a mad lady called Alice.
Marsh Street	a street leading to a marsh near Hungate.
Mucky Peg Lane	now Finkle Street.
Thursday Market	the Golden Lion has gone and the shops have changed hands but the Three Cranes and what is the Roman Bath remain. The square was a slave market in late Roman times. During the Civil War Cromwell's army *'shot well nigh forty Hot Fiery bullets'* into the square, one of which *'slewe a maide'*. The sign on The Three Cranes pub in the square is designed to mislead: the pub is named after the lifting gear used by stallholders rather than anything ornithological. Previous names of the Roman Bath are the Cooper, the Barrell Churn and the Barrell in the late 18th century and the Mail Coach after that for 140 years.

Other Curious Yorkshire Streets

Yorkshire delights in curious and intresting street names. They are by no means confined to York; here is a small selection from the rest of the county.

HULL
Where better to start than in **The Land of Green Ginger**, joyously named after the herb garden here? Less aromatic was **Rotten Herring Street** which speaks, and smells, for itself – something which has characterised the city for centuries with its frozen fish industry. But we may be jumping to conclusions: John Rotenhering lived here in 1350 and has **Rotten Herring Staith** named after him. Who knows if he ever stank of rotting fish? **Whitefriargate** (Carmelites) and **Blackfriargate** (Dominicans) evidence Hull's religious, monastic past. You played bowls in **Bowlalley Lane** and made daggers in **Dagger Lane** (**Daggardlane** in the 14th century).

BEVERLEY
There's a **Bull Ring** and a **Hengate** hinting at the livestock bought and sold here. **Walkergate** is nothing to do with hikers but tells us about the cloth fulling which went on; **Wednesday Market** and **Saturday Market** are self explanatory while **Toll Gavel** is the place were tolls were collected (Old English toll + gafol = tribute, rent). **Flemingate** is where the people from Flanders tended to live while **Loundress** or **Londoners Lane** (and **Londiners Street** in 1660) is the place for London folk. As in York, gates are everywhere with **Keldgate** (the site of a spring from Old Norse kelda), **Ladygate** (where the church of Our Lady is) and **Lairgate** leading to a barn, from Old Norse hlatha. You may not have wanted to go down **Hellgarth Lane** (a haunted field or denizen of criminals), or indeed **Lurk Lane** – a somewhat unsalubrious part of town, frequented by unsalubrious characters.

HEDON
Occupations abound with **Fletcher Gate** (Middle English flessher for butcher); **Bakster Gate** (Old English baecere for baker) and **Souttergate** (Middle English souter for shoemaker).

MARKET WEIGHTON
Dogs were kept in **Hungate**.

MASHAM
Badger Lane has nothing to do with badgers – rather it signifies the market there where people were badgered.

PICKERING
Saltergate was at the end of the salt road from Saltburn for local salt workers.

RICHMOND
The Frenchness of Richmond is reflected in *Frenchgate* – a French and Scandinavian compound name. **Bargate** signifies barley crops while **Ankirkirk** is church of the anchorites. **Gallowgate** is of course the doomy one way street leading to the gallows.

RIPON
More cheerful are **Blossomgate** and **Horsefair** – both self-explanatory.

SCARBOROUGH
The town has its **Carter Gate** – the street of the carriers, **Sandgate,** the road to the beach and, delightfully, **Dumple Street** indicating a hole in the river bed or pond (from Old English dumpel or dump).

REDCAR
Rocket Street describes the lifeboat rocket station here.

KNARESBOROUGH
Chain Lane and **Tentergate** are areas of a particular industry although less obvious are **Dumb Pots Lane** and **Sweet Bits Lane**. Tentergate is an area associated with weavers, mainly of linen, the cloth being stretched out to dry on tenter frames (cf. 'to be on tenterhooks', from old French tendre, to stretch). Originally, this was part of the separate township of Scriven-with-Tentergate. In **Gracious Street**: there have been (and still are) several places of worship on or near Gracious Street – United Reform Church, Quaker, Methodist and Anglican – it has been incorrectly assumed that 'gracious' is an appropriate name derived from the presence of these chapels and churches. The name, however, is derived from Anglo-Saxon gracht hus (literally 'ditch houses'), and refers to houses built on the town's main ditch, or defensive moat, which became an open sewer. This ran along what is now Gracious Street, and which in the 19th century was even called Grace Church Street. **Gallon Steps**: the 96 steps leading from the bottom of Kirkgate to Waterside do not, as is sometimes said, derive their name from water being carried up from the river (see Water Bag Bank), but are named after Mr Richard Nicholas Gallon, born in 1789, who lived in the house at the top, Nidd Pavilion, and later moved to Hawkshead, Cumbria, where he died in 1834. **Finkle Street** is the original name of what in the 18th century was called **Swine Market**, from the many pigs sold here. There are Finkle Streets in many other northern towns, and the name could be derived either from a Viking word meaning 'angle', 'corner', or a Middle English form of 'fennel'. **Bond End**: the name for the once-distinct community at the bottom of High Street originates from the fact that the boundary of the outer area in which serfs or bondsmen once lived was situated here. **Jocky Lane** derives its name from the fact that a horse dealer once had his stables here. (The earliest use of the word referred to a dealer rather than a rider.) Because there had once been a synagogue here, it had also been known as **Barefoot Lane** or **Ten Faith Lane**. **Scotch George Lane** is said to be derived from that of a Scottish cattle drover who regularly passed through Knaresborough. **Water Bag Bank** is the only fully cobbled street in the town. Its name arises from the fact that leather bags of water were for centuries carried up here from the River Nidd, usually slung across the backs of donkeys and horses. In addition, women – just like Jack and Jill – carried pails of water up the hill, at a half-penny a time.

Other Knaresborough names: **Chaffey Dam**, also known as Chappy Dam, and originally 'Chapman's Dam', referring to the mill it served. This is a weir on the Nidd with an ancient right of way across the river marked by stepping stones, although attempts to get this right restored by Knaresborough Town Council have so far failed. **Nanny Goat Hole** was a shelter on the way down the crag, where goats once grazed, below the castle. It was used to house a searchlight during the Water Carnival, and was well-known to 'courting' couples. Sir Harold Mackintosh, the toffee magnate from Halifax, lived in Conyngham Hall from 1924 to 1942, breeding prize dairy cattle in the extensive grounds. He presented to the people of Knaresborough a small wooded area in nearby Bilton Fields, nicknamed '**Toffee Park**'. **Foolish Wood** is the wood overlooking the Nidd, opposite Conyngham Hall, which was part of the royal hunting ground. Its odd name is probably derived from 'foal-house close', suggesting this was where horses were bred. Other woods are **Icehouse Wood** and **Dog Kennel Wood**.

Claro was the name of the wapentake (the old subdivision of a shire) which included Knaresborough, as well as Harrogate, Boroughbridge and Ripon, extending as far as Middlesmoor to the north west and Wetherby to the south. Though wapentake is a Viking word (a show of weapons for voting), Claro is a Norman name connected with Claro Hill, about 4 miles to the north east of Knaresborough. Claro is possibly derived from Old French clarion – a trumpet or bugle, which was used to call people together.

Roman Settlements in Yorkshire

CALCARIA (Tadcaster, North Yorkshire) fort
CAMBODUNUM (Slack, West Yorkshire) fort = CAMULODUNUM
CATARACTONIUM (Catterick, North Yorkshire) fort and town
COLONIA [AURELIA?] EBORACENSIUM or **EBORACUM** (York; c.A.D.211-217) *colonia* and legionary fort
DANUM (Doncaster, South Yorkshire) fort
DELGOVICIA (Millington) signal station
DERVENTIO (Malton, North Yorkshire) fort and town
ISURIUM BRIGANTUM (Aldborough, North Yorkshire) walled town
LAGENTIUM (Castleford, West Yorkshire) fort
LAVATRAE (Bowes) fort
MAGLONA (Greta Bridge), fort
OLENACUM (Elslack, near Skipton West Yorkshire?) fort
PETUARIA [PARISORUM] (Brough on Humber) town
VETERAE (Brough in Stainmore) fort
VIROSIDUM (Brough by Bainbridge, North Yorkshire) fort

OTHER ROMAN SITES INCLUDE:

Adel (West Yorkshire), settlement
Castleshaw, fort
Cawthorne, practice camp
Drax (North Yorkshire)
Elslack, fort - possibly the same as Olenacum above
Filey, (North Yorkshire), signal station
Goldsbrough, (North Yorkshire), signal station
Healam Bridge, posting station

Huntcliff, (North Yorkshire), signal station
Newton Kyme (North Yorkshire)
Ravenscar, (North Yorkshire), signal station
Rossington (South Yorkshire)
Scarborough, (North Yorkshire), signal station
Templeborough (South Yorkshire)
Thornton-le-Street, posting station
Wensley (North Yorkshire)
Winteringham (Humberside)

Wapentakes in Yorkshire

The three Yorkshire Ridings were sub-divided into smaller administrative units called 'wapentakes' corresponding to the Anglo Saxon 'hundred' in other counties. The word, from vapnatak as in the Danelaw, means 'taker –up of a weapon', the right to bear arms and the badge of a free man who was consulted on issues of local government at civic meetings and who would make clear his assent by brandishing his weapons. It is from Old English wǣpen(ge)tǣc, itself from Old Norse vápnatak, from vápn 'weapon' + taka 'take'. Some of these wapentakes , such as Agbrigg (Wakefield) and Skyrack (Leeds) are still reflected in local place names. The word became obsolete around the year 1900. The Borough and county of Kingston upon Hull (Hull) was never in any wapentake.

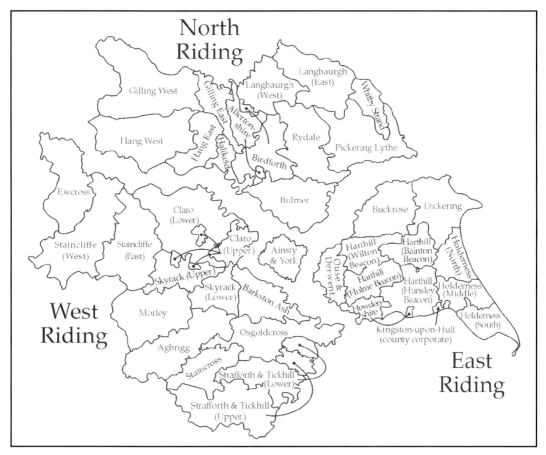

The wapentakes of Yorkshire shown in their ridings. York acted as the capital of Yorkshire and its location at the confluence of the three ridings, it along with the wapentake Ainsty had its own neutral area which was not part of any of the three ridings.

Yorkshire and 1974 Local Government Reorganisation

The botched 1974 local government reorganisation left the county administration as follows:

CLEVELAND - part of the old North Riding centred on Middlesbrough and including Hartlepool from Co. Durham

HUMBERSIDE - much of the East Riding and parts of the old West Riding (Goole-Snaith area), centred on Beverley. This later became North Humberside but in 1996 reverted to being called the East Riding of Yorkshire.

NORTH YORKSHIRE - much of the North Riding (most of The Dales area, Malton, Pickering, Scarborough, Whitby etc), the northern parts of the old West Riding (Ripon, Skipton, Settle etc), and the most northerly parishes of the East Riding centred on Northallerton.

SOUTH YORKSHIRE - the southern part of the old West Riding, with four Metropolitan City or Borough Councils (Barnsley, Doncaster, Rotherham and Sheffield).

WEST YORKSHIRE - the rest of the old West Riding, with five Metropolitan City or Borough Councils (Bradford, Calderdale [Halifax], Kirklees [Huddersfield], Leeds and Wakefield).

Some fringe areas were exiled from Yorkshire altogether: Dent/Sedbergh area to Cumbria; Barnoldswick/Slaidburn region to Lancashire; the area around Saddleworth to Greater Manchester; Bowes/Ronaldkirk area to Durham.

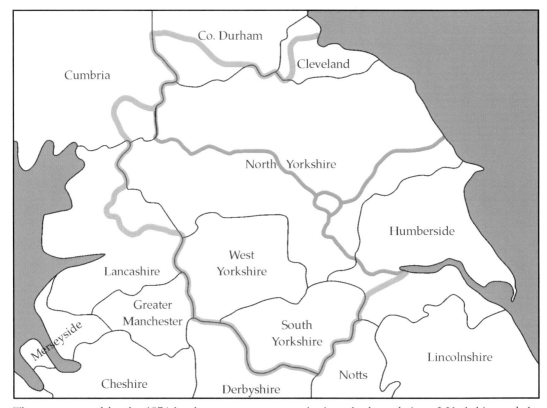

The areas created by the 1974 local government reorganisation, the boundaries of Yorkshire and the ridings are overlain.

Rivers of Yorkshire

There are 25 rivers of at least 12 miles in length within the boundaries of the four counties of Yorkshire. Here are all the officially designated rivers including the shortest main river in England, the River Bain at 2.5 miles. Most of these rivers lie completely within the county boundaries, except for: the Ribble, which empties into the Irish Sea at Lytham; the Rother, whose source is in the Peak District; the Greta, which flows into Lancashire to join the River Lune; the Tees, which flows within County Durham and forms part of the boundary with North Yorkshire, and the Ryton, most of which is in Nottinghamshire.

Rank	Name	Length		Rank	Name	Length	
1	Ure	118 km	73.3 miles	25	Gypsey Race	25 km	15.5 miles
2	Swale	117.8 km	73.2 miles	26	Cover	22 km	13.7 miles
3	Derwent	115.1 km	71.5 miles	27	Colne	20.6 km	12.8 miles
4	Don	114.1 km	70.9 miles	28	Skell	19 km	11.8 miles
5	Aire	114 km	70.8 miles	29	Riccall	18.36 km	11.4 miles
6	Wharfe	97 km	60.3 miles	30	Rother*	16.77 km	10.4 miles
7	Nidd	95.45 km	59.3 miles	31	Loxley	16 km	9.9 miles
8	Tees*	88.4 km	54.9 miles	32	Skirfare	15.24 km	9.5 miles
9	Ouse	84 km	52 miles	33	Worth	15.2 km	9.4 miles
10	Calder	71 km	44 miles	34	Laver	15 km	9.3 miles
11	Humber	61.9 km	38.5 miles	35	Holme	13.86 km	8.6 miles
12	Rye	61.5 km	38.2 miles	36	Ryburn	11.4 km	7.1 miles
13	Dearne	51.9 km	32.2 miles	37	Sheaf	9.6 km	6 miles
14	Wiske	46.9 km	29.1 miles	38	Kyle	9.31 km	5.8 miles
15	Hull	46.84 km	29.1 miles	39	Spen	8 km	5 miles
16	Leven	46.2 km	28.7 miles	40	Dove, Sth Yorks	7.91 km	4.9 miles
17	Esk	45 km	28 miles	41	Greta*	7.55 km	4.7 miles
18	Ribble*	38.48 km	23.9 miles	42	Rivelin	6.81 km	4.2 miles
19	Seven	34.9 km	21.7 miles	43	Doe	5.92 km	3.7 miles
20	Foss	31 km	19 miles	44	Dibb	5.2 km	3.2 miles
21	Dove	30.22 km	18.8 miles	45	Twiss	4.17 km	2.6 miles
22	Went	26.7 km	16.6 miles	46	Bain	3.95 km	2.5 miles
23	Washburn	26 km	16.2 miles	47	Ryton*	3.4 km	2.1 miles
24	Foulness	25.51 km	15.9 mi				

* River lies partly outside Yorkshire; the length is the distance within the county.

Dales in the Yorkshire Dales

ARKENGARTHDALE
Grid Ref: – SE 039993. Arkengarthdale runs approximately north west to south east and is the valley of the Arkle Beck; it is the northernmost of the Yorkshire Dales and a subsidiary dale to Swaledale, which it meets at Reeth. It takes in many other small streams such as Great Punchard Gill, Roe Beck, Fagger Gill, Annaside Beck, and William Gill as it passes through delightfully named small settlements such as Raw, Arkle Town, Langthwaite (where a back road leads to Booze), Eskeleth and Whaw. Lofty Tan Hill Inn is in the dale which was originally called Arkil's Garth, after Arkil, an 11th century Viking chieftain.

BARBONDALE
Grid Ref: - SD 655827. Barbondale is on the western fringe of the Dales; its largest settlement is the village of Barbon which is three miles from Kirby Lonsdale and two miles from Casterton. The Ease Gill cave system runs beneath Leck Fell, Ireby Fell, and Casterton Fell - a huge underground cave system which runs for 41 miles and is not only the most complex but the longest in Britain.

BIRKDALE
Grid Ref :- NY851018 Birkdale is at the end of Swaledale and is one of the smallest of the Dales; the hamlet of Birkdale is two miles from Keld with nearby waterfalls like East Gill (NY896011) and Currack Force (NY888016), which is supplied by Stonesdale Beck. Kisdon Fell rises to 1,636ft.

BISHOPDALE
Grid Ref: - SD956818. A side dale on the south side of Wensleydale which extends for some six miles (10 km) south west from Aysgarth. There are three villages in the dale: West Burton, Thoralby and Newbiggin. West Burton claims to have the largest village green in England. J.M.W. Turner spent a lot of time here painting the landscape. The Bishopdale Beck flows through the dale to join the River Ure just over one miles east of Aysgarth. The B6160 road follows the river to the watershed at Kidstones Pass where it continues to Cray and Buckden in Upper Wharfedale. Newbiggin is home to the 300 year old coaching inn, The Street Head Inn.

CHAPEL-LE-DALE
Grid ref: SD739769. Wide u-shaped Chapel Le Dale stretches from Ingleton to the Ribblehead Viaduct. The Ribblehead Quarry Nature Reserve features a 1.5 mile walk through a Viking age settlement. Other points of interest include White Scar Caves, Great Douk Cave, the Ingleton Waterfalls , and St. Leonard's Church whose graveyard contains some of the workers who lost their lives building the Settle to Carlisle Railway. Douk is a common name in the Yorkshire Dales. Examples include Low Douk on Ireby Fell, Douk Gill Cave near Horton in Ribblesdale, Dowkabottom Cave in Littondale, and High Douk Cave near Great Douk Cave. One meaning of the name is "damp, wet, misty", but William Carr in his 1828 book on the dialect of Craven gives the meaning as "To bathe, to duck".

CLAPDALE
Grid Ref :- SE014887. Clapdale lies in the Craven Fault zone, and marks the division between the sandstone rocks of the Bowland area and the limestone of the Ingleborough area. The Ingleborough Estate contains the showcase Ingleborough Cave; famous Gaping Gill, Britain's biggest pothole with the longest unbroken underground waterfall is there; and Alum Pot.

COVERDALE
Grid Ref: – SE 071795. Coverdale is in the far east of the Yorkshire Dales and takes its name from the River Cover, a tributary of the River Ure. The dale runs south west from the eastern end of Wensleydale to the dale head at Park Rash Pass, between Great Whernside to the south and Buckden

Pike to the north with a number of moorland crossings in between, including that of Deadman's Hill - named after the discovery of the headless corpses of three Scottish pedlars in 1728. The dale gives its name to Coverdale cheese. West Scrafton, has a mere 40 houses of which ten are Grade II listed. The Manor House is 16th century and was the home of Lord Darmley, who later became Mary, Queen of Scots husband.

DEEPDALE
Grid Ref: - SD895796. Deepdale lies to the north west of Whernside; the village of Dent has the highest railway station in the country.

DENTDALE
Grid Ref: – SD703871. Dentdale is in the north-west of the Yorkshire Dales National Park in Cumbria (it used to be in the Ewecross Wapentake of the West Riding, but was transferred to Cumbria in 1974); it is the valley of the River Dee, but is named after the village of Dent. The dale runs east to west starting at Dent Head a railway viaduct on the Settle-Carlisle Line. Dentdale is one of the few Yorkshire Dales that drains westwards towards the Irish Sea. The dale can boast over 200 listed buildings and structures which include the railway viaducts, bridges, barns, a farmhouse, mileposts and telephone boxes; the Church of St Andrew in Dent is Grade I listed.

GARSDALE
Grid Ref: – SD 74530 89561. Garsdale, the Dale that Died, Garsdale, means 'Garth's valley'; it too was part of West Yorkshire until 1974 when it was transferred to Cumbria. The dale is the valley of the Clough River. A statue of Ruswarp, a fourteen year old collie dog stands at the railway station. Ruswarp belonged to Graham Nuttall, the first secretary of the Friends of the Settle–Carlisle Line. In January 1990 Nuttall and Ruswarp went missing in the Welsh mountains; Ruswarp was found on the fell in April 1990 next to his owner who had died eleven weeks earlier. The dog had to be carried off the fell and The Royal Society for the Prevention of Cruelty to Animals awarded Ruswarp their Animal Medallion and collar for 'vigilance' and their Animal Plaque for 'intelligence and courage'. Danny Bridge is the site of a 17th century mill on the "old road", before joining the River Rawthey near Sedbergh.

KINGSDALE
Grid Ref: – SD 70222 78740. Kingsdale is on the western edge of the Yorkshire Dales National Park with Whernside to its east and Gragareth to its west. Kingsdale is drained by the south westward flowing Kingsdale Beck which becomes River Twiss before joining the River Doe at Ingleton to become the River Greta.

LANGSTROTHDALE
Grid Ref: – SD 881764. Langstrothdale has three hamlets: Beckermonds, Yockenthwaite and Hubberholme.

LITTONDALE
Grid Ref: – SD 93307180. Littondale has the River Skirfare flowing through it; its source is the confluence of Foxup Beck and Cosh Beck at the hamlet of Foxup. The dale is replete with bronze and iron age settlements. The superb Falcon Inn is in Arncliffe.

MALHAMDALE
Grid Ref: – SD 900629. The upper reaches of the valley of the River Aire, famous for spectacular limestone scenery at the head of the valley at Malham and above the spectacular 260' ice age formed Malham Cove. Villages in Malhamdale include Kirkby Malham, Airton and Bell Busk. In the Domesday Book, Malham is Malgun, meaning "settlement by the gravelly places".

NIDDERDALE
Grid Ref: – SE 15946 65669. Nidderdale is the upper valley of the River Nidd which at first flows south underground then rises to form several reservoirs including the Gouthwaite, before it turns east, finally joining the River Ouse. Pateley Bridge is the main town with other settlements including Wath (meaning 'ford'), Ramsgill, Lofthouse and Middlesmoor ("moorland in the middle of two streams": the River Nidd and its tributary How Stean Beck) all above Pateley Bridge and Bewerley, Glasshouses, Summerbridge, Dacre, Darley, Birstwith, Hampsthwaite and Kettlesing below.

RAYDALE
Grid Ref: – SD 91963 87910. Raydale is on the south side of Wensleydale and can boast the shortest river in England, the Bain , a mere 2.5 miles long. There are three hamlets in the dale: Countersett, Marsett and Stalling Busk, along with the village of Bainbridge. Marsett's name is first recorded in 1283 as Mouressate and is derived from old Norse meaning the shieling of a man named Maurr. In Countersett the Boar East and West were originally one farm, and before that a pub there was called The Boar Inn which sported the date 1667 above the door, along with a Latin inscription which translated as "Now mine, once thine, but whose afterwards I do not know". Stalling Busk means "clearing in the forest for stallions".

RIBBLESDALE
Grid Ref: SD816640. Ribblesdale starts at the confluence of the Gayle Beck and Cam Beck near Ribblehead Viaduct and then flows into the river Ribble, with Ribblesdale ending above Hellifield. The Ribble is the only river in the dales which flows westwards - for a total of 75 miles before emptying into the Irish sea between Lytham St. Annes and Southport. Towns and villages in Ribblesdale (from north to south) include Selside, Horton-in-Ribblesdale, Stainforth, Langcliffe, Giggleswick, Settle, Long Preston and Hellifield. Giggleswick means dwelling or (dairy) farm of a man called Gikel or Gichel', an Old English or Middle English personal name which may be probably a short form of the biblical name Judichael + wīc. Opposite the Craven Arms Hotel (once the Old Station Inn) is a plague stone. The Church of St Alkelda is here, an obscure Anglo-Saxon saint associated with Middleham.

SWALEDALE
Grid Ref: – SD 97636 98304. Swaledale runs from west to east, from the high moors on the Cumbria–Yorkshire boundary at the watershed of Northern England to Richmond. Nine Standards Rigg, the ridge with nine ancient cairns, rises on the watershed at the head of Swaledale. To the south and east of the ridge there a number of smaller dales: Birkdale, Little Sleddale, Great Sleddale and Whitsundale which converge to form the narrow valley of upper Swaledale at Keld. From there the valley runs south then turns east at Thwaite whence it takes in Muker, Gunnerside, Low Row, Healaugh and Reeth.

WALDENDALE
A side dale of Wensleydale. The name Walden is first recorded in 1270 and comes from the Old English wala denu, meaning "valley of the Welshmen".

WENSLEYDALE
Grid Ref - SD 874898. Not the usual naming after the river here but the old name of Yoredale can still appears on some maps. The dale now takes its name from Wensley, once the market town for the dale. Wensley comes from Woden's ley, or meadow of the pagan god Woden. Castle Bolton here is where Mary, Queen of Scots was incarcerated: she escaped and headed towards Leyburn but lost her shawl on the way; hence the name 'The Shawl' for the cliff edge that runs westward out of Leyburn. Hawes is the highest market town in England, first recorded in 1307, and famous for cheesemaking, and its rope making since 1725, where church bell ropes, bar ropes and banister ropes are made.

WHARFEDALE

Grid Ref - SE 0740 6254. The part from the River Wharfe's source to near Addingham is known as Upper Wharfedale, the first stunning fifteen miles of which is Langstrothdale, including the settlements of Beckermonds, Yockenthwaite and Hubberholme, the last famous for its church where J. B. Priestley is buried.

The Ten Highest Mountains in the Yorkshire Dales

	Height		Location
Whernside	736m	2,415 feet	Ribblehead SD738814
Ingleborough	723m	2,372 feet	Chapel-le-Dale SD740745
Great Shunner Fell	716m	2,349 feet	Thwaite SD848972
High Seat	709m	2,326 feet	Mallerstang NY801012
Wild Boar Fell	708m	2,323 feet	Mallerstang SD757988
Great Whernside	704m	2,310 feet	Upper Wharfedale SE002739
Buckden Pike	702m	2,303 feet	Upper Wharfedale SD960787
Gregory Chapel	695m	2,280 feet	Mallerstang NY802002
Pen-y-ghent	694m	2,277 feet	Ribblesdale SD838733
Hugh Seat	689m	2,260 feet	Mallerstang SD808991

In the UK a mountain is defined as a summit over 2,000 feet 610 metres high.

Yorkshire Lakes

	Area		Region
Hornsea Mere	189 hectares	467 acres	East Riding of Yorkshire
Lake Gormire	5.6 hectares	14 acres	North Yorkshire
Malham Tarn	62 hectares	153 acres	North Yorkshire
Scarborough Mere	16 ha / 6.5 ha*	40 acres / 16 acres*	North Yorkshire
Semerwater	40 hectares	100 acres	North Yorkshire

* Before and after Scarborough Mere was partially drained by the construction of the York to Scarborough Railway was built in 1845.

Yorkshire Waterfalls

	Drop	River	Grid Reference
Aysgarth Falls	30 metres*	Ure	SE014887
Beezley Falls	30 metres*	Doe	SD705746
Catrake Force	6 metres	Swale	NY892013
Catrigg Force	6 metres	Ribble	SD832671
Cautley Spout	198 metres*	Rawthey	SD681975
Clapham Falls	110 metres	Wenning	SD746695
Cote Gill Waterfall	4 metres	Skirfare	SD933692
Cotter Force	1.5 metres	Ure	SD848920
Currack Force	3 metres	Swale	NY888016
East Gill Waterfall	4.5 metres	Swale	NY896011
Force Gill Waterfall	6 metres	Ribble	SD758820
Gordale Scar Waterfalls	10 metres, 5 metres	Aire	SD915641
Hardraw Force	30 metres	Ure	SD869916
Hellgill Force	10 metres	Eden	SD778965
Janet's Foss	4 metres	Aire	SD911633
Kisdon Force	30 metres*	Swale	NY898010
Linton Falls	10 metres*	Wharfe	SE001633
Mill Gill Force	6 metres	Ure	SD939915
Pecca Falls	35 metres	Twiss	SD695749
Posforth Gill Waterfall	7 metres	Wharfe	SE078565
Scaleber Force	15 metres	Ribble	SD841625
Stainforth Force	2.5 metres	Ribble	SD818671
The Strid	Special†	Wharfe	SE064565
Swinner Gill Waterfalls	3 metres	Swale	NY910007
Thornton Force	15 metres	Twiss	SD695753
Uldale Force	15 metres	Rawthey	SD729965
Wain Wath Force	1.5 metres	Swale	NY884015
Waterfall Gill	4 metres	Aire	SD985568
West Burton Falls	6 metres	Ure	SE019867
Whitfield Gill Force	8 metres	Ure	SD934922

* total drop with more than one waterfall.

† The Strid is not really a waterfall but a dramatic narrowing of the River Wharfe which upstream is about 10 metres wide. The full flow of the river is channeled through a gap about 2 metres wide and very deep with a ferocious undercurrent. The narrowness of the channel has encouraged foolhardy visitors to jump it. However, failure is fatal and there are no recorded survivors of a fall into The Strid.

Some Interesting Yorkshire Pubs

'there is nothing which has yet been contrived by man, by which so much happiness is produced, as by a good tavern or inn'.

Doctor Johnson

Pub names, like the names of towns and villags, hills, rivers and dales, often tell us much about local history in the vicinity, famous local people and local topography. Here is a selection of some of the more interesting pubs in Yorkshire with a tale to tell. Some are still with us, others are long gone – but these too are just as vocal about the past as those whose doors remain open.

In 1875 Yorkshire could boast some 10,000 pubs. Now there are significantly fewer with time being called for the last time all the time. The message I offered in my book on the pubs of Harrogate and Knaresborough is just as valid here: *So, if there is a message to take away from this book it is simply put the book down, get up, go out and call in at your local for a pint or two and help preserve and extend this most British of social institutions. Once the pub, your favourite pub, has gone, it's often gone for good.*

But don't take it from me - in the words of a cautionary Hilaire Belloc (1870 –1953)
When you have lost your inns drown your empty selves for you will have lost the last of England.

In the beginning pubs, particularly pubs out in the country, brewed their own ale in brewhouses next to the pub; women did most of the work: Madam Bradley of Northallerton and Nanny Driffield of Easingwold are legends n their own brewhouses; "Brewsters," or "alewives" brewed ale in the home for domestic consumption and commercial sale, albeit on a small scale. These brewsters made a substantial contribution to the family income. It was good ale which attracted neighbours into their houses and led to the birth of the public house. Stingo, Knockerdown and Rumtum were famous Yorkshire brews with reputations as far south as London's Marylebone. Hopped ale was imported from Flanders around 1400 after which time hops were grown in England for beer production: ale usually has a lower hop content than beer.

At the same time hostelries were set up by the roadside catering for travellers. This had started with the Romans locating *tabernae* on their extensive road network and continued apace with merchants plying between markets, long distance drovers, commercial travellers, monks commuting from monastery to monastery, pilgrims (as exemplified by *Chaucer's Canterbury Tales*) and all manner of other people moving from village to village or from town to town. The Wild Man on the A64 near Tadcaster was a good example. The lords of the manor sometimes provided refreshing and sustaining beer house facilities for the workers in their fields. Ale was an important part of the Yorkshire diet as it was affordable and unpolluted compared to water. It is estimated that the average adult drank up to eight pints a day.

Things started to change in the 17th century when in 1657 turnpikes led to a huge increase in the number of horses and coaches full of passengers criss-crossing the county. Turnpikes demanded coaching inns for board and lodge for the drivers and passengers, and stabling for the horses, which required changing every fifteen miles or so. The railways 200 years later brought the next seismic change with the establishment of railway inns at stations; the third development was the now ubiquitous car and the transportation of goods by road which led to a need to cater for day-trippers, business people, long-distance lorry drivers and other travellers – often in the very pubs which once served coach and railway travellers.

The first common brewers were the Nesfield family of Scarborough established in 1691; the end of the 18th century saw the emergence of the common brewery; this was boosted by the Beerhouse Act in 1830, with names from the 19th century like Hull Brewery, John Smith's, Sam Smith's, Tetley's, Timothy Taylor's and Theakston's all still very much alive today. Beer brewing had moved out of the home and was an industry in its own right supplying a growing number of public houses and hotels. Just look at Tadcaster.

The aim of the Beerhouse Act was to encourage people to drink beer rather than spirits. Any householder who paid the poor rate could sell beer, ale or porter by buying an excise license but did not a need justices' licence; spirit selling retailers did. Beer sellers had to promise to give correct measures, maintain good order, to allow no drunkenness or gambling and not to dilute the beer! Hmmm. They were only allowed to sell beer after 4.00 in the morning or after 10.00 at night. However, not everyone liked the Act: many beerhouses emerged from the back streets of large cities and became working class drinking dens. *The Leeds Mercury* of 23rd October 1830 reported, "We receive from many quarters grievous complaints of the demoralising effects of this Act, which has, by making beer cheap, led to an increase of intoxication".

Pub signs and the names and the images depicted on them are an intriguing subject all of their own. The Romans started it all with a welcoming sign showing a bunch of vine leaves to denote a *taberna*. As with any other commercial enterprise, pubs used signs or symbols to signify the nature of the business going on within. The barber's pole and the pawnbroker's balls still survive to this day: the reason for all this symbolism was that most people could not read until the end of the 19th century, so words would have been quite useless: a sign, however, spoke volumes. From 1393 it was the law for innkeepers to display a sign: pub owners accordingly invented names and signs to differentiate their pub from the one up the road: the sign set it apart from other inns and taverns in the locality; it might also advertise what might be found inside (for example cold meats or board games as well as ale), or indeed the political leanings of the landlord. Coats of arms reflect the custom adopted by noblemen where they displayed their banners outside the inn to show that they might be found within. York's imposing gallows sign at **Ye Olde Starre Inne** spanning Stonegate is a very rare surviving example of these literally un-missable pub indicators.

Royal Oak was a supporter of Charles II (he hid in one at Boscobel after the battle of Worcester in 1651 before restoring the monarchy in 1660); Punch Bowl indicated a Whig; Marquis of Granby reflected the philanthropy of said Marquis. Chequers denoted board games while The Board proclaimed that cold meats were on offer inside – the board being what the meats were served on, hence 'board and lodge'.

In 1553 the number of pubs was restricted by law: London was allowed forty, York a mere eight and Hull a miserable three. Legislation so universally, yet happily, ignored and unenforced would be hard to find: in 1623 there were still 13,000 licensed premises in England.

In her 1698 *Through England On a Side Saddle in the Time of William and Mary* the enterprising and fearless Celia Fiennes called in at Leeds on her trip round the kingdom and gives us a fascinating insight on the price and strength of beer here, agonising as to whether her bar meals should be on the house or not.

> Leeds is a Large town…their ale is very strong, but for paying this Groat for your ale you may have a slice of meate Either hott or Cold according to the tyme of day you Call, or Else butter and Cheese Gratis into the bargaine; this was a Generall Custom in most parts of Yorkshire but now they have almost Changed it, and tho' they still retaine the great price for the ale, yet Make strangers pay for their meate, and at some places at great rates, notwithstanding how Cheape they have all their provision. There is still this Custome on a Market day at Leeds, the sign of ye bush just by the Bridge, any body yt will goe and Call for one tanchard of ale and a pinte of wine and pay for these only shall be set to a table to Eate wth 2 or 3 dishes of good meate and a dish of sweetmeates after. Had I known this and ye Day wch was their Market I would have Come then but I happened to Come a

day after ye market, however I did only pay for 3 tankards of ale and wt I Eate, and my servants was gratis.

A few years later Daniel Defoe, in his *A Tour Through the Whole Island of Great Britain*, agrees - although he is not so obsessed with the bar meals: inns and beer played an integral role in the lucrative wool and textile industry in Leeds:

'formerly the cloth market was kept in neither part of the town, but on the very bridge it self; and therefore the refreshment given the clothiers by the inn-keepers, of which I shall speak presently is called the Brigg-shot to this day… The clothiers come early in the morning with their cloth; and as few clothiers bring more than one piece, the market being so frequent, they go into the inns and publick-houses with it, and there set it down… by half an hour after eight a clock the market bell rings again; immediately the buyers disappear, the cloth is all sold, or if here and there a piece happens not to be bought, 'tis carried back into the inn, and, in a quarter of an hour, there is not a piece of cloth to be seen in the market'.

Incidentally, Defoe wrote much of his Robinson Crusoe in **The Rose and Crown** in Halifax's Back Lane, according to his Leeds publisher, Edward Baines. The full, somewhat prolix title of the book is *The Life and Strange Surprising Adventures of Robinson Crusoe, of York, Mariner, Written by Himself.*

Pubs, then, were not always just pubs. Many doubled up as coroners' and magistrates' courts, as markets, morgues and as smugglers' dens; others were also blacksmith's, cobblers or carpenters – often the landlord's day job. **The Denmark Arms** in Scarborough was also a grocers until its closure. Appropriately enough **The White Boar** in Huddersfield was also a butchers; fiddling the customer has always happened: in 1734 the landlord here, John Walker, was fined for giving short measures. **The Beaumont Arms** at Kirkheaton near Huddersfield doubled as an undertakers. **The Three Nuns** at Mirfield was where the nuns brewed their own ale. **The Cricket Inn** in Sheffield's Hyde Park had its own cricket pitch from 1826, as has **The Strafford Arms** at Stainborough nearby. **The Victoria Park Hotel** in Sheffield had a bowling green and 'an American bowling alley' in the mid 1800s. **The Crooked Billet** at Ryhill near Hedon housed a slaughterhouse. Best of all, though, was **The Humber Tavern** in Paull east of Hull; here in 1836 Trinity House decided that 'lights be exhibited in the windows of a public house at Paull as a temporary expedient until the erection of permanent lights.'

Wellington's Beerhouse Act of 1830 saw licensed premises double in ten years with 25,000 new licenses issued within three months of the legislation. It also galvanised the rise and rise of the common brewery, brewing beer and selling it to other outlets rather than for oneself. In 1823 Hull had 274 inns serving a population of 44,924 making one pub per 164 people; York was even better provisioned with 194 inns for 22,529 inhabitants: one for every 116 residents. Take children out of the equation and the figures are even more astonishing. Tadcaster takes the biscuit in 1837 with 24 inns and taverns and eleven beerhouses: 35 places to drink for a population of 2,400 providing one pub for every 70 people – more than twice the national average at the time. At its peak Sheffield in 1863 had 560 inns and hotels with 682 beerhouses and over 600 off-licences. Beerhouses naturally proliferated here around the steel mills and heavy engineering factories: a common sight was boys wielding broomsticks with cans suspended full of beer for the thirsty workers.

Some of Yorkshire's pub names are arcane and obscure. Before we embark on the a-z pub crawl here are a few of the puzzling ones, in no particular order, although we might as well begin with **The Puzzle Hall** at Sowerby Bridge which denotes the puzzles inside available to drinkers which puzzled all. **The Folly** outside Halifax remembers the 270 feet high folly built by John E Wainhouse to annoy his neighbour. **The Salmon Leap** (formerly **The Station Hotel**) at Sleights denotes the salmon leap on the River Esk there while **The Three Legs of Man** in Leeds describes the Isle of Man coat of arms. Hull's **Goat and**

Compasses is a corruption of the Puritan motto 'God encompasses us' while the city's **Ravenser** remembers the village on the Humber engulfed by the sea in 1346. Bell-ringing is commemorated in **The Ring of Bells** in Barnsely. The nickname (Peter) of the landlady of **The Just Peter Inn** (once **The Railway Inn**) provides the name for this curious pub in Holme on Spalding Moor. Between York and Malton is **The Spitalbeck Inn**, but there is no beck to be seen: the original inn was next to the Spital Beck a mile down the road at Barton Hill. In earlier times coaches would stop at the inn to collect two fresh horses to help the existing team haul its load to the top of the much steeper hill. Part of the building which became the inn was used as a hospital for Cromwellian soldiers during the siege at Scarborough Castle in the Civil War. Despite the image painted on its sign **The Bruce Arms** at West Tanfield has nothing to do with Robert the Bruce; it was originally named after the Bruce family, famous northern landowners. **The Triangle Inn** in Sowerby Bridge is vaguely mathematical, named as it is after the triangular piece of land on which the nearby village of Triangle is situated. In Triangle itself is **The White Bear**: the Triangle Cricket Club was founded at the pub as was the Triangle Reading Society; the pub was used as a Coroner's Court. Other **White Bears** prowl around Barnsley, Masham, Sowerby Bridge, Skircoat Green and, confusingly, Cow Green in Halifax. One bear which did no prowling was **The Old White Beare** at Norwood Green near Halifax from 1533: this pub was named after a ship which fought the Spanish Armada. There was a **Leopard** in York slain by the Luftwaffe in the 1942 Baedeker raid; and one in Calverley (later **The Thornhill Arms**) dating back to 1673 and named after the three leopards on the coat of arms of the Weavers' Company. North of York, Haxby and the contiguous village of Wigginton are a veritable safari park with their **Tiger**, **Red Lion** and **Black Horse**. Another **Tiger** was in Hedon; there is a **Blue Lion** at East Witton. At **The Wolf** in Luddenden built in 1653, the Inn was said to be a rendezvous for army recruiting officers in the early 18th century; in 1745, Janet, a Scottish maid at the inn gave sanctuary to a soldier from Bonnie Prince Charlie's army who was being pursued by the English army. In 1877, the property was acquired by the Luddenden Co-operative Society; the Luddenden Working Men's Club & Institute was also here from 1880 until 1946. Foxes abound, with or without the hounds: one **Fox** is in Holgate in York, another was in Low Petergate dating from the 15th century but demolished in 1958; its other names were **The Lord Byron** and **The Beech Tree**.

Here are some quintessentially Yorkshire-named Yorkshire pubs. The Wapping Spring brewery and the spring which watered it in Outlane just outside Huddersfield gave its name to **The Wappy Spring Inn**. The brewery closed in 1957. **The Who Could A' Thowt It** in Brighouse was the Masons' Arms until 1870. **The Who Could A' Thowt It** in Southowram was formerly Clough Head Cottage at Clough Head, Sunny Bank Lane and also known pithily as **Who Would a Thowt It, Ba Gum Who'd A' Thowt It**, and **Ba Gum Who Wad A' Thowt It** in the 1860s. There was a passage between the cellars of the pub and the cottage next door which provided a quick escape for illegal drinkers. The pub closed in 1933; when it was demolished the stone and roof slates went into the rebuilding of Coventry after the Second World War. **The Queen O'Towd Thatch** at South Milford dates from 1720 and means nothing more than the queen with an old thatched roof – a feature which endured until the early 1900s. **The Ram's Head** at Denshaw was popularly known as **T'Owd Tupps**. **The Needless** got its name from the magistrate (depicted on the sign) who declared that another pub on the Morley-Batley road was 'needless' as there were already two. **Needless** prevailed, however, and became one of the many pubs in which Dick Turpin downed his last pint before incarceration. It was also called **The Cardigan Arms**. The **Q in the Corner** in Sheffield was famous for its blind fiddlers while **The Warm Hearthstone** nearby was well known for encouraging drinkers to dip their own bread into dripping from the pub's roasts. In Barnsley, **The Gyngleboy** is named after the slang term for a coin and later for someone who jingles coins in their pocket. **The Tom Treddlehoyle** at Pogmoor was local author Charles Roger's pen name. The uniquely titled 18th century **Lettered Board** is in Pickering on Smiddy Hill.

The Samuel Plimsoll in Sheffield commemorates the man who saved many a seafarer's life when he did away with the 'coffin ships' and introduced his famous load line. Another life-saver is remembered by **The Davy Lamp** at Thrybergh near Rotherham. A male version of Knaresborough's **Mother Shipton**

has been awarded eternal life in the sign of **The Hermit Inn** at Burley in Wharfedale (formerly **The Woolpack**); the hermit in question is the prophesying Job Senior – the bastard son of a wealthy Ilkey landowner born in 1780. Senior also had the special skill of being able to sing tenor, treble, alto and bass all in the same hymn. When his wife died, he was blamed and her relatives destroyed his house and stole all his money leaving him no choice but to become a hermit. **The Henry Jenkins Inn** at Kirby Malzeard remembers the man of that name who died in 1670 aged 169.

The Floating Light stood on the scenic A62 over Standedge, opened in 1940 and closed around 2000. The name derives from lights used by workers digging the canal tunnel – the longest in Britain – that runs beneath. **The Nont Sarah's** pub at Scammonden above Huddersfield is named after aunt Sarah, the licensee some 150 years ago. At Ogden **The Causeway Foot** used to be known as **The Buck Inn**, **The Goose Inn** and **The Peat Pitts** in 1789 after the nearby peat pitts. **The Naked Man Inn** in Settle dates from 1663; it is happily matched with **The Naked Woman** one mile up the road in Langliffe dating from 1660. Less happily both are long closed. The now shut **Whale Fishery** in York took its name from the licensee Christopher Bean who was a harpooner on Hull boats in the Arctic and created a vivid sign representing a minitiature carved whaling boat. The Leeds coaching inn **The Bull and Mouth** was a corruption of Boulogne Mouth popularised by Henry VIII when he captured Boulogne Harbour. **The Feoffees** (try saying it after a few pints) in Sheffield was built on the site of a 1726 poor school – feoffees being the term for the charitable trustees. **The Old Silent** at Stanbury near Haworth gets its name from the fact that Bonnie Prince Charlie hid there and the locals maintained silence for a couple of weeks so that he could make good his escape.

In 1881 **West Bottom Tavern** in Halifax's Hob Lane was a row of three cottages for workers in the local quarries, the middle one of which was a beer house. The name was changed to **The Hobbit** after restoration in 1975. Also around Halifax **T' Wheel Hoile** was also known as **Old Coley Mill Inn**. It opened in 1830 and closed in the 1920s. The pub stood near Coley corn mill which fell into disuse, leaving only the wheel hole once the dangerous mill wheel had been removed. **The Whiskam Dandy** was named after the hamlet of Whiskam Dandy. A less obvious railway hotel not called The Railway or The Station is the **L & Y.R. Hotel** in Knottingley signifying the Lancashire and Yorkshire Railway. **The Running Man** in Halifax is a vivid reminder of the odious Halifax gibbet; freedom, and life, could be won by running a certain distance from the town. Failure, though, meant the gibbet after all and gave rise to the desperate refrain '*From Hull, Hell and Halifax, Good Lord Deliver Us*'. There were four pubs called **The New Delight** around Halifax: one survives at Wanstalls; the name is taken from *Milton's Paradise Lost*:' *Heav'n's last best gift, my ever new delight*' - Eve addressing Adam at Book V, 19. Once it was called **The Travellers' Rest**. **The Church Steps** in Dewsbury is the only pub in Britain built on consecrated ground while **The Postcard** in Holmfirth is named after the comic post card firm, Bamforth, based there. **The Flouch Inn** from 1827 near Penistone is very odd: it was originally **The New Inn** but when the name was changed to **The Plough**, parts of the lettering, namely part of the p and part of the g, fell off…

Pubs named after local industry and the occupations they spawned are, of course, extremely common, and we have already seen a number of Yorkshire examples. Here is a small selection of the less usual; some are gone, some are still with us: **Brassmoulders Arms** (Leeds); **Boatman's Rest** (Barnsley); **Brickmakers Arms** (Hull); **Butchers Arms** (Batley); **Carriers Arms** (Morley); **Clothiers Arms** (Leeds); **The Cobblers** (Pontefract); **Colliers Arms** (Elland); **Coopers Arms**, **Jolly Sailors**, **Miners** and **Millers Arms**, **Hammer and Stithy** – a name for an anvil (Ossett); **Engineers Arms** (Hull); **Electricians Hotel** (Huddersfield); **Fellmongers Arms** (Leeds); **Foresters Arms** and **Graziers Arms** (Wakefeld); **Horsebreakers Arms** (Hutton Sessay); **Jet Miners Arms** (Great Broughton); **Joiners Arms** (Hampsthwaite); **Nailmakers Arms** (Sheffield); **Ostlers Arms**, **Plasterers Arms** and **Skinners Arms** (Leeds); **Spinners Arms** (Colne Bridge); **Yarnspinners Arms** (Bradford); **Fishermans Hut** (Leeds); **Shepherd's Boy** (Dewsbury); **The Shears Inn** (Hightown, Huddersfield).

The Plummet Line in Halifax opened in 1898 and still retains its fine tiled nameplate. It is, of course, named after the builders' weighted line. Halifax can also boast **The Pot O' Four** – the pot used by wool combers to heat their combs. **The Whisket** in Todmorden was originally a beer house built by William Fielden - a basket-maker; whisket is a name for a basket. **The Collier** at Elland recalls the boats that shipped the coal and not the men who dug it; the nearby **Barge and Barrel** evokes similar memories. **The Slubbers Arms** in Huddersfield gets its name from slubber, a person or machine which slubs, i.e. works carelessly – here, a reference to textile workers. **The Veterinary Arms** at Hunmanby is so named after the vet who supplemented his fees with the selling of ale.

Nothing unusual about the name of **The Globe** at Raistrick; however, in 1910 the landlord hanged himself during the lunchtime session; his wife carried on serving until the session was over before she called the police.

Less inviting pubs are: **The World's End** in Knaresborough - owned by Charles Blenkhorn, who also ran the nearby pleasure boats, hotel and café. He was also town postmaster; his sister was postmistress. At one time the pub sign is said to have depicted an earthquake with a bus falling into the River Nidd and the pub collapsing; **The Cemetery Arms** in Leeds and **The Black Swan** at Leyburn which has a man-trap on the wall are just as cheery. At South Kirby **The Travellers** doubled up as the village mortuary.

We can see that many Yorkshire pubs are imaginatively named. More importantly, they are often descriptive of local history and topography, in much the same way as town and village names, the names of hill, rivers and dales. No book on Yorkshire place names could be complete without reference to the pub names which fascinate and delight us. Here then is the pub name crawl to end all pub name crawls. A word of caution: a numer of these pubs are closed or have been inflicted with a change of use so please do check the latest situation if setting out to visit. The current climate would indicate that this is a fluid situation in more ways than one with pubs closing (a few reopening) all the time.

THE 1900TH, YORK
Started life as **The Golden Lion**, originally home to a wealthy local cotton trader and mill owner, and first licensed to sell ale in 1771. In 1971, the year of York's 1900th anniversary, the pub was modernised and re-named "The 1900th. However in 1983, the pub reverted to its original name, The Golden Lion, by popular request.

THE ADMIRAL HAWKE HOTEL, BOSTON SPA
One of the many English pubs named after Edward Hawke, (1705 –1781) famous for his service during the Seven Years' War - particularly his victory over the French at the Battle of Quiberon Bay in 1759, heading off a French invasion of Britain. Admiral Hawke can also be found at Hessle. Other warlike names are legion and include **The Admiral Duncan** at Wakefield (defeated the Dutch at Camperdown); **The General Rawdon** at Luddendon Foot (fought with Monck in the Irish Rebellion and aided Charles II in 1660); and **The General Elliot** in Leeds who defended Gibraltar in 1779.

AIRE OF THE DOG, BURLEY
Other pubs there include **The Cardigan Arms**, **The Merry Monk**, and **The Haddon Hall** which was used as a setting for *The Beiderbecke Tapes*.

THE ALBION, LEEDS
Near Armley Gaol, this 1860s pub is world famous as the model for the pub in 00 gauge model train sets. It was originally two shops, one of which became a beer house called **The Fleece**; the other became **The Albion Hotel**.

THE ALICE HAWTHORN, NUN MONKTON

The Alice Hawthorn Inn has stood on Nun Monkton's village green for over 220 years. The Anglo Saxon name for the village is Monechtone; the eighteen acre green is one of England's largest and one of the last working greens in Yorkshire; in keeping with the name of the pub, livestock still graze contentedly there.

The old pub is named after one of the greatest English race mares we have known. Born in 1838, Alice Hawthorn won 51 races (and ran one dead heat) out of 71 races and was placed in ten others in just five seasons including two victories at the Doncaster Derby and Queen's Vase Cup. She won fourteen other cups and eighteen queen's plates; you can find paintings of this "Queen of the turf" around the pub. The pub was originally called **The Inn** and then **The Blue Bell**. There were at least three pubs in the village in the past: **The White Horse** was opposite on the other side of the green where White Horse House now stands.

An alternative derivation of the name holds that one day, a locally bred horse was in difficulties foaling and was helped out by a young girl walking down by the river. The owner of the horse, grateful that she had managed to save the foal, asked the girl to name the horse. She could not think of an appropriate name, other than her own name - Alice Hawthorn. A less romantic derivation has us believe that Alice was the name of the landlord's mistress and the foal was born under a hawthorn bush.

To commemorate the foal, the pub took on this more interesting name, The Alice Hawthorn Inn. Her foals also went on to become Derby winners themselves. The Alice Hawthorn Inn has remained open for over 200 years, except for two years, between 2007 and 2009, when it was closed for a sensitive restoration.

There are many pubs named after famous racehorses: Yorkshire alone has more than thirty. There is another **Alice Hawthorn** in Wheldrake near York; there is the **Flying Dutchman** in Summerbridge on the road from Knaresborough to Pateley Bridge – the sign here originally showed the ship of that name but was changed to depict the racehorse when it won the Derby and St. Leger in 1849; other Fying Dutchmen are, or were, in Wombell and York. The **Altisidora** in Bishop Burton near Beverley commemorates the 1813 St. Leger winner; the landlord staked eveything he had plus the inn on Altisidora winning – before that the pub was named the **Horse and Jockey** and **The Evander** – another racehorse. There is the **Cleveland Bay** at Redcar; **The Little Wonder** in Harrogate (now closed) named after a 50-1 Derby victor in 1840; it was the 'Little' Wonder because it only stood fifteen hands high and cost its owner a mere 65 guineas. **The Barefoot** (closed) in York; **The Revellers Arms**, 1818 St. Leger winner (Yafforth); **The Non Plus Inn** (Morton on Swale); **Charles XII** (of Sweden) at Heslington, York who had to run the 1839 St. Leger twice after a dead heat and then walk home from York to Doncaster. **The Beeswing** at East Cowton near Northallerton won the Doncaster Cup in 1840, 1841 and 1842, as well as the Ascot Gold Cup – the oldest horse in 1842 to win both races; there is another Beeswing in York. York too has **The Winning Post** and **The Gimcrack Hotel** – the Gimcrack is a race at York in turn named after the horse which won 27 of his 36 races over seven seasons; he won his last race in 1771, age eleven and is celebrated in George Stubbs' famous painting. There is also in York **The Knavesmire** and **The Chase** which sported an eight feet saddle on its sign. **The Bay Horse** in Monkgate was once **The Bay Malton** named after a horse which flourished between 1764 and 1767. **Eclipse** (formerly **The Black Horse**), **Old Ebor** in Nunnery Lane, **Tam O' Shanter** in Lawrence Street (although it may have something to do with Burns' poem) and **The Froghall** in Layerthorpe complete our York line-up. **The Why Not** in Sheffield's Burngreave reminds us of the 1894 Grand National Winner; **The Well Run Dimple** in Fargreave must surely have been a racehorse too. **The Nancy** in Burton Pidsea takes its name from the horse which won twelve out of its thirteen races around 1850, including the Chester Cup. In Sheffield (where there is no racehorsing tradition) the 1847 Derby winner at 5-1 is celebrated by **The Cossack** and by the 1872 winner at **The Cremorne**. **The Voltigeur** at Barton was a winner at York and was the 1850 Derby winner. At Crakehall near Bedale **The Bay Horse** was first called **The Octavian** which along with **The Revellers** at Yafforth was a St. Leger winner.

THE ANCHOR, TADCASTER

Tadcaster is a town of breweries (three no less) and pubs. The first building in Bridge Street used to be the Anchor, originally the **Hope and Anchor**, used by boatmen working on the river; **The Golden Lion**, a coaching inn, was nearby, now gone. The lion is the Lion of Flanders, emblematic of the fact that the hop was introduced to England from Belgium. The Golden Lion specialised in heavy baggage wagons, known as slow coaches. **The White Swan**, however, has survived – at one time owned by a Joseph Middleton who lived through the reigns of six monarchs: George III, George IV, William IV, Victoria and Edward VII. He was born in 1815 just before the Battle of Waterloo and died in 1901. The green tiled **White Hart** was nearby at No. 22. **Hope and Anchor** derives from the Letter to the Hebrews (6:19): "We have this as a sure and steadfast anchor of the soul, a hope."

THE ANGEL COMMERCIAL INN, TADCASTER

Known in Tudor days as **The Red Hart** it still retains some of its Tudor architecture in the doorway; the Angel closed in 1855 to make way for **The Londesborough Arms**. Next door was **The White Horse**, a coaching inn hit hard by the arrival of the railways and closing temporarily in 1840. However, Lord Londesborough needed somewhere to accommodate his guests on race days and so those whom he could not accommodate at home at Grimston Hall were, after 1855 when he reopened it and renamed it **The Londesborough Hotel**, offered rooms here. Matthew Kidd was landlord of the Angel when it was sold to Lord Londesborough; part of the deal was that Kidd became landlord of the Londesborough. It finally closed in 1976 to become the offices of Sam Smith's brewery.

THE ARABIAN HORSE, ABERFORD

The only pub in the country named 'The Arabian Horse', which dates back to the first arrival of Arabian Horses for the racehorse bloodstock. The horses, on their way to Middleham, were stranded in Aberford due to bad weathe; people flocked from miles around to see the 'Arabs'. At this point the name was changed from **The Bay Horse** to **The Arabian Horse**. There were nine pubs in Aberford at one time.

Horses generally grace many a pub. We had **The Flying Horse** in Pontefract (closed and once called **The Corporation Arms**), and **The Rocking Horse** in Wakefield.

THE ASS IN THE BAND-BOX, NIDD

At Nidd the pub gloried in the delightful name of the Ass in the Band-Box. It was built in 1712 and sported a sign bearing a coat of arms depicting a unicorn (ass) and crown (band-box). In 1800 this was repainted to show Napoleon sitting on an ass, sailing on the high seas in a band-box on his way to invade England. With yet more inevitability the pub became known as 'My Arse in a Band-Box'.

THE BAY HORSE, TADCASTER

A tale of smiths of one sort or another. Originally known as **The Smith's Arms** in the 18th century, early 19th century records show the pub to have included a smithy and was owned by John Houseman, a blacksmith. It remained in the family until 1844 when it was sold with barn, stable, garth and orchard. John Smith, one of the local brewers, bought it in 1858 and then sold it on to Lord Londesborough in 1867. Another of the three Tadcaster brewers is, of course, Sam Smiths.

THE BAY HOTEL, ROBIN HOOD'S BAY

The Bay Hotel goes back to 1828 when it began life as **The New Inn**, then **The Robin Hood´s Bay Hotel** and subsequently, The Bay Hotel as it is to this day. The hotel features in the first feature film produced by J. Arthur Rank, partly shot on location at Robin Hood´s Bay. The film was *The Turn of the*

Tide and was based on the book *Three Fevers*, by Leo Walmsley. The Bay is the only pub in the country which has the dubious distinction of having a ship wrecked against its walls. In 1838 the brig *Romulus* came crashing against the pub wall with its mast smashing straight through one of the windows.

THE BIG 6, HALIFAX

The Big 6 dates from 1852 when John Horsfall built twenty back-to-backs, known as Green Terrace or "Horsfall's Houses" now Horsfall Street. In 1857 John converted one of the back-to-backs into a beerhouse while two other cottages were used as a brewshop and stables. At this time they brewed their own ale and John's younger brother William ran the pub for him. The original name was **The Bowling Green** but it became known as The Big 6 around 1894. By the 1880s the pub was the focus of the local community and from 1874 the "Bowling Green Free & Easy Society" met there every Sunday night, run as a Friendly Society or a Savings Club. From the early 1880s until after the First World War the pub was the venue for the local Chrysanthemum Show – all blooms had to displayed in Big 6 bottles. In 1894 William Henry and his brother George went into business as Hop Ale Brewers. The pub became known as the Big 6 after the Big 6 Mineral Water & Hop Ale Company or possibly because William Henry lived at No.6 Horsfall Street. From 1908 George Horsfall, a virtual teetotaller, was in charge of the pub 'and ran it with an iron fist'. The Bowling Green became known as "the silk hat place"; George banned drunkenness and all games, while women were discouraged.

THE BILL O'JACKS, SADDLEWORTH MOOR

The Bill O'Jacks was demolished to make way for the Yeoman Hay reservoir, just up the road from **The Isle of Skye**, but not before it was the setting for a grisly, yet unsolved murder. On April 2nd 1832 a landlord and his gamekeeper son, Thomas and William Bradbury, were violently murdered at The Bill O' Jacks or **The Moorcock**, reported at the time as "*one of the most diabolical murders ever committed... a scene of bloody carnage that sent shockwaves through the local community and beyond. According to witness accounts at the inquest, blood covered the floor, furniture, walls and stairs of the pub as if there had been a violent struggle, "The walls and flags streaming with gore*" according to one colourful contemporary newspaper report.

Bill O' Jacks exemplifies the custom of naming somebody with reference to their father. Bill or William Bradbury was son of Jack Bradbury and hence was known as Bill O' Jacks. In the same way Thomas Bradbury would be Tom O' Bills as on on the gravestone in Saddleworth Church. Other examples are **Bill O' Nats** at Meltham which was another **New Inn** but became known as Bill O' Nats because landlord Bill Dyson was the son of Nathaniel.

There were more unspeakable goings-on at **The Cross Keys** at Uppermill near Saddleworth when the curate lodger in a drunken rage poked out the eyes of a woman with a red hot poker. He is remembered in the bar which was named Buckley's Kitchen after him.

THE BINGLEY ARMS, BARDSEY

Yorkshire's first pub – and the UK's oldest – was the ale house in which Samuel Ellis started brewing in AD 953 at Bardsey to the north of Leeds; it has survived to this day under the guise first of **The Priest's Inn** and then of the Bingley Arms, keeping up the tradition and heritage started by Ellis and the Kirkstall Abbey monks who drank there on the way to St. Mary's Abbey in York. From around AD 1000 a local court was held at The Priest's Inn with offenders escorted to the pillory across the road, opposite the church. Inside the chimney, there are two priest holes dating back to 1539 and an 18th century Dutch oven. The Ellis family remained in control until 1780; the ARP accidently blew up the beer house in 1942.

THE BIRCH HALL INN, BECK HOLE

A time warp you won't want to leave…Algernon Newton RA painted the sign on the Birch Hall Inn – one of the few inn signs to be painted by a member of the Royal Academy. He lived in the village at **The**

Lord Nelson Inn. A notice in the Birch Hall describes the ancient game of quoits which is still played on the village green in a local league. Each quoit is 5½ pounds in weight and the hub to be reached is 11 yards away, so the advice on the notice is quite apt: "the throwing of the quoit is a test of skill, judgement and strength." The two bars are either side of the village shop which is an integral part of the pub. The pub has been called everything from Brick Bat to Birch Hat: the birch element is probably a reference to trees growing around the pub when it was built, or a connection with the custom of hanging a 'birch besom' over the door to signify that the building was an ale-house. Hall is an old word for a meeting place of whatever size or construction.Beck Hole is part of the Duchy of Lancaster; some of the cottages around the green date back to 1728.

THE BLACK BULL, REETH
Reeth once had three pubs: **The Black Bull**, **The King's Arms** and **The Buck Hotel**. The Black Bull is the oldest dating from 1680 and is famous for its upside-down sign: it was inverted after a dispute with National Park authorities over the pub's external rendering and remains so today. **The King's Arms**, or "**Middle House**" goes back to 1734.

THE BLACK SWAN, HELMSLEY
William and Dorothy Wordsworth stayed here in 1802 on the way to visit William's future wife, Mary Hutchinson at Gallows Hill in Brompton-by-Sawdon, near Scarborough. Dorothy tells us in her diaries that they "slept at a very nice inn and were well treated." All three stayed there again on the journey back from the wedding. On this occasion Dorothy's diaries tell us, "My heart danced at the sight of its cleanly outside, bright yellow walls, casements overshadowed with jasmine, and low, double gabled-ended front." The pub has no name on the sign, the wooden swan speaks for itself, recently turned round to hide the weathering the other side has endured. Five other inns existed in 1823: **The Board** (now **The Feversham Arms**), **The Crown**, **The New Inn** (a posting-house in Borogate), **The Golden Lion** and **The Royal Oak** in Market Place.

THE BLACK SWAN, YORK
The Black Swan is in Peasholme Green; former coaching station, seriously haunted and also known as *The Mucky Duck*, it is one of the oldest licensed houses in York. Originally, though, it was the home of William Bowes, former Sheriff, Mayor and MP between 1417 and 1428. It still has a fine oak staircase and a magnificent Delft fireplace. The upstairs room was the venue for illegal cock-fights; the grill used by the guard to watch the stairs can still be seen. General Wolfe's family lived here; it was the HQ of the York Layerthorpe Cycling Club from 1834. **The Leeds Arms** (closed 1935) was next door on the corner of Haymarket; **The Woolpack** was over the road.

BLIND JACK'S, KNARESBOROUGH
Blind Jack is the nickname of John Metcalf, who was born in 1717 in a cottage (demolished in about 1768) near Knaresborough parish church and was a veritable jack of all trades. He attended school aged four, but at the age of six was struck by smallpox, which left him completely blind.

An intelligent boy with prodigious determination and energy, despite his disability he led an active life climbing trees, swimming, hunting and gambling. At fifteen, he was appointed fiddler at the Queen's Head in High Harrogate. Later, he earned money as a local guide (mainly by night), eloped with Dolly Benson, daughter of the landlord of **The Royal Oak** (later **The Granby**) and, in 1745, marched as a musician to Scotland, leading Capt Thornton's 'Yorkshire Blues' to fight Bonnie Prince Charlie's rebels.

Blind Jack is best known for his work as a pioneer of English road building. His extensive travels, and the stagecoach he ran between York and Knaresborough, had made him all too familiar with the appalling state of English roads. Soon after a new Turnpike Act in 1752, he procured a contract for building a 3 mile stretch of road between Ferrensby and Minskip. Then he built part of the road from Knaresborough to Harrogate, including a bridge over the Star beck, and went on to lay around 180 miles of road in Yorkshire, Lancashire and Derbyshire. The specially-constructed viameter he used to measure his roads can still be seen in the Knaresborough Courthouse Museum.

Following Dolly's death in 1778, he went to live with his married daughter in Spofforth. Here, after many active years in business and as a violin player, he died in 1810, leaving behind four children, twenty grandchildren and 90 great-and great-great grandchildren. A tombstone in Spofforth Churchyard pays tribute to the remarkable achievements of 'Blind Jack of Knaresborough'; he was commemorated with a bronze statue by Barbara Asquith in Knaresborough marketplace in 2009.

THE BLUE BELL, YORK
This, York's smallest pub and one of the best, is in Fossgate. It was built in 1798 when the back of the pub faced on to Fossgate and the front was in Lady Peckett's Yard. The Rowntrees were responsible for physically turning it around in 1903, no doubt because one of their temperance-preaching Adult schools was in Lady Peckett's Yard. York City FC held their board meetings here; in the Second World War it served as a soup kitchen. Women were barred from the public bar until the 1990s. Drinking is encouraged in the narrow corridor where a drop-down seat gives some rest to the weary.

THE BLUE PIG, FAGLEY, NEAR BRADFORD.
The gents' toilets are in Pudsey although the pub is in Fagley. The delightful name comes from the man who was washing down the pig sties here and added a dolly blue in emulation of his mother during the weekly wash. He decided to give the pigs a scrub at the same time – hence blue rinsed pigs.

THE BOARD INN, KNARESBOROUGH
The Board dates back to the 1630s, and is now a shrine to all things Leeds United, and vinyl. The name would have clearly indicated to travellers arriving in Knaresborough from the York road that, apart from a bed, cold meats were available here – served on wooden boards, hence the phrase board and lodge. The pub features some attractive Tower Brewery stained glass windows. Differentiation collapsed in Scarborough which had eleven **Board Inns** at one time – four of them in Quay Street. Bridlington has one **Board Inn**.

THE BOAR'S HEAD, RIPLEY, NR HARROGATE
The main buildings in Ripley are Ripley Castle, the *hôtel de ville* and the old coaching inn, the Boar's Head. A 19th century member of the Ingilby family tore down the existing village and rebuilt it, modeled on an Alsatian village with an "hôtel de ville" style town hall.

King Edward III stayed several times in Knaresborough Castle nearby, most notably in January 1328 after his marriage to Queen Philippa in York. In 1355, he was attacked by a boar that he had just wounded, and was thrown from his horse. His life was saved by Thomas Ingilby who slew the beast; Ingilby later received a knighthood, and a boar's head was henceforth included in the Ingilby coat of arms and provided the name for this Ingilby-owned hotel and bar. The name above the door is Sir Thomas Ingilby Bt.

BOWMAN'S COMMERCIAL HOTEL, HOWDEN
Two of the pubs here were Bowman's Commercial Hotel & Posting House and **The Wellington**. Until 1851 Bowman's was **The Nagg's Head**, while the Wellington changed its name from **The White Hart** in 1823 after the famous battle. When the Yorkshire Show was held here in 1864, Bowman's expanded at the back to accommodate a smithy, 85 horses and a further eighteen bedrooms.

THE BRIDGE INN, GRINTON
The Bridge Inn - a former coaching inn dating back to the 13th century – is opposite the church of St. Andrew, known as the 'Cathedral of the Dales' and goes back to the 12th century, founded by William de Ghent, a relative of William the Conqueror. Observant visitors will have noticed the sheep and guitar

on the pub's chimney; sculptor Mike Kutz replaces the instrument every year (always a last minute secret) to coincide with the start of each Swaledale Festival. Previous years have featured a French horn and a cornet – someone stole the cornet. Licensee Andrew Atkin tells an eye-watering story about the positioning of the French horn – not publishable here.

THE BRIDGE INN, RICHMOND
In Bridge Street at Green Bridge (now a private house). The Bridge was originally called **The Tile Sheds Inn**. Its claim to be the oldest pub in England (proudly painted on the front wall of the pub at one time) may be a little exaggerated. At one time Richmond had 60 pubs. These included such exotically named houses as **The Cleaver**, or **Chopping Knife**; **Dainty Davy** (a racehorse); **The Gaping Goose** and **The Bishop Blaize**, formerly called **The Elephant**. This last one underlines the importance of wool to the town and to Swaledale – Bishop Blaize being the patron saint of woolcombers. In 1921 Richmond also had two temperance hotels, both in Market Place: Varey's and The Albany.

THE BRIGADIER GERARD, YORK
A private residence and the Gas Works Social Club were other uses for this school building which was extended and converted into **The Brigadier Gerard** in Monkgate in 1984. The name comes from the famous racehorse which won seventeen of its eighteen races – the single defeat was at York in 1972. The horse in turn was named after Brigadier Etienne Gerard, the hero in Arthur Conan Doyle's *Exploits of Brigadier Gerard*, a series of short stories originally published in *The Strand* magazine between 1894 and 1903.

THE BRITANNIA, TADCASTER
The Britannia was owned by John and William Dyson next to **The Coach and Horses** (originally **The Half Moon**). A 1901 advert shows us that it was keen to attract the emerging cyclists' market, calling itself the *"Cyclists House – Dinners, Teas and Refreshments provided for Cyclists and Parties"*. William Dyson was an owner of river barges. The pub was named after their 90 ton keel boat which shipped the first ever cargo of John Smith beer to Hull for delivery to Amsterdam where it won a gold medal in 1895. Baron Londesborough sold The Britannia in 1873 to John Smith's for £900: *"Public House…stables, cowhouse and shed, cottage and warehouse, in occupation of Ann Dyson."* There is another **Britannia** at Loftus.

THE BROWN BEAR, SHEFFIELD
The Brown Bear is one of Sheffield's oldest pubs housed in an 18th century Grade II listed building. The pub is decorated with theatre posters from the nearby Crucible Theatre and Lyceum Theatre.

THE BUM-ROYD
see *The Victoria*

THE BUMPER CASTLE, YORK
The Bumper Castle in Wigginton Road was built by William Johnson, landlord of **The Three Cranes** (qv) in York until 1846. His widow took over on his death in 1879. She was the oldest licensee in the UK when she died aged 102 in 1907. It is now an Indian restaurant.

THE BURTON STONE INN, YORK
The stone in front of the pub with its three holes may have been a rallying point for soldiers before going off to war, or it may be a plague stone. Its holes would either have held a cross or have been filled with vinegar and coins deposited: the money allowed those quarantined beyond to buy food; the vinegar acted as a disinfectant. It used to be called **The Plough**.

THE BUSBY STOOP, NEAR THIRSK
This pub is eerily associated with Busby's stoop and the Dead Man's Chair – an oak chair that was cursed

by the murderer Thomas Busby, coiner and drunkard, before being hanged and gibbeted next to the pub at Sandhutton for the murder of his father-in-law, Daniel Auty in 1702. The inn took its name from the post or stoop on which his chained-up remains could be seen. The is haunted by Busby's ghost: wartime bomber pilots thought it unlucky to sit there. In 1972 the chair was hung from the ceiling of Thirsk Museum to stop people sitting in it and being fatally cursed as a consequence. No one has sat in the Busby Stoop Chair since.

THE BUSFEILD ARMS, EAST MORTON, NEAR BINGLEY
Always famously misspelt, this pub was made from three cottages and was once **The Hare and Hounds**. It is also famous for its mention in Charlotte Brontë's *Jane Eyre*.

THE CALCARIA, TADCASTER
The Calcaria pub in Westgate is named after the Roman name for Tadcaster and means place of the lime burners, indicating the local importance of quarrying going as far back as Roman times, at the very least. The pub was originally called **The Fleece**.

THE CAT AND BAGPIPES, EAST HARLSEY, NORTHALLERTON
The Cat and Bagpipes, is devoid of cat. It is derived from the Latin 'catphractes', cavalry troops who wore iron breastplates, body armour adopted later by Scots border bandits. In the days of the border raids the skirl of bagpipes evoked the warning cry 'The Cats are coming!' The name and sign are a throwback to these times. There used to be a Cat and Bagpipes near 10 Downing Street.

THE CAYLEY ARMS, BROMPTON
The invention of the aeroplane can be seen in the sign of **The Cayley Arms** at Allerston and Brompton. Sir George Cayley it was who in 1799 engraved a design for a fixed-wing aircraft. Cayley got his coachman to pilot a glider across Bromton Dale in 1853 and was only thwarted from greater things by the lack of a viable engine. The coachman resigned. William and Mary Wordsworth were married here in 1802. **The Barnes Wallis** – named after the inventor of the Dambusters' bouncing bomb is at North Howden, near Goole.

THE CAYLEY ARMS, ALLERTON
The Allerston **Cayley Arms** was first called **The Osbaldestone Arms** after local Squire George, (1786–1866), one of the most celebrated, yet eccentric all-round sportsmen of all time. The website (www.artwarefineart.com/gallery/portrait-george-osbaldeston-1786-1866-known-squire-osbaldeston) tells us that:

> 'He was educated at Eton from 1802 until 1803, when he was expelled. He matriculated at Brasenose College, Oxford in 1805 but his unruly behaviour (including pouring hot gravy over the head of a fellow student) meant that he just avoided being sent down, leaving Oxford without a degree in 1807. To compensate he was skilled at billiards, cricket, shooting, rowing, tennis, horse-racing, carriage-racing, and especially fox-hunting. He was reputed to have a son, by a Miss Green, a Lincoln prostitute, but the child was sent abroad. At cricket, he first played at Lord's in 1808 and bowled and batted for the All England team. He rowed competitively, with success from boyhood to middle age. He was a famous shot, both at game birds and at live pigeons. He rode at least one horse to death. In 1831 he rode an endurance horse race against time, covering 200 miles in ten hours, for a bet of 1,000 guineas, which he won easily, inspired by the famous exploit of the 17th century highwayman 'Swift Nick' Nevison, who rode from London to York in 15 hours. The same year he fought a duel on Wormwood Scrubs with Lord George Bentinck over a gambling debt, following a race in which Osbaldeston probably bent the rules; neither was hurt'. Gambling was Osbaldeston's downfall; he lost about £200,000 on horses. He lived 'a life

of plunder'. At one county ball he was said to have seduced both the daughters of the house in one evening.

The pub was renamed **The Fox Covert**.

THE C.B. HOTEL, ARKENGARTHDALE
Takes its short name from Charles Bathurst 18th century lord of the manor and lead mine owner whose lead pigs are all stamped with his initials, like the 1750 pub.

THE CHEMIC TAVERN, LEEDS
The early 19th century Chemic Tavern got its name from nearby Johnston's Chemical Works, which produced Vitriol – sulphuric acid – up to the 1890s which would have been used by the tanneries and dyeworks of the Meanwood Valley.

CHEQUERS INN, OSMOTHERLEY
800 feet above sea level, the turf fire in the Chequers – a 300-year-old drover's inn – is reputed to have been burning constantly for 200 years. The sign says "Be not in haste, step in and taste – Ale tomorrow for nothing." The sign disappeared in 1965, later turning up in Northallerton and was eventually re-installed in 1984. Chequers was patronised by smugglers, one of whom is said to be buried under the fire. Osmotherley was also noted for the alum, jet, coal and ironstone mines nearby. The origin of the pub name Chequers is interesting; it may relate to to the Wild Service Tree or Chequers Tree (*sorbus torminalis*) the fruit of which are also called chequers and were used as a flavouring for beer before the introduction of hops. Alternatively, it may be derived from the coat of arms of a local landowner; this name and the accompanying sign originated in ancient Rome when a chequer board indicated that a bar also provided financial services. The checked board was a counting aid and is the origin of our word exchequer. Nearby on the drovers' road were **The Limekiln House** (closed 1890) and **The Dialstone House**.

THE CLEVELAND TONTINE INN, NEAR NORTHALLERTON
A product of the coaching days: in 1804 the Yarm to Thirsk turnpike was opened on the route of the London to Sunderland mail coach; the subsequent growth in traffic created a demand for a hostelry to refresh passengers and horses; and led to the building of The Cleveland Tontine. The building was financed by way of a tontine – an old business practice where a group of investors sink money into a venture. As the consortium members die, the shares are divided between the remaining investors until there is one investor left who by then has inherited 100% of the shares. Tontines are now illegal as they seemed to be accompanied by a number of 'unnatural' and suspicious deaths.

With the arrival of the railways the Tontine become a private residence known as Ingleby House and after Second World War was bought by Camerons brewery of West Hartlepool, as it was then. A restaurant, ballroom and cellar bar were built in. There was also a Tontine in Sheffield until the demise of the coaching trade.

THE COACH AND HORSES, HARROGATE
The Coach & Horses opened around 1827 at the junction of Tower Street and West Park, and was one of eight public houses in the area. These included **The Brunswick Hotel** at the southern end of West Park, now private residences called Prince of Wales Mansions; at the northern end was **Mr Muckle's Vaults**. Tower Street was home to **The Albert Hotel** and **The Coach Maker's Arms**, opposite what is now **The Tap & Spile**, which was called **The Belford**. Next door to the Coach and Horses was **The Golden Lion**, and then **The Obelisk**, which was rebuilt in 1838 as **The Commercial**, before becoming **The West Park Hotel** in 1899. Between the Commercial, a coaching inn, and the Brunswick was **The Clarendon**, enlarged and adapted in 1847. **The Lancaster House Hotel** was described in 1830 as being

'fitted up in a most elegant manner'. By the end of the 19th century the Coach & Horses had expanded so much that there were seven doors at the front of the building.

In 2015, after the death of local author David Nobbs, the pub was renamed **Nobbs' Retreat**. David Nobbs played an enormous part in the local community and to celebrate this landlord John Nelson completely transformed his pub. Tables were covered with photos of him and with the covers of his many books. Beers were rechristened after the more famous novels and his most popular quotes were written on blackboards. The pub was renamed Nobbs' Retreat and also carried the name Sunshine Desserts, the fictitious company which Reggie Perrin worked for. The pub sign was set up so that David's widow, Susan, could pull a cord and see some of the letters fall off – in imitation of scenes in the TV series when letters from the name were seen to regularly fall off.

COCHRANES WHARF, SELBY

Andrew Cochrane founded a shipyard in 1884 at Beverley, but then moved his firm in 1898 to Selby, where they built trawlers and coasters for the Hull and Grimsby fishing fleets. In the First World War the yard built 90 steam trawlers for private owners and 70 steam trawlers for the Admiralty, which were used as minesweepers, gunboats and barges. In the 1930s work reverted to trawlers, harbour tugs and coasters. In the Second World War the yard was employing 500 people and built 21 Admiralty rescue tugs, 30 harbour tugs and numerous trawlers and a lighthouse. Greenpeace's *Rainbow Warrior* was built in Selby in 1957. She was built from the hull of the deep-sea fishing ship *Ross Kashmir*, later the *Grampian Fame*, launched by Cochrane in 1957. The name lives on in the Cochranes Wharf pub at the end of Galgate.

THE COD AND LOBSTER, STAITHES

This pub has fourteen inch thick walls supported by steel rods to prevent a further repeat of the three times it has been partly washed away by the North Sea. The pub's website states:

> 'The pub has felt the wrath of the waves on at least three occasions. The last in the great storm of 1953 when the front was washed away and the fishermen looked on in sorrow as the precious bottles of brew bobbed about on the retreating foam [along with the kitchen, scullery and two bedrooms]. Locals will tell you that, until very recently, one had to wait for a retreating wave before making a dash into or out of the bar to avoid getting your feet wet! As the sign says: "In rough weather please use the other door"!

THE COMMERCIAL, EASINGWOLD

The Commercial Inn is on the site of the old **Unicorn**. The Unicorn here (there was another on Long Street) is but one of thirteen hostelries referred to in a broadsheet entitled *A Peep at the Publicans of Easingwold* and performed in the 1820s by a Mr Smith at the Theatre. **The Green Tree** is another and described as the place 'where the Scotchman may meet with his clan' – drovers no doubt. In Market Place is **The Angel**, **The York** (once **The Talbot**) and **The George**. A thatched Tudor public house, **The Blue Bell**, now demolished, was run by Anne Harrison, better known as Nana Randan. She was permitted by her friend Thomas Salvin to use the 'chief seat' in the parish church. Her grave is near to the church door; legend has it that if at midnight you run round the church three times and spit on her grave she will rise from it. **The Jolly Farmers** nearby also had a thatched roof.

Long Street was nothing if not short of inns and taverns. They included, at one time or another, **The Unicorn**, **The New Inn**, **The Horse Shoe**, **The Green Tree**, **New Rose & Crown**, **Old Rose & Crown** (now Nos 83-87), **The Sun** and **The Punch Bowl** (now No 41); **The Royal Oak**, **The Bay Horse** and **The Fleece** at the Thirsk end which survive only as the names on the houses which replaced them. Alcohol and Long Street sometimes did not mix, it seems: Tom Cowling died from excessive drinking at the Royal Oak in 1825 and William White, a joiner, suffered the same fate when he carelessly downed a pint of rum instead of ale in The Unicorn. Thomas Gill tells us that at The New Rose & Crown Frank Sellars 'writhing under the anguish of disappointed love in his ardent attachment to Miss Fanny Thorpe, a pretty dressmaker in the town, hung himself in the coach house' (*Gill's Family Almanack*, 1872). In 1838 a lovelorn Mary Scaife from Ripon hanged herself in the kitchen of The New Inn; a verdict of Temporary Insanity was returned.

The Jolly Farmers stood at the top of Spring Street. Private Ted Webster, son of the landlord, was posted to South Africa in 1900 - an Easingwold Volunteer forming part of the King's Own Yorkshire Light Infantry. This extract from one of his letters home gives an idea of the conditions endured there: '*There is a strong Boer commando 15 miles from here, and a lot of snipers all round...the country is stinking with dead animals lying about in the veldt. Every place where we camp we have to bury some or else burn them. The whole place is infested with flies*'.

THE COVER BRIDGE INN, NEAR LEYBURN.
An ancient travellers' inn on the monk road from Jervaux Abbey to Middleham. The pub is famous for two good reasons: it was where monks took refuge during the destruction of Jervaux Abbey in the Reformation: not only did they enjoy a pint or two of ale but they kept alive the recipe of Wensleydale cheese. It was also where the first formally recorded game of cricket took place in 1706. The 300th anniversary was celebrated in 2006 in grand style with a festival of cricket and a flypast by the Red Arrows and a Spitfire and Hurricane with musical accompaniment provided by the band of the Royal Regiment of Fusiliers.

THE CRAVEN HEIFER, SKIPTON
This Craven Heifer (1807-1812) was bred by the Rev. W. Carr in 1807 on the Duke of Devonshire's estate weighing in at 312 stone 8 lbs and measuring from the tip of her nose to her rump 11 feet 4 inches. A wonderful animal. She was bought by Mr. John Watkinson of Halton East for £200 and taken to Smithfield by a Mr G. Pickop and a Mr J. Kitchen. The journey to London took 73 days from the 19th November to 30th January 1812, during which time she was proudly shown at towns and cities on the way. Sadly, the Craven Heifer met an ignominious end when she was competed for in a cockfight.

THE CROFT SPA HOTEL, CROFT
Croft is famous as the place where Lewis Carroll spent much of his childhood; the hotel was close to Halnaby Hall where Lord Byron spent his honeymoon after his marriage to Lady Annabella Milbanke in 1815

THE CROSS KEYS, YORK
The crossed keys is a common symbol in York, particularly in the vicinity of the Minster: they are St. Peter's keys to heaven, the St. Peter to whom York Minster is dedicated - the Cathedral and Metropolitical Church of St. Peter in York. St. Peter's keys are prominent in York Minster's logo. The area around the Minster was the Liberty of St. Peter: in medieval times, this was administered by the Dean and Chapter of the Minster and not by the Lord Mayor. The walls enclosing the Liberty were twelve feet high broken only by four guarded gates; inside were the Archbishop's Palace, the Dean's house and houses for the Canons, the Treasurer and the Precentor (together they form The Chapter) and St. William's College.

THE CROWN, HARROGATE
Built originally in 1740 by Joseph Thackwray, great uncle of the owner of Montpellier Square and Gardens, it was renovated in 1847 and again in 1870. Thackwray was given permission to buy the Crown hotel by King George III in 1778. In 1784 the head waiter, William Thackwray was making so much money that he was able to buy The Queen Hotel nearby. Thackwray was no fool: as noted, in 1822 he discovered a number of new wells, one of which was a sulphur well called the Crown Well and another

he channelled into the back yard of the Crown. This led to an Act of Parliament giving Harrogate powers to protect their mineral waters against such piracy.

Lord Byron stayed in 1806 with 'a string of horses, dogs and mistresses'. Whilst here he wrote *To a Beautiful Quaker*, inspired it seems when he happened to notice a pretty Quaker girl nearby. The first stanza of the poem is taken from the first edition of *Fugitive Pieces* published in 1806:

> *Sweet girl! though only once we met,*
> *That meeting I shall ne'er forget;*
> *And though we ne'er may meet again,*
> *Remembrance will thy form retain.*
> *I would not say, "I love," but still*
> *My senses struggle with my will:*
> *In vain, to drive thee from my breast,*
> *My thoughts are more and more represt;*
> *In vain I check the rising sighs,*
> *Another to the last replies:*
> *Perhaps this is not love, but yet*
> *Our meeting I can ne'er forget.*

Elgar visited in 1912. In the Second World War the Government requisitioned the Crown for the Air Ministry – they finally vacated in 1959.

THE CURRIERS' ARMS, SELBY
The Cash Boot Co and Beasley's fruit and vegetables shop replaced the Elizabethan Albert Hotel, previously known as the Curriers Arms, signifying its proximity to the tanneries, which were at the rear of the building.

THE CUTLERS' ARMS, ROTHERHAM
Another good example of a pub named after a local industry. The Cutler's Arms is a Grade II listed Edwardian Pub described by CAMRA as the most 'ornate surviving Edwardian Pub in Yorkshire.' Original features include leaded stained glass windows, original tiles and parquet floor and bar.

THE DERAMORE ARMS, HESLINGTON
There were three alehouses here in the 18th century: in 1823 there were **The Robin Hood** and **The Ship**, by 1840 renamed **The Bay Horse** and **The Fox** respectively. The Bay Horse was then rebadged **The Charles XII** after the winner of the 1839 St. Leger flat race. The Fox was later called **The Ship**, **The Yarburgh Arms**, **De Yarburgh Arm** and renamed again in 1967 as The Deramore Arms after George Deramore, on succeeding his brother as second Baron Deramore in 1890.

THE DOCK GREEN, LEEDS
The Dock Green, named of course after the famous television programme, was built in 1903 at a cost of £6,408 – as a police station house. It was sold in 1961 to a brewery when it became the Dock Green and was opened by Jack Warner who played George Dixon of Dock Green in the TV series. George Dixon made his debut in the film *The Blue Lamp* in 1950; at 26 minutes this was short lived as he was shot by the villain played by Dirk Bogarde.

THE DRAGON HOTEL, HARROGATE
First records of the Dragon (named after a Charles II racehorse) go back to 1764 when the owners, the Liddals, won the famous Dunmow Fitch; this entailed married couples going to Dunmow, Essex and swearing that for a year and a day they had never had a quarrel and never wished themselves not married.

The hotel was also called **The Green Dragon** and was owned between 1827 and 1830 by Thomas Frith, father of the painter W.P. Frith. In 1870 it became High Harrogate College and was demolished in the 1880s to make way for Mornington Crescent.

Many of the hotels in Harrogate grew out of farmhouses: the popularity of the town as a spa rather took it by surprise and many visitors were initially accommodated in extended farmhouses with meals comprising produce from the farms. **The Dragon**, **Granby** and **Queen** all were originally farms.

THE DROPPING WELL INN, KNARESBOROUGH

Also known as Mother Shipton's Inn, Mother Shipton herself featured on the copper sign above the door. The Dropping Well estate was run by a Mrs Comer and her five daughters in the early 20th century until they were forced to leave when the Slingsby family lost the estate to pay the costs of the Slingsby Baby Case in 1916. The Slingsby Baby Case was the popular name given to the lawsuits involving a member of the Slingsby family and his American wife regarding whether their son was adopted or if he was naturally theirs and so legally entitled to the Slingsby inheritance. They lost their case, and in 1916 the Slingsby Estate, covering much of Knaresborough, was sold off by public auction.

The last direct male descendant in the Slingsby line, Sir Charles of Scriven Hall was a keen huntsman, and, unfortunately, is remembered as much for his tragic death during the York and Ainsty fox-hunt on February 4th 1869 as anything else. A fox was spotted at Monkton Whin and pursued for a full hour. When Slingsby crossed the River Ure near Newby Hall at Stainley House between Harrogate and Ripon, in a flat bottomed boat used for maintenance at the hall, the horses in the crowded ferry-boat became restless. Saltfish, Slingsby's horse, kicked the horse of Sir George Wombell. Saltfish leapt from the boat dragging Slingsby with him: the boat capsized and within minutes eight horses and six men, including Sir Charles, were drowned. Saltfish survived. The funeral at Knaresborough Parish Church was the largest in the town's history, with at least 1,500 mourners arriving on foot, as well as ten coaches of dignitaries and 53 private carriages.

Born in 1488 (so fifteen years before Nostradamus) in a cave next to the River Nidd, the legendary Mother Shipton (née Ursula Southeil) is synonymous with Knaresborough, and with the art of prophecy. Suffering from what was probably scoliosis, and variously branded a witch and the devil's daughter, her predictions have included the downfall and demise of Cardinal Wolsey, the Gunpowder Plot, the Great Fire of London, her own death, and, happily with no success, the end of the world in 1881 and 1991. She did not appear in records until 1641 when, living in York, she predicted that the disgraced Cardinal Wolsey, who planned to be enthroned as Archbishop in 1530, would see York, but never reach the city. Wolsey got as far as Cawood Castle, and from the tower saw York Minster in the distance, vowing he would have Mother Shipton burnt as a witch, but he was arrested on a charge of high treason, and died on the journey south. This first printed version of the prophecies spread the fame of Mother Shipton throughout England.

In 1667, a fictionalised account of her by Richard Head says she had been born (after her mother had been seduced by the Devil in disguise) at Knaresborough, 'near the Dropping Well'. Head's publication contains the first of many fabricated prophecies attributed to Mother Shipton, all written after the events (eg the defeat of the Spanish Armada). Forgeries were taken a stage further by the Brighton bookseller Charles Hindley, who in 1873 confessed that he had fabricated prophecies about modern inventions and the one that had caused much alarm:

Then the world to an end shall come
In eighteen hundred and eighty one

William Grainge noted that in 1848, when the Knaresborough Viaduct collapsed, locals had started saying that Mother Shipton had always predicted that 't' big brig across t' Nidd should tummle doon twice, an' stand fer ivver when built a third time' – a garbled version of which still survives, linked with the end of the world.

Up to about 1908, a cottage near Low Bridge attracted tourists as the birthplace of Mother Shipton. The cave near the Dropping Well, though associated with her from Victorian times, was not publicised as her actual birthplace till about 1918. Further afield the prophetess became a figure of folklore. For 200 years or so, she was familiar as a puppet who smoked a real pipe. A moth has been named after her: *callistege mi*, which apparently bears a profile of a hag's head on each wing. She became a popular character in pantomime, her part played by men, including David Garrick in 1759, making her the first real pantomime dame. By 1770, at Covent Garden, Mother Shipton's spectacular transformation scenes also led to her incarnation as the first fairy godmother.

Despite claims by numerous other towns, Knaresborough is where Mother Shipton was born – to Agatha during a violent thunderstorm. The Dropping Well is one of Britain's oldest tourist attractions; the earliest known description is by John Leland, the antiquary of Henry VIII. After his visit in about 1538, he wrote of *'a Welle of a wonderful nature, caullid Droping Welle. For out of the great rokkes by it distillith water continually into it … what thing so ever ys caste in and is touched of this water, growth ynto stone.'*

A tourist attraction since 1630, the Petrifying Well has intrigued visitors with its seemingly magical ability to change everyday objects into stone by depositing layers of calcite on them. Seven hundred gallons of water flow through every hour and it takes approximately six months to 'petrify' a teddy bear, for example. Today, the well features a highly imaginative array of articles, some of which are in the museum. Nowadays, the overhang is regularly scraped to prevent collapse, as happened in 1704, 1816 and 1823.

THE DRYSALTERS, LEEDS
The name comes from the occupation of its first licensee in 1834 – one Joseph Lee, who was listed as a *'drysalter, oil dealer, preparer of peachwood, camwood, cotton manufacturer and victualer of the Drysalters Arms'*.

THE DUKE OF CUMBERLAND, COTTINGHAM
Other pubs here include **The King William IV**, **The Cross Keys**, **The Railway**, **The Fair Maid** and **The Blue Bell** – typical fare for a typical English village, although Cottingham is exceptional in that it is home to thousands of Hull University students and the Cross Keys in particular has suffered their depradations for many a decade. Up the road at Skidby is **The Half Moon**, in the shadow of the famous windmill. The Duke of Cumberland referred to defeated the Jacobite Army at Culloden. His nickname was 'Butcher Cumberland'.

THE DURHAM OX, CRAYKE
The Durham Ox was a notable hostelry on the drover's road from Scotland to the meat markets of the south and London. Crayke's other (long gone) pub was **The Rose & Crown**. It was known locally as **The Crown**, and before that was named **The Greyhound**. A third pub is named in an 1820 trade directory: **The Horse & Hounds**. The Durham in Durham Ox reminds us that Crayke was in the Bishopric of Durham.

Bulls were everywhere. Others include **The Castle Howard Ox** (York); **The Blackwell Ox** (Carlton and Sutton-on-the-Forest); **The Wensleydale Heifer** (West Witton); **The Airedale Heifer** (Mirfield) and **The Craven Heifer** (Heckmondwike, Ilkley, Stainforth, Barnoldswick and Skipton). Then there is **The Chained Bull** at Moortown, Leeds.

THE DUSTY MILLER, MYTHOLMROYD
The name has nothing to do with the history of this 18th century pub but the Coiners restaurant there

has. Although it is disputed, it is claimed that the pub was the haunt of local counterfeiters, or coiners in 1769. William Dighton, the Halifax excise officer, and Robert Parker set out to end the scam but Dighton was shot in the head for his troubles. Parker continued and eventually the coiners and the murderers were hanged. Dighton lives on in the eponymous pub in Halifax which changed its name in 1970 from **The Wheatsheaf**. The Dusty Miller was also a post office in 1853. In the 1990s it was renamed **Portman & Pickles**.

THE ELEPHANT AND CASTLE, BARNSLEY
Named after the coat of arms of the Cutlers Company. Some say a corruption of the words "Infanta of Castile".

THE EUGENE ARAM, KNARESBOROUGH
The long-gone Eugene Aram was named after the ill-fated Eugene Aram who was born at Ramsgill in Nidderdale in 1704; he moved to Knaresborough in 1734 and set up a school at the top of High Street, in White Horse Yard, now Park Square. A self-educated scholar and linguist, Aram was proficient in Latin and Greek, Celtic and Hebrew as well as in advanced mathematics. Things took a turn for the worse for Aram when he was implicated in a fraudulent scheme along with a flax-dresser, Richard Houseman, and a young cordwainer, Daniel Clark. On February 7th 1744, Clark disappeared; it was assumed that he had absconded with some valuables. Aram paid off his debts and left Knaresborough. However, that was not the end of the matter: in August 1758, a skeleton was unearthed on Thistle Hill. Houseman, accused of Clark's murder, denied that the remains were Clark's – 'this is no more Clark's bone than it is mine' and eventually confessed that Clark was, in fact, buried in St. Robert's Cave; Houseman alleged that he had seen Aram strike Clark.

Aram was traced to King's Lynn, where he was an usher in a school; he was arrested and brought back and imprisoned in York Castle. A sophisticated defence speech failed to save him and he was found guilty at York Assizes; on August 6th 1759, he was sentenced to swing in York, and later hung on the gibbet in Knaresborough, near the **Mother Shipton Inn**. Body parts were stolen as relics. Two writers made Eugene Aram well known to Victorians – Thomas Hood, in *The Dream of Eugene Aram: Murderer* (1831), which vividly describes his guilty conscience, and Edward George Bulwer (Lord) Lytton in a work of pure fiction, *Eugene Aram*, which attempts to exonerate him. The 1875 Memoirs of the *Celebrated Eugene Aram With the "Gleamings" After Eugene Aram Unexpectedly Gathered After the Publication of His "Memoirs"*, by Norrisson Cavendish Scatcherd and Thomas Hood, introduces a disaffected, and hard-up, Mrs Aram to the witness box; she was also infatuated with Houseman: 'until her pecuniary resources failed her, she was mute; and then, after some grumbling, she turned the full tide of her wrath on her unfortunate husband. Her gossip, from the account we have of it, was that of a faithless, incredible, and frivolous woman. As to the murder, she could, at most, only speak from suspicion'.

THE FALCON, ARNCLIFFE
Step back in time and enjoy good beer the way it used to be served: in someone's front room, from a jug straight into your foaming glass. The Falcon has been in the same family for 140 years. It was the original Woolpack in *Emmerdale*: is that a good thing?

THE FAUCONBERG ARMS, COXWOLD
The Fauconberg Arms, is named after the Fauconberg Hospital, a 1662 almshouse for "ten poor and infirm men", now old people's homes. The pub bears the somewhat self-deprecating motto: "*Bonne et Belle Assez*".

THE FERRY BOAT INN, SPROTBOROUGH
Walter Scott wrote *Ivanhoe* here, which gave birth to **The Ivanhoe**; it boasts its own cricket pitch. There is no Roman Catholic church in the vicinity so mass is held in **The Newton**.

THE FOUR ALLS, OVINGTON, NEAR RICHMOND

Dates back in parts to 1800. The Four Alls name derives from the four universal aphorisms: The King (or queen) rules for all; The Priest prays for all; The Soldier fights for all; The Ordinary Man or farmer pays for all. There is one in Hull too. Sheffield went one further with **The Five Alls**, adding the lawyer pleading for all and replacing the common man with John Bull.

THE FOX AND HOUNDS, CARLTON-IN-CLEVELAND

Canon John Latimer Kyle had been vicar in Carlton for 49 years by the time of his death in 1943. He bought the Fox and Hounds pub next door to the vicarage managing it with the same enthusiasm and vigour as he did his ministry. To fend off the inevitable criticism he met from church colleagues he agreed to impose a six-day licence whereby the inn remained closed on Sundays. He was also responsible for setting up one of the first youth clubs in the country – over the stables at the inn. The pub closed in 1969 and is now a private house. There is another pub of the same name at West Witton.

Country pubs, of course, reflect country life and sports. For example there is **The Badger Hounds** at Hinderwell, **The Bedale Hunt** at Melmerby and Harrogate's **Claro Beagles Hotel** and **The Fox and Coney** at South Cave.

THE FRENCH HORN, BEVERLEY

A long lost but delightfully named pub which stood in Highgate. It may have been the same place as **The Greyhound** at the northern corner of Ladygate and Dog & Duck Lane, opposite **The Dog & Duck Inn**. Dog and ducks pubs refer to the old and nasty sport of setting a duck loose (with wings pinioned) on a pond and letting dogs race in after them – and tear them to shreds; diving was the only hope. **The Royal Dog and Duck** at Flamborough, however, extinguished any cruel past: it got its regal name from the visit of Prince Louis of Battenberg (father of Earl Mountbatten of Burma) in 1900. **Talbots** (for example at Middlesbrough and Malton) signify a now extinct breed of large hunting dogs. Middlesbrough FC was formed at **The Talbot**.

THE GAPING GOOSE, GARFORTH

Some of the interior decor dates from the 1930s with Art Deco features on the windows and doors and a mosaic tiled entrance lobby. Not much goose or gaping in evidence.

THE GARDENERS ARMS, HARROGATE

'A pint of really well kept beer to drink at leisure while reading a book by the fire is, I think, my idea of what I like best about pubs. No TV. No music. No 'place to be seen'; If you want an 'upmarket refreshment experience', don't come here'.

The Gardeners is an old alehouse occupying an old building dating from 1698: stone-built, with stone-mullioned windows, stone-flagged floors and stone slate roof. Time has not changed its quintessentially 18th century original look, or its essentially domestic atmosphere. The two main rooms are still either side of the old central entrance corridor. The parlour, to the right with serving hatch, has solid walls and probably was the publican's own private 'best room'. The Piggery to the left boasts a huge fireplace. Behind the parlour is a small bar with a snug yet smaller still.

The splendid sign shows a gardener hard at work toiling on his land, flanked by two maidens bearing the fruits of his labours; the motto reads: *'In the sweat of thy brows shalt thou eate thy bread'*. An outhouse in the large garden once housed the Franklin Brewery, itself taken over from the pub's original brewery and now the Daleside Brewery in Starbeck.

The tap room, to the left of the corridor has old bench seating and an ancient hearth. The rear rooms, including the serving area and the games room, are former domestic quarters. For most of its history the Gardeners belonged to the Mountgarrett estate which finally sold it in the 1970s to long-standing tenant,

Maurice Johnson. It has been in brewery ownership for just over a decade.

There is a **Gardener's Arms** in Hull, near the university.

THE GENERAL TARLETON, FERRENSBY

A former 18th century coaching inn, named after the notorious British general who fought in the American War of Independence. It was claimed that General Sir Banastre Tarleton, 1st Baronet (1754 – 1833) was guilty of massacring Continental Army troops at the Battle of Waxhaws who were in the act of surrendering; he became known as 'Bloody Ban' and 'The Butcher', a nickname which has stuck in popular culture for rebel propaganda purposes. An account by an American field surgeon named Robert Brownfield tells that a Colonel Buford raised a white flag of surrender, "expecting the usual treatment sanctioned by civilized warfare". While Buford was calling for mercy, Tarleton's horse was hit by a musket ball and fell – this gave the impression to the loyalist cavalrymen that the rebels had shot at their commander while pleading for mercy. The Loyalists attacked, dispensing "indiscriminate carnage never surpassed by the most ruthless atrocities of the most barbarous savages." Tarleton's men then stabbed the wounded where they lay.

The Loyalists and British regarded Tarleton as a skilful leader of light cavalry and praised him for his tactical prowess and determination, even against superior numbers. His green uniform was the standard of the British Legion, a provincial unit put together in New York in 1778. Tarleton was later elected a MP for Liverpool and became a leading Whig politician. Tarleton's cavalry went by the name of 'Tarleton's Raiders'.

Before all this, Tarleton was educated at the Middle Temple, London and University College, Oxford University in 1771 in preparation for a life in law. In 1773 his father left him £5,000 which he frittered away on gambling and women - mostly at the Cocoa Tree club in London. In 1775 he bought a commission as a cavalry officer in the 1st Dragoon Guards and soon showed his worth as a skilful horseman and leader of men, working his way up to Lieutenant Colonel. He was a staunch supporter of the slave trade and became notorious for his derision for and mockery of the abolitionists. His portrait was painted by both Reynolds and Gainsborough. Tarleton in Georgia USA features in F. Scott Fitzgerald's *The Ice Palace*.

THE GEORGE, BARMBY MOOR

Barmby has enjoyed a number of pubs over the years: The George existed in the late 17th century, and an inn, run by the occupant of Barmby Moor House, was open on the road to the south of the village in 1770. About the same time Thomas Heard (d. 1824) established The Barmby Moor House, also known as **The Bunch of Grapes**, and later **The Wilmer Arms**, which closed in the 1850s. The Boot & Slipper opened around 1823, known then as **The Boot & Shoe**.

THE GEORGE, PIERCEBRIDGE

The George is famous for the clock that inspired American composer Henry Clay Work to write his famous *My Grandfather's Clock* after he visited in 1878 and heard the story of the clock. The owners were the Jenkins brothers – on the death of the first, the clock which hitherto had kept good time, began to run slow. The clock later stopped at the precise moment of the second Jenkins's death and never ticked again. All long case clocks were henceforth called 'grandfather' clocks. The clock – stopped – can still be seen there.

THE GEORGE AND DRAGON, TADCASTER

Originally at 18 High Street it was first called **The Black Swan** and then **The George** - all before 1830. It was owned by the Chantry chapel of St. Nicholas' in St. Mary's church around 1548 and featured a 1592 stained glass in the window which pictured a Tudor Rose with the initials WK – the sign of the George who belonged to the Chantry of St. Nicholas – hence the name? The square archway to the right was knocked down in the 1900s after a drayman was decapitated while delivering in his horse and cart.

THE GEORGE AND DRAGON, YARM

The king of all railway pubs: on February 12th 1821, a meeting was held at the George & Dragon Inn successfully calling for a Bill to grant permission to build the Stockton & Darlington Railway. In 1890 *Bulmer's Directory* listed twelve inns in Yarm: **Black Bull**, **Cross Keys**, **Crown Inn**, **Fleece**, **George and Dragon**, **Green Tree**, **Ketton Ox**, **Lord Nelson**, **Red Lion**, **Three Tuns**, **Tom Brown**, and **Union** and **The Cross Keys** next to the Leven Bridge. A number survive, including the 'Ketton Ox', named after the famous ox bred near Darlington and noted for its cock fighting; and the 'George and Dragon'.

THE GEORGE HOTEL, YORK

One of York's coaching inns, serving Hull, Manchester and Newcastle, in Coney Street opposite **The Black Swan** and the offices of the *York Courant* until 1869 when the inn was tragically knocked down to make way for Leak & Thorp; in 1867 it was called **Winn's George Hotel**. There was an earlier inn on the site called **The Bull** but the landlord, Thomas Kaye, replaced this with the George in 1614. Famous guests included Anne and Charlotte Brontë in May 1849 en route to Scarborough; they stopped and visited the Minster. Four days later, Anne died of consumption aged twenty-nine.

John Taylor, the Water Poet, stayed here in 1622 and waxed lyrical in his *A very merrie, wherry –ferry voyage or York for my money*. Elsewhere he praised the landlord: honest Mr Kayes in Cunneystreet. *He entertan'd me well, for which I thank him, And gratefully amongst my friends I'll rank him.*

THE GOLDEN BALL, YORK

The Golden Ball dates back to the late 18th century with its first mention in newspapers of 1773. Charles Dickens may well have drunk here: Mr Micawber from *David Copperfield* is based on a Richard Chicken, a feckless character who in 1847 worked in the same railway office as Albert Dickens, Charles' railway engineer brother. Chicken, who lived opposite the pub, was also an actor and at one time a self-styled Professor of Elocution and Lecturer on Defective Annunciation. The pub was increased in size in 1883 when the old "Jail Lane" was widened to become what is now Cromwell Road. The jail, and gallows, used to be at the bottom of the street at Baile Hill. John Smith's bought the pub in 1902 and in 1929 their refurbishment included the unique bar-side seating alcove.

THE GOLDEN FLEECE, YORK

The ancient *Golden Fleece* still survives (with its impressive golden sheep hanging above the door) on Pavement. The pub is reputedly haunted, home to no fewer than seven ghosts. Earliest mention is in the City Archive of 1503; it originally belonged to The Merchant Adventurers' who named it to celebrate and refresh their thriving woollen trade. In 1702, John Peckett, Lord Mayor, owned it. The building has no foundations which accounts in part for its lop-sidedness. The sign was blown down in 1900 or so causing the sheep to lose its legs and its head.

THE GOODFELLOWSHIP INN, HULL

Opposite the university, it was Philip Larkin's local when he lived in Newlands Park, and where he sometimes spent his luchtimes when working at the university library.

THE GOTE GATE INN, WITHERNSEA

This pub is about 450 years old and has been called the rather less colourful **Alexandra** since 1938. It was originally named after a farm here called Got Gate House – got being old Norse for ditch or stream, gate a street. The sign showed a goat but apparently this was just to add interest and has nothing to do with the etymology.

THE GRANBY HOTEL, HARROGATE

Harrogate's reputation for fine hotels grew from a need to accommodate the increasing numbers of visitors to what was quickly becoming one of Europe's finest spas. Former names of the Granby include

The Sinking Ship (not just a case of bad branding but a reference to the defeat of the Spanish Armada) and **The Royal Oak** – Royal Oak was its name when Blind Jack of Knaresborough played his fiddle there and Harrogate's first theatrical productions were held in the barn. It was renamed the Granby in 1795. Blind Jack allegedly eloped with the landlord's daughter on the eve of her wedding to another man in the 1830s. Guests have included Lawrence Sterne and Robert, Clive of India. The Granby is now Granby Court Care Home.

THE GRIFFIN, LEEDS
The 1872 Grade II-listed Griffin on Boar Lane was previously known as **Bar Censsa** and before that **The Griffin Hotel**, one of the top hotels in Leeds; it closed in 1999. The Gothic revival building boasted a unique Potts clock at the corner of the building with the hours ingeniously replaced by the words 'Griffin Hotel'. For many, though, the Griffin will be cherished as the place where Leeds United was born. The current pub is on the site of the earlier Griffin Hotel, a coaching inn from at least the 17th century; it was rebuilt as a railway hotel, for the Leeds New Station which opened in 1869 owned by the joint London and North West and North East Railway Companies. Another pub with an interesting clock is **The New Inn** in Barwick-in-Elmet which, instead of numbers on the dial, bears the sonorous words 'No Tick'.

GUY FAWKES ARMS, SCOTTON
There used to be four pubs in Scotton. **The Bay Horse** pub can be seen on late 19th century Ordnance Survey maps down the road from **The Star Inn**, now known as the Guy Fawkes Arms, roughly opposite the Methodist Chapel. Then there was **The George IVth** and another, on the junction of Ripley Road and New Road leading into Scotton, called **The Fox and Hounds**.

Born in York in 1570, Guy Fawkes moved to Scotton in his late teens when his widowed mother married Dionis Baynbrigge (Dennis Bainbridge) of Scotton, a Catholic who resided at Percy House, Scotton, and also at Scotton Old Hall. Guy had been brought up a Protestant, but the illegal Catholic religion of his new relatives led to his conversion. In 1593 he moved south, and eventually joined the Spanish Army then fighting in the Netherlands.

As Captain Guido Fawkes he had a distinguished military record, and his expertise with explosives attracted the plotters to him in their attempt to assassinate James I. It has been claimed that the plot was made around a table in a Knaresborough inn, but this is, in fact, is an antique bought in modern times by the owner of Scotton Old Hall. Guy Fawkes, under the pseudonym Johnson, a servant to Thomas Percy, smuggled 36 barrels of gunpowder under the House of Lords, in time for its royal opening on 5th November 1605. Just before midnight, he was arrested, 'booted and spurred', about to flee, with a watch, lantern, tinderbox and slow fuses. He was 'interviewed' by King James in his bedchamber, taken to the Tower to be tortured, and finally 'hanged, drawn and quartered' as a traitor on 31st January 1606. Though his effigy is still burnt in effigy on 5th November ('Plot Night', as it is called in parts of Yorkshire), no guy is ever burnt at St. Peter's, his old school in York, or on the public bonfire in Scotton.

HALES BAR, HARROGATE
One of the most historic and oldest pubs in Harrogate, Hales Bar is the town's only traditionally gas-lit bar. Its origins hail as far back as the earliest days of the town's rise as a leading spa resort and was one of the first inns to cater for spa visitors after sulphur wells were first established in the mid-17th century. Sulphur springs still bubble beneath the cellar and their unique smell occasionally percolates up to the bar area.

There are records from the 17th century to inns close to the Old Sulphur Well, mostly from the Pannal Constable, who noted that he went to 'sulfer wells to cease quarrels'; probably it was **The Bell**, **Promenade** and **White Hart Inns** which were implicated in this anti-social disorder.

Hales Bar took over the licence of the Promenade when the latter closed in 1840 and was bought by the brewer and developer Thomas Humble Walker for £1,220. Mr Walker extended the old Promenade Inn during the 1840s: the older building was converted into a house, the newer part became an inn which initially took the name of the new landlord, Hodgson. In about 1882, Hodgson was replaced by William Hale.

Tobias Smollett drank here when in May 1766 he visited Harrogate, the setting for part of his novel *The Expedition of Humphry Clinker*. Hales was a favourite too of Sir John Barbirolli when the Hallé Orchestra was in town; some interior scenes for *Chariots of Fire* were set here.

THE HAMMER AND HAND, HUTTON LE HOLE

The Hammer & Hand beerhouse was built in 1784 by Emmanuel and Betty Strickland and bears the inscription "By Hammer and Hand all Arts do Stand'. It was next door to a blacksmith's which later became **The Crown Inn**. The well-named Boxing Tom (Tom Proud) was landlord in 1870.

THE HARK TO BOUNTY, SLAIDBURN

Parts of this pub goes back to the 1300s, although most of the existing fabric dates from the 16th century. The inn was called **The Dog** until 1875, when the squire of the village, who doubled-up as the Rector, had a pack of hounds. One day while out hunting, he called at the inn only to be disturbed by 'a loud and prolonged baying from the pack outside'. Above the din of the other hounds the squire's favourite dog, Bounty, could be heard prompting him to call out.... "Hark to Bounty!" Upstairs is the Courtroom used as the local court from the early 19th century until the mid 1930s. This was the "Moot" Court which dealt with local matters such as land transfers and disputes in addition to the punishment of local offenders. **The Hark to Rover** is at Kirkstall and **The Hark to Mopse**y is at Normanton.

THE HARK TO MOPSEY, NORMANTON

There are two possible etymologies. One is that the landlord had a nagging and loud-mouthed wife called Mopsey who could be heard by passers by; they would routinely say "Hark to Mopsey!" So the inn became known by that name. Alternatively, the landlord was given a foxhound puppy to train. The puppy was called Mopsey and, whenever the huntsmen and pack passed the inn, the pup would emit a distinctive bark or bell. Bell means a baying produced by hounds. The passing huntsmen would, therefore, remark "Hark to Mopsey."

THE HARK TO ROVER, KIRKSTALL

The name apparently comes from medieval times when monks from the abbey lived in a house nearby. One night it caught fire but a dog's insistent barking woke a monk who shouted the alarm - "Hark to Rover". This woke the other monks who extinguished the fire. An alternative derivation holds that the name comes from a local legend concerning a barmaid, Mary, who worked at **The Star and Garter**. She was implicated with a lover who was involved with a gang of highwaymen who had waylaid and killed a man at Kirkstall Abbey. When she saw her lover burying the body, she wailed and screamed so loudly that Rover her dog, back in her cottage, heard her and barked incessantly. Robert Southey tells the story in his poem *The Maid of the Inn*.

Other Hark To's include **The Hark to Nudger** in Dobcross.

THE HAWORTH ARMS, HULL

A fine student pub which competes for the substantial student market with **The Gardeners Arms** just up the Cottingham Road. Probably named after the location of the Brontë parsonage. Nick Drake once played upstairs; the refurbished first floor venue is now called Drake's Bar.

THE HENRY PEACOCK, STARBECK, HARROGATE

Of the two public houses on the High Street - **The Prince of Wales** and the Henry Peacock, the latter, originally **The Harrogate Hotel**, was renamed after the master of the local workhouse during the 19th century and is currently closed.

> 'Henry Peacock was born in poverty, and spent his life not quite getting out of it. He first came to Starbeck in 1825 with his wife Elizabeth, as master and matron of the workhouse, for a joint salary of £50 a year. After having run the Aldbrough and Boroughbridge workhouse for the previous three years, the Peacocks were noted to have viewed Harrogate as an opportunity to "better themselves"'.
>
> *Starbeck- A Journey through the Past* by Stephen G Abbott

The workhouse here was known euphemistically as 'The House of Industry' and 'The Castle of Industry'. There is a kind of irony in naming a pub after Peacock when we remember that one of his edicts as master of the local workhouse was the prohibition of alcohol. Nothing unusual about that, but transgression for 'bringing into the house or drinking any spirituous liquor' was met with the toughest of punishments and hypocrisy: transgressors were 'contained in a dark room and allowed nothing but bread and water the next day'.

Peacock was dismissed from the workhouse in 1838 and remarried (his wife had died in 1837); his new bride was a Mrs Waudby, a widow who owned **The Brunswick Hotel**. It was not long before Peacock took over as landlord.

THE HOP GROVE, YORK
The Hop Grove on Malton Road has been around since 1857 at least. Records refer to it under the name **The Hop Pole Inn** in 1889 and 1893. This was replaced in the 1930s by the present building. For a short period from 1997 it was renamed the **The Stockton-on-the-Forest** after the nearby village.

It comes as no surprise that beer, brewing and inns themselves feature frequently in pub names. There is a **Cock and Bottle** in York (formerly **The Plumbers Arms** and **Duke's Place**), **The Corporation Brewery Taps** in Doncaster, **The Hogshead** at Woodhouse near Sheffield and the amusing **Jack and Gill** in Allerton. You might have wanted to slip in the tiny **Slip Inn** north of York (now gone) although the pub of the same name on the city's Ouse refers to the river traffic; failing that drop in at **The Drop Inn** in Guisely or go to **The Local** in Leeds or one of Hull's two **Full Measures**. **Pig and Whistles** (as in Pudsey) signify the mug into which your beer was poured from the jug (for example in Leeds). **The Boy and Barrels** at Selby and Mexborough is Bacchus, the Roman god of wine sitting on a tun of ale.

THE HULL CHEESE, HULL
Possibly a reference to strong and thick beer brewed in Hull or that exported from Burton through the port of Hull. According to John Taylor (1578 – 1653) self-styled "The Water Poet"

> "[Hull cheese] is much like a loafe out of a brewer's basket; it is composed of two simples—mault and water, … and is cousin-germane to the mightiest ale in England".

The phrase 'you have taken Hull cheese' means you are drunk. Similar expressions include 'he hath been hit by the barn-weasle'. There has been an inn on this site since the late 18th century; the Cheese was called **The Paragon Hotel** and gave its name to Hull's Paragon Street and Paragon Station.

THE JOHN F. KENNEDY HOTEL, DEWSBURY
Once **The Turk's Head**.

THE JOLLY SAILOR, CAWOOD
At one time Cawood supported eighteen pubs – only three are left: **The Jolly Sailor**, **The Ferry Inn**, and **The Castle** – all indicative of the town's history with sailors on the river, a ferry and the castle.

THE JOSEPH HANSOM, YORK

Joseph Aloysius Hansom (1842-1900), the architect and inventor of the Patent Safety Cabriolet that bears his name, was born at 114 Micklegate and christened in the Bar Convent chapel. He suffered from severe depression and shot himself in his office on 27th May 1900. A pub in Market Street was named after him. Architecturally, Hansom's best known work is probably the majestic neoclassical Birmingham Town Hall. The Hansom Cab was so common a sight that Disraeli called it 'the gondola of London'. Recently renamed **The Robert Burns** – one of its former names.

THE KETTON OX, YARM

The oldest of Yarm's pubs – there were nineteen at one time. The Ketton Ox is named after the famous shorthorn bred by Charles Colling of Ketton, near Stamford. It weighed in at 220 stone; Colling refused an offer of £2,000 for it in 1801. The pub is not all about big bulls: there is also the cock-fighting rooms upstairs concealed behind the bricked-up windows after cock fighting was made illegal in 1849. One cock-fighting pit would be left empty to fool the authorities, while the fighting continued unabated in another. There were secret stairs and a hidden chute down which dead or mutilated cocks were despatched. A room called The Morgue was where dead bodies dredged from the Tees would be kept for post-mortem examination.

THE LAMB AND FLAG, LEEDS

Named after the crest of the Merchant Tailors – highly appropriate in a tailoring city like Leeds. Other Lamb and Flags may derive from lambs and flags depicted on the arms of the Knights Templars. It was a popular religious symbol featuring the Agnus Dei (lamb of god) holding the red cross flag representing the resurrection of Christ before it was the flag of England. This was the emblem of the Middle Temple which was given a charter in 1608 to occupy lands formerly owned by the Knights Templar.

THE LEEDS ARMS, TADCASTER

Owned by the Earl of Egremont who sold it to York brewers Bulmers in 1828 when it was called **The Angel**; the sale included a cow house, pigsties, coalhouse and stables. It was renamed **The Drovers Arms** in 1844 to reflect its position on a road frequented by drovers and acquired in 1875 by Hotham & Co who went on to establish Tower Brewery; it was then bought by John Smith's in 1885. In 1880 it had become the Leeds Arms, was demolished in 1933 and replaced with the present building.

THE LIFEBOAT INN, SPURN HEAD

The second Lifeboat Inn at Spurn was built largely from the bricks from the demolished lifeboat cottages around 1860; chalk was dumped here to protect the inn. The first Lifeboat Inn, or **Tavern**, or, according to the Ordnance Survey map, **The Lifeboat Hotel**, was a converted barracks and home to the master of the Spurn lifeboat station. Apart from selling drink and provisions, the master, in common with his fellow crew members, made money from loading gravel from the beaches onto ships.

THE LION INN, BLAKEY RIDGE

At the highest point of the North York Moors, this remote 16th century icon stands at 1,325 feet. It was established in 1553 or 1558 when it is recorded that the traditional bunch of green leaves was hung outside the pub after a brewing session to welcome travelers. Farmers from Commondale, Danby and the Fryups, established a market for surplus corn at Blakey Inn delivering and selling to the horse breeders and stable owners of Ryedale. In the 1870s a Mrs. Potter kept it as the Lion Inn until she married George Morgan, the mining engineer of the nearby Sherrif Pit. The custom the miners brought was demanding. The ale is no longer served in half gallon jugs, but it is still a wonderful pub.

THE LIQUORICE BUSH, PONTEFRACT

Gven the town's status as the world capital of liquorice production and the fact that it is the host of the annual Liquorice Fair, it comes as no surprise to find a pub called The Liquorice Bush. Previous names have been less interesting: **The Tankard** and **The Central**. Pontefract also has **The Ancient Borough Arms** once known as **Brices Vaults** from 1860 after Brice and Butler, the chemists.

THE LORD COLLINGWOOD, UPPER POPPLETON
Named after Vice Admiral Cuthbert Collingwood (1748 – 1810) an admiral in the Royal Navy, and a colleague of Lord Nelson's in several of the British victories in the Napoleonic Wars. On Nelson's death at Trafalgar Collingwood assumed the command of the British fleet.

THE LOWTHER HOTEL, GOOLE
The Lowther, in Aire Street, was the first building to be built in New Goole by Sir Edward Banks, in 1824; it was originally called **The Banks Arms Hotel** but was renamed in 1935, after Sir Edward died, in honour of Sir John Lowther, chairman of the Aire & Calder Navigation when the canal first opened.

The town was bombed by Zeppelins in the First World War: the mass grave for the victims of a raid which destroyed a theatre is in the cemetery of St. John's. Sixteen people died on 9th August 1915: ages ranged from eight months to 74 years. This was the second time all the windows at the Lowther were smashed... The Riot Act was read from there in April 1880 during an election-day riot: the Lowther was the Tory headquarters and fights broke out as Liberals surrounded the hotel and tried to gain entry. All the windows were smashed and police reinforcements were called.

MAJOR TOM'S, HARROGATE
Opened February 2014 and named, of course, after Major Tom in David Bowie's *Space Oddity*. It seems to always have been a place of entertainment in one form or another: it was a dance hall in the early 1920s, a place for rest and recuperation for the troops in the 1940s and it was a nightclub in the 1970s. It may also have been a masonic lodge at some point. Before it was refurbished as Major Tom's it served time as an antique centre with a number individual traders under one roof. The upstairs was split into about ten different shops and it had a small café. Now there is a vintage shop downstairs and a record shop upstairs with the bar/cafe.

THE MALLYAN SPOUT HOTEL, GOATHLAND
Named after the waterfall – the tallest in the North York Moors at 70 feet, the hotel dates back to 1892. Goathland was of course the setting for the village of Aidensfield in the popular soap, *Heartbeat*. The name Aidensfield was arrived at after a visit to St. Mary's Church nearby where members of the crew admired stained glass pictures of St. Aidan.

THE MARQUIS OF GRANBY, KNARESBOROUGH
Lieutenant-General John Manners, Marquess of Granby PC, (2nd January 1721 – 18th October 1770) was commander in chief of the British army from 1776 to 1770 and an M.P. for Grantham from 1754 to 1768. When Granby, serving in the Blues and Royals, was sent to Paderborn in northern Germany to command a cavalry brigade he led a charge at the Battle of Warburg and is said to "have lost his hat and wig, forcing him to salute his commander without them". This instigated a British Army tradition whereby non-commissioned officers and troopers of the Blues and Royals are the only British army soldiers who may salute superior officers without wearing headdress.

Granby was one of the first commanders to appreciate and understand how crucial welfare and morale were for the troops. Most of his portraits show him mounting a horse, or helping the wounded. The reason why he so frequently appears on pub signs is his philanthropy: he gave financial assistance to many of his wounded soldiers to start a new life and help them set up as innkeepers.

THE MAYPOLE, CLIFTON, YORK
The Sign of The Maypole used to be on Clifton Green named after the maypole which stood there. Sadly,

there is more to its reputation than the innocent pleasure of dancing round a decorated pole. In 1647 sisters Elizabeth and Helen Drysdale were executed at York for poisoning the beer of their lovers here with oxalic acid; the men died, the girls hanged and the girls' bodies were later given up for anatomical dissection. In 1649 another woman was hanged after being found guilty of burning down the pub.

THE MOON AND SIXPENCE, WHITBY
Named after Somerset Maugham's *The Moon and Sixpence*; he explained this with "if you look on the ground in search of a sixpence, you don't look up, and so miss the moon".

THE MORELY DASHERS, MORLEY
The Morley Dashers is so named after the piece workers who took finished cloth from Morley to Leeds and then dashed back for more.

THE MORRITT ARMS, GRETA BRIDGE
Famous for its literary and fine art associations, the present Morritt extends back to the late 17th century when it was a farm; some of the farm outbuildings were were converted into the hotel and surrounding buildings. With the days of coaching, Greta Bridge became the second overnight stop for the London-Carlisle coach, bringing with it many visitors and a demand to cater for them. There were soon three inns at Greta Bridge, including The George, situated on the bridge on the other side of the river, and **The New Inn**, now Thorpe Farm, and **The George and Dragon**.

Charles Dickens visited Greta Bridge in 1839 to research *Nicholas Nickelby* and highlight the scandal of cheap boarding schools. Dickens stayed at The Morritt with Hablot K. Browne (better known to us as illustrator Phiz) – and in the novel made it the meeting place between Nicholas and Wackford Squeers. In what must be one of the first 'five star' hotel reviews this is how he described his stay in a letter to his wife Kate soon after arrival on a blizzardy Yorkshire night:

> I was in a perfect agony of apprehension, for it was fearfully cold, and there were no outward signs of anybody being up in the house. But to our great joy we discovered a comfortable room, with drawn curtains and a most blazing fire. In half an hour they gave us a smoking supper and a bottle of mulled port (in which we drank your health), and then we retired to a couple of capital bedrooms, in each of which there was a rousing fire halfway up the chimney. We have had for breakfast, toast, cakes, a Yorkshire pie, a piece of beef about the size and much the shape of my portmanteau, tea, coffee, ham, and eggs; and are now going to look about us.

Between the end of the 18th century and beginning of the 19th Turner and Cotman painted many of the picturesque spots in and around the River Greta. Sir Walter Scott's epic poem, *Rokeby*, is set close to The Morritt. The famous York architect John Carr, designed the bridge near to the hotel.

The association with Dickens lives on in The Morritt with the unique mural of Dickensian characters in The Dickens Bar. In 1946 John Gilroy, famous for his advertising images for Guinness, completed the mural as a favour to Major Morritt, the then owner.

NELLIE'S, BEVERLEY
Officially **The White Horse** in Hengate it acquired the name Nellie's from the days before 1976 when the pub was owned and run by the Collinsons family. Francis Collinson bought the pub form the church in 1927 and her daughter Nellie managed it until its sale to Samuel Smith's. The pub was originally a coaching inn; records go back before 1666; it is the second oldest surviving Inn in Beverley after **The Sun Inn**, opposite Beverley Minster. However, Nellies has preserved most of its original features, 'including gas lights and chandeliers, small individual rooms, rickety stone and wooden floors, and open

fires'. Unlikey as it sounds, Sam Smith's modernised the place in 1976 installing its first bar –before that your beer was served on the kitchen table. The sign was a rocking horse above the door and there was a well in the yard. Nellie's lover was Suitcase Johnny, so named because of the freqency with which Nellie kicked him out.

Not to be outdone, nearby **The Royal Standard** on North Bar Within from 1546 was known as **Dolly's** – after Dolly Wilde, veteran landlord there. Previous names were **The Boot Hotel**, and **The Turf Hotel** on account of Beverley races.

THE NEW BEEHIVE, BRADFORD
This pub displays 'Arts and Crafts' interior design at its best with its five gas-lit bars, extensive oak panelling, high ceilings, and huge mirrors . Three of the rooms boast open fires which together with the 58 gas lamps create a truly atmospheric ambience.

THE OLD BALL, LEEDS
Named after balls delivered at Horsforth Cricket club pitch next door.

THE OLD BELL TAVERN, HARROGATE
The tavern's name refers to the fact that until 1815 an earlier inn, **The Bell**, occupied the site. The original Bell Tavern was one of the early 17th century alehouses which served visitors to Harrogate's world famous Old Sulphur Well which lies beneath the dome of the Pump Room museum opposite. It was sometimes called **The Blue Bell**, because of the colour of its sign; the inn was also a stage in the York to Harrogate coaching journey; the 'machine' had its York terminus at **The Black Swan** in Peasholme Green there arriving 'in time for dinner'. **The Bell Tavern** closed in November 1815, after which the property was a private residence until 1846 when the site was cleared for the building of Royal Parade; the original Bell's cellars were incorporated into the new building. A set of historic drawings showing the original Bell Inn are on display in the Old Bell bar lobby area. In 2001 the ground floor of No.7 Royal Parade was merged into the tavern. This was originally the world famous Farrah's Harrogate Toffee shop: the room has been restored with the centrepiece comprising the original Farrah shop display unit – a fascinating museum of Farrah memorabilia.

The aim, and the unique selling point, of Original Harrogate Toffee was to cleanse the palate of the putrid taste of Harrogate's sulphur water. Original Harrogate Toffee is similar to both butterscotch and barley sugar and uses three different types of sugar, butter and lemon to give a unique texture and flavour. It is still made in copper pans and packaged in the recognisable trade-mark blue and silver embossed tins. According to a newspaper clipping on the wall President Bill Clinton visited the pub during a trip to Britain: he downed a Diet Pepsi.

YE OLDE BLACK BOY, HULL
The oldest pub in Hull, dating from 1729. The site of the Black Boy (but not the pub) can be found in early Hull rentals; the first property was known as Gastryk House. In 1336 Richard Taverner came into possession of a tenement, a gift of William de Gastryk to Richard's father, Hugh. The Black Boy only occupies part of the Gastryk House site. The name first appears in 1748 when a deed involving William Hayton, baker, mentions the Black Boy to the south of his land.

OLD MOTHER REDCAP, SHEFFIELD
Old Mother Redcap was what "ale wives" who brewed the beer in beer houses were called.

THE OLDE OAK INN, COWTHORPE, NEAR HARROGATE
Named after the gigantic oak tree here. According to a history of Knaresborough, "*The leading branch fell, by a storm, in the year 1718; which, being measured with accuracy, was found to contain five tons and two feet of wood.*

Before this accidental mutilation, its branches are said to have extended their shade over half an acre of ground; thus constituting, in a single tree, almost a wood itself'.

The entire tree contains 70 tons of wood and is said to be between 600 and 1600 years old. In the 1880s 95 children and their vicar assembled in the tree's hollow and sang hymns from within.

THE OLD RED GINN, BRADFORD
The headquarters of Bradford Northern Rugby League club after the split from the Union. The name comes from a hoist used in the local collieries.

YE OLDE STARRE INN, YORK
York's oldest licensed public house, serving us since at least 1644. The striking gallows sign of the Olde Starre Inne still stretches across the street, originally erected in 1733 by landlord Thomas Bulmer who was obliged to pay the owner of the building over the street on to which it joined - 5s rent per year. In 1886 it read '***Boddy's Star Inn***'; the pub is named after Charles I – popularly known as '*the Old Star*' and was used as a Civil War morgue, field station and operating theatre by the Parliamentarians, much to the disgust of the Royalist landlord. The cellar is 10th century and the well was once the only source of clean water in the area.

YE OLDE WHITE HARTE, HULL
The pub was originally a house built in the Artisan Mannerist style similar to nearby Wilberforce House, probably in the 1620's. The pub dates from around 1700 so stories regarding the 'plotting room' and its association with Charles I and the start of civil war simply do not fit. The famous skull on display here is interesting.

The skull is a youth's. A slight fracture indicates he died from a blow to the head sustained when an angry sea captain, drunk on French brandy, belted him with the butt of his pistol. The boy's body was secreted under the staircase where it remained undiscovered until after a fire sometime in the 19th century. Some contend that the skull was found in the attic during renovations in 1881 and that it belongs to a serving girl who was seduced by the landlord and her body hidden up there to avoid scandal and the wrath of the landlady.

This White Harte is in Silver Street; there is another **White Hart**, a former gin palace, in Alfred Gelder Street with a magnificent and very rare ceramic bar. The white hart was the badge of King Richard II.

THE ORIGINAL ALFRED MOODIES, WAKEFIELD
Also known as **Moody's Vaults** and **The Hole in the Wall** it was originally a wine merchants shop. **The Redoubt** here was named after a Royal Navy warship; before, it was **The Drovers' Inn** and **The Spotted Cow**. **The Royal Oak** sees the start of the annual World Coal Carrying Championship. At nearby Sandal **The Three Houses** was where Swift Nick – John Nevison- was arrested on his rapid ride from London. No sign of Dick Turpin.

THE PACK HORSE, LEEDS
Has been going since 1615. It was part of the estate of the Manor of Whitkirk owned by the Order of St. John of Jerusalem as evidenced by the Templar Cross on the front wall. In the 18th century it was nicknamed **The Slipin** and was home to a dancing academy from 1750. **The Ship Inn** is in the next yard.

THE PALMER FLATT HOTEL, AYSGARTH
The name of this hotel derives from its position on the site of a medieval hospital where ill pilgrims returning from the Holy Land Crusades were treated. These patients often carried palm leaves back with

them as mementoes and as symbols of their pilgrimage – and so became known as 'palmers'. The existing building dates from the 18th century and in 1854 was described as *"a wayside hostelry of truly rural appearance, but possessing excellent accommodation and liquors, for the numerous parties of visitors to the Falls, by whom it is much frequented in the summer months"*. The current owners have, sadly, renamed the pub the dull and commercially correct **Aysgarth Falls Hotel** – devoid of and stripped of any history.

THE PEACOCK INN, LEEDS
Opposite the Leeds United football ground, the pub gave the club its original nickname – not the other way round. Elland Road has been the home of Leeds United AFC since the club was founded in 1919; previously the ground was occupied by Leeds City FC and Holbeck Rugby Club. Bentley's Brewery owned it under the name of the Old Peacock Ground, after the nearby pub – hence the club's nickname, the Peacocks.

THE PHOENIX, YORK
In George Street near Fishergate Bar, the original name until the mid 1800s was **The Labour in Vain**. The sign depicted a white woman vigorously scrubbing a black baby to make it white, in vain. The inscription read '*You may wash him and scrub him from morn till night; your labour's in vain, black will never come white*'. The more prosaic new name derives from the Phoenix Iron Foundry which stood nearby. Fishergate Bar had been walled up in 1489 as punishment for the locals who had rioted against a tax levied to pay for a war against Brittany; it was reopened to provide access to the new cattle market in 1827.

THE PODGER, LEEDS
This name comes from a small engineering firm called Archibald's, which closed in the 1950s when the land was bought by Tetley's to create a new pub in Garforth. The brewery asked Mr Archibald to suggest a name. He came up with The Podger, after a tool his firm invented.

THE POLAR BEAR, HULL
The Polar Bear (like **The Botanic** next door) gets its name because it stood opposite the old Hull Zoological Gardens, on the corner of Spring Bank and Princes Avenue. The Polar Bear is famous because it is one of only eleven pubs nationwide that still has a ceramic bar now grade II listed.

THE PORTMAN AND PICKLES, HALIFAX
Takes its name from two Halifax celebrities: Eric Portman and Wilfred Pickles.

THE POSTGATE, EGTON BRIDGE
Nothing to do with posts or gates, but the site of the house of Father Nicholas Postgate on which the pub stands (one of the last of the English martyrs to be hanged, at York in 1679). With the Popish Plot still fresh in the minds of Protestants, Father Postgate was discovered baptising a child in Whitby in 1678 and committed to York Castle on the evidence of three women. On the day of his execution the 82 year old '*was strangled by the hands of the comon hagman, his brest opend and his hearte cut out, the little blood remain in his aged trunk spilt upon the ground*'. The Whitby excise man at whose house the baby was baptised drowned himself in the Devil's Dump, a pool at nearby Sleights.

THE PUSH INN, BEVERLEY
Records go back to 1717, and in later years became the shop of apothecary and spirit merchant's James Mowld Robinson. Accoding to Jan Crowther in her *Beverley in Mid-Victorian Times*:

> ... and surely the most versatile of all – James Mould Robinson, who was a maltster, sold wines and spirits, brewed beer, both for consumption off and on the premises, dispensed medicines and operated as a surgeon, acted as an insurance agent, and sold corn. In 1851 Robinson lived over the shop, but by 1867 he had moved to a more elevated address in North Bar Without.

The name "Push Inn" was apparently taken from a sign on a door of the inn and has become its official name. Better to push in than to be pushed out. It is reminiscent of other jokily named inns such as **The Nobody Inn** in Doddiscombsleigh and Grantham.

THE QUIET WOMAN, YORK

The long-gone Fishergate pub had a sign depicted a woman carrying her decapitated head. Nagging woman meets her fate? A common name often accompanied by sexist rhymes along the lines of "Here is a woman who has lost her head/She's quiet now – you see she's dead".

THE RAGGALDS INN, MOUNTAIN, NEAR BRIGHOUSE

Once a staging post for the cloth industry at 1,200 feet. It was notorious for gambling and illicit (all night) drinking. Alfred J. Brown regales it thus in his Four Boon Fellows: *Now here's to the inn with the rollicking name And the stiffest of sack and the fattest of game*! Nearby is **The Withens** at 1,392 feet, the highest pub in Yorkshire until Tan Hill was imported into the county, famous for its cockfighting and knurr and spell, poor man's golf. It was built to cater for local quarry workers. Quarries also influenced **The Stone Chair** and **The Delvers** near Halifax.

THE RAILWAY HOTEL, TADCASTER

What was **The Bull and Dog** coaching inn changed its name to The Railway Hotel in 1837 when it was acquired by the Wharfedale Brewery of Wetherby from the 6th Duke of Devonshire, and when the rise of the railways was on the horizon. In 1856 the then landlord Godfrey Braim was the victim of an early rail accident: he died in a collision at Church Fenton while returning from the Market Weighton Agricultural Show. Full details can be found on his tombstone in St. Mary's Church. Braim's successor, William Proud, eying the rise of the railways, established a shuttle coach service to Bolton Percy Station *"to meet every train during the day."*

THE REINDEER, DONCASTER

This 200 year old horse coaching inn was just one of many interesting pubs in Doncaster. Others include **The Red Lion** which opened in 1742 and was where the name of the classic St. Leger was decided on – it was named after the servant who suggested the race to the Marquis of Rockingham, the race's sponsor. Indeed there are a plethora of race related pubs here: **The St. Leger Tavern** (1822) formerly **The Three Jolly Blacksmiths**; **The Horse and Jockey** (1815); **The Turf Tavern** (1826) where racehorses were bred in the stables and the first ever horsebox was deployed to transport Elis, the 1836 St. Leger winner, back to Goodwood – drawn by six horses. **The Ridgewood** is named after a 100-7 St. Leger winner while **The Beechers Brook** recalls the notorious Aintree fence.

THE ROMAN BATH, YORK

Formerly **The Mail Coach**, **The Barrel Churn**, **The Cooper**, **The Barrel**, the pub is now named after the Roman bathhouse excavated here in 1930 and which is partly visible, including cold room: *frigidarium*, hot room: *caldarium* and underfloor central heating system: *hypocaust*. Tiles stamped Legio VI and Legio IX have been uncovered recording legions which were stationed at *Eboracum*.

THE ROYAL STATION HOTEL, HULL

Features in Philip Larkin's *Friday Night at the Royal Station Hotel* as a place where "*silence laid like carpet*". Other Larkin haunts include the **Goodfellowship**, **The George Hotel**, **Ye Olde Black Boy** and **Ye Olde White Hart**.

THE SAIR INN, LINTHWAITE, NEAR HUDDERSFIELD

There are a number of theories competing to explain this unusual name. Originally it was known simply as **The New Inn** but later it took on the less simple **t' Saah**: a happy pig on the sign would suggest that saah was really sow; others say it is sour – as in a response to 'how's the beer?' Others still say it is after the name of an owner John O' T' Saah who lived near a stream and saah means, onomatopoeically, a rushing sound. See also Bill O' Jacks.

THE SCARBROUGH INN, LEEDS

Named after a former owner (and not the resort, which has a different spelling). It stands on the site of a mediaeval Leeds manor house that was rebuilt in 1765 as a most desirable residence. Henry Scarbrough bought the property in 1826, when it became known as **The Kings Arms**. In the late 1890s, Fred Wood established The Scarbrough Hotel pub. He organised talent nights here in the large concert hall and any act showing potential was put on at his City Varieties in Leeds. Some people call it **The Scarbrough Taps**; no one seems to know why – apart from the blindingly obvious beer taps.

THE SHIP INN, ALDBOROUGH

The Ship's interior can still boast a good deal of seasoned hard old timber which may well have come from ships; as with the land-locked **Ship Inn** at Strensall serving the Foss Navigation, and **The Ship Inn** at Acaster Malbis (associated with ferry across the Ouse from Naburn) the pub echoes the importance of river traffic, in this case downstream from Boroughbridge.

The Ship was probably a monastic or church rest house at one time, serving St. Andrew's Church opposite. The hostelry probably grew out of a 16th century farm which had its own beer house-cum-brewery. This Ship may be the pub mentioned in the Aldborough parish records for 1596, when a man hired a gun from another man in a pub, gave him two pence to fire a shot, crossed the road over to the church and took a pop over the minister's head. The shot, thankfully, missed but achieved its intention of putting the fear of God in the minister.

We know that it was known as the Ship in the 17th century, evidenced by a token copper coin in existence, dated 1671, which shows a ship in full sale with the inscription "John Briggs in Aldborough his half penny". A John Briggs owned an acre of land in Aldborough at that time. Traders and landlords often issued small copper coins in the reign of Charles II when small change was in short supply. The antiquary William Smith, writing in 1884, believed that the coin depicted the Ship at Aldborough.

The Blackburn family ran the inn for more than 130 years: Thomas Blackburn in 1712, another Thomas Blackburn in 1747, his son Richard in the early 19th century and Ellen Blackburn as late as 1844.
The very inland **Sailor** at Bolton Abbey is called after the sailor's employment agency which existed in the village.

THE SHIP INN, SALTBURN

The seaside town of Saltburn once had four inns - **The Seagull**, **The Dolphin**, **The Nimrod** (where the mortuary stood) and The Ship which dates back to the late 1500s and still serves today. The inn itself was the focus of the local smuggling trade with its most famous landlord John Andrew, known locally as the 'King of Smugglers'. His was a sophisticated operation. Contraband was hidden in a nearby stables in a void under a stall. If a search was expected this stall was occupied by a mare that kicked at strangers. It is said that there were also tunnels connecting the pub to nearby houses.

Until 1881, the Ship Inn was used as the local mortuary for the many victims of drowning awaiting post-mortem from frequent shipwrecks washed up on the beach. Hurricane lamps were still being used in the inn in the 1940s.

The Three Mariners in Scarborough performed a similar morbid role; the buxom figurehead from a wrecked Norwegian ship was erected above the pub's door from which Elvira, as she was known, would descend and warn the town's sailors when a storm approached.

Ships, of course, are all over the place – usually but not always at coastal pubs. To name a few we have, or had, **The Bonny Boat** (an eskimo kayak brought back from a whaling expedition in 1612) in Hull; **The Oberon**, also in Hull; **The Steam Packet** (Goole); **The Sloop** near Snaith; **The Frigate** in Marske; Whitby has its **Cutty Sark**; Hessle its **Ferry Boat Inn** and Bootferry its **Ferry**. There is **The Ship Ahoy** in Bridlington and **The Gipsy Moth** in Selby commemorating Sir Francis Chichester's epic circumnavigation in 1967. **The Newcastle Packet** recalls the importation of north east coal in Scarborough from 1732 in the pub the sailors drank in; the pub dates from 1230 and was once the customs house.

THE SKYRACK, LEEDS
Named after the local wapentake.

THE SLIPWAY, YORK
The Ouse Navigation Trustees built the slipway at Clementhorpe in 1836 which gives its name to the pub there, The Slipway.

THE SNICKELWAY INN, YORK
A 15th century pub named after the famous snickelways (alleys and backstreets) which characterise the city. It was once a brothel as well as being the Royalist powder magazine during the English Civil War. It was originally called The Anglers – nothing to do with fishermen but because it was close to the Minster stonemasons' yard – an angler being a geometrist working on the stones. This follows a long tradition of the pub being named after artisans: previous names include **The Painters' Arms**, **The Square & Compass** and **The Board**.

THE SPACEY HOUSES HOTEL, PANNAL
The recently demolished 19th century Spacey Houses Hotel and pub was on the Pannal side (west), of the A61, named after the coaching inn on the Spacey Houses side, or east side, of the road, which had been converted into a farm house and is now private housing. The hotel had its own brewhouse, the Old Spacey House Brewery Pannal, owned by J. Holmes throughout the 1900s. It was all sold to Tetley's in 1960.

THE SPITE AND THE MALICE, OTLEY
One day in the mid 1800s William Parkinson went for his usual pint at **The Travellers**, converted in 1853 from a row of terraced cottages. In 1852 cottages at the the other end of the terrace had been licensed and became **The Roebuck**. On that fateful day, Parkinson decided to try The Roebuck for a change, after which he headed for his usual Travellers, but he was met with a torrent of abuse from the landlady who told him to return whence he came. Somewhat upset, Parkinson went back to the Travellers, spluttering 'there's nowt but spite and malice up here'. The Travellers became known as **The Malice** and the Roebuck **The Spite**. The Travellers closed down but The Spite lived on and in 1980 was required by magistrates to clarify its name – The Roebuck officially became The Spite.

THE SPOTTED HOUSE, BRADFORD
Probably named after the reference to it as 'The House at the Spot' in 1504. In the 19th century it had a bowling green, tennis courts and a swimming pool. JB Priestley drank here – when he was not drinking at **The George** in Hubberholme. He is buried in the graveyard there. The Spotted House is Priestley's '*haunt of rare souls*'.

THE SQUINTING CAT, LUND HOUSE GREEN, HARROGATE
One of Britain's more intriguing pub names, that of the Squinting Cat in Pannal, built around 1720 as a smithy but converted to a coaching inn in which the dining room was used to repair coaches. The name derives from a former landlady known as 't'owd cat': she was in the habit of squinting out of the window

from behind the curtains to scrutinize customers as they approached; in doing so she gave the pub its nickname, **The Cat**. So, in 1930 when the pub was refurbished it was renamed the Squinting Cat. Recent modernisation has erased all of the pub's former innate charm and character.

There are many other feline inspired pub names, not least **The Red Cat Inn**, in Harrogate. **The Cheshire Cat** at Ellesmere Port is the first reference we have (from 1770) to the phrase 'grinning like a Cheshire Cat'; **The Burmese Cat**, in Melton Mowbray, is a result of a brewery chairman whose wife bred Burmese cats. There is a **Whittington and Cat** in London and one in Hull in deference to Dick, and to his cat with **Puss in Boots**, for example, in York and Stockport; a cat turns up on the **Whittington Stone** at Highgate, London and **The Whittington Cat** at Whitehaven. **The Cat I' Th' Well** near Halifax gets its name from the Catywell Brook and not a cat. Similar, but very different, is **The Blinking Owl** at Boroughbridge.

THE STAR, BRIDLINGTON
Named after the star which guided the three wise men to Bethlehem. There is another **Star** at Harome.

THE SUN INN, LONG MARSTON
Undoubtedly the most famous visitor to this pub would have been Oliver Cromwell, around the time of the famous and decisive Civil War battle at Marston Moor in 1664. The pub itself is named after Edward VI, and has long been populated by ghosts which include Cromwell himself, lots of Royalist troops and Prince Rupert of the Rhine fleeing on horseback.

THE SWAN AND TALBOT, WETHERBY
This building was sold for £1,510 in the great Wetherby sale. The Swan and Talbot coaching inn has the dubious distinction of receiving a direct hit from a German incendiary bomb during the Second World War. It went through the roof and two floors, only to burn itself out on the cellar floor. The inn was originally called **The Dog and Swan** and was permitted until 1611 to bear the coat of arms of the Swann family from Askham Manor in Askham Richard. The dog in question was a talbot hound, a hunting dog similar to the beagle and now extinct. The name was then changed to the Swan and Talbot.

THE SWAN ON THE STRAY, HARROGATE
The Swan on the Stray used to be called **The Black Swan**, hence the sign; it was extensively refurbished before its reopening in February 2010. There has been a Black Swan on this site in High Harrogate since at least the latter part of the 18th century. In 1815 there is a record revealing that "the workhouse committee refreshed itself liberally at the Black Swan, receiving a bill from Landlord Joseph Waite for £5 6s 10d". Alright for some.

Other ornithological pubs flock to Yorkshire. They include **The Phoenix** near Barnsley (and York) and **The Dotterel** near Filey. **The Eagle and Child** (Conisborough and once in York) comes from the coat of arms of the Earl of Derby while **The Swan with Two Necks** (Leeds and Wakefield) is a corruption of the Vintners Company crest – the swan with two nicks. Tadcaster has **The Jackdaw**, **The Old Falcon** and **The Falcon**. **The Red Rooster** is in Brighouse while Sheffield has its **Pheasant**. Ex birds are also represented: **The Pigeon Pie** is at Sherburn, is listed and dates from 1800. **The Wrens** in Leeds is a favourite with the Opera North crowd at the Grand Theatre nearby; despite the wrens on the sign, it has nothing to with the bird though – named as it is after Mrs Wren, the first landlord.

THE SWORDSMAN, STAMFORD BRIDGE
Named after the fighting in the crucial battle here in 1066 before the even more crucial battle at Hastings. In the early autumn of 1066, Harold Godwinson's English throne was under serious military threat on two fronts: from Harald Hardrada (with Harold's disaffected and exiled brother, Tostig Godwinson) in the north and from William of Normandy in the south. York capitulated to the Vikings and left Harold

in a quandary: to meet Hardrada in battle and then go on to deal with William or to head south immediately. In the event Harold came north and joined battle with Harald here at Stamford Bridge winning a total and militarily impressive victory.

Stamford Bridge has never been short of public houses. **The Three Tuns**, recorded in 1823, is lost to us but **The Bay Horse** and **The New Inn**, mentioned in records in 1823 and 1840 respectively, remain open. The New Inn was renamed The Swordsman in 1974 to celebrate the town's Viking heritage. **The Jolly Sailors**, mentioned in 1840, was possibly **The Hope & Anchor**, known from 1851 and last recorded in 1892. **The Three Cups** on York Road is reputedly on the site of a camp for soldiers waiting to take part in the battle; an ancient, 23-foot-deep draw well, discovered during building works in the 1960s, can still be seen today through a porthole in the floor.

Other belligerent Yorkshire pubs include **The Standard Inn** after the 1138 battle of that name near Northallerton; and **The Crooked Billet** (a twisted branch used as a poor man's walking stick or as a weapon) after the exceedingly bloody War of the Roses battle at Towton in 1461. It is the meeting place of Towton Battlefield Society, whose aim is to preserve the skills and craft of the traditional longbow. York has its **Trafalgar Bay** and Halifax its **Trafalgar**; there is a **Crimea Tavern** at Castleford and a **Crimea Inn** near Huddersfield; **The Balaclava Inn** was in Norton and **The Inkerman Tavern** in Hull. An **Alma Inn** at Sowerby Bridge is named after the victory at Alma in the Crimea. Rotherham's **Tabard** denotes the sleeveless tunics worn by heralds while **The Cat and Bagpipes**, a corruption of cateran, at East Harlsey reminds us of the marauding, freebooting Scots. Darsfield near Barnsley has **The Longbow**. Todmorden celebrates two ships involved in a naval battle outside Boston Harbour during the American War of Idependance: **The Chesaspeake and Shannon** which opened in 1813. The outcome was that *The Shannon* captured *The Chesaspeake* and towed her to Halifax, Nova Scotia where she was commissioned into the Royal Navy. There is a **Dunkirk Inn** at Denby Dale. **The Light Horseman** in York from 1830 echoes to the building of the cavalry barracks nearby in Fulford Road.

THE TAN HILL INN, REETH

The Tan Hill Inn from 1737 is the highest inn in the British Isles at 1,732 feet. It dates to the 17th century; during the 18th century it was used as an inn by coal miners. The last mine on Tan Hill closed in 1929. The pub is also one of Britain's most isolated although it used to be surrounded by miners' cottages, until these were demolished in the 1920s. The mining industry is reflected in the pub's earlier name, **The Kings Pit**. **The Cat Hole** near Keld was similarly remote and has been called 'the loneliest inn in the world'.

THE THREE ARROWS, BOROUGHBRIDGE

We know lot more about the pub here than we do about the stones which it commemorates. No one really knows for sure where the stones came from, how many there originally were, what they were for ,and who placed them and when. What we do know is that they are Neolithic gritstone monoliths, 18ft, 22ft and 22ft 6in tall, the last being taller than anything at Stonehenge. They have been variously called The Devil's Bolts, The Three Greyhounds and The Three Sisters but are today usually named either The Three Arrows or The Devil's Arrows. The origin of the latter comes from the end of the 17th century: Old Nick, irritated by an insult from Aldborough, threw the stones at the village from How Hill, south of Fountains Abbey but the arrows fell short by a mile. You should know that walking twelve times around the stones anti-clockwise will raise the Devil. The missing fourth arrow was, according to John Leland, used for the foundations of Peggy Bridge over the River Tutt at St. Helena in Boroughbridge.

THE THREE CRANES, YORK

The sign on The Three Cranes pub in St. Sampson's Square is designed to mislead: the pub is named after the lifting gear used by stallholders rather than anything ornithological.

THE THREE LEGGED MARE, YORK

This York pub is named after a triangular type of industrial gallows which despatched three felons at once; one was in use at the Knavesmire until 1801; it was removed in 1812. There is a replica of the 'wonkey donkey' in the beer garden of the pub in Low Petergate - there is no future in riding the three legged mare. The pub is owned by the York Brewery which started brewing in 1996 – the first local brewers since the closure of Aldwark based Hunt's in 1956. The brewery's other York pubs are **The Last Drop Inn** in Colliergate; **The Yorkshire Terrier** in Stonegate and **The Tap Room** in the brewery itself in Toft Green. In Leeds the Brewery has Mr Foley's Cask Ale House opposite Leeds town hall.

THREE MARINERS INN, SCARBOROUGH

The pub is one of Scarborough's oldest, dating back to the 1300s. It is certainly one of the most haunted—by a headless woman, who warns fishermen of impending doom and disaster. The pub is now a museum charting the history of smuggling in the area; it was linked to the shore by a series of caves and tunnels and features secret cupboards, false floors and hidden rooms. There is even a very small window used as a look out down Quay Street. Over the years the Three Mariners has revealed some of its secret past: a concealed room has been discovered there which contained a keg of gunpowder; a small boy broke through some plaster one day to find himself trapped in a small cupboard—only his cries revealed his whereabouts.

THE THREE MERRY LADS, SHEFFIELD

The Three Merry Lads was originally a farm but was converted into a pub around 1837. It was owned by the Marsden family who named it after their three sons.

THE THREE PIGEONS, HALIFAX

This English Heritage Grade II listed building dates from 1932 and retains most of its original Art Deco interior. It is also listed as one of the UK's top ten most architecturally important pubs by Camra.

THE THREE SWANS, SELBY

The official crest of Selby Abbey shows three swans; they live on in the name of the pub at the end of Church Lane. The story of the abbey starts from when Benedict sailed up the River Ouse and spotted three swans alighting on the bank close by. This he took to be an omen – a sign of the Father, the Son and the Holy Ghost – and immediately planted a cross and built a wooden hut there. William the Conqueror's Governor of York, Viscount Hugh, spotted the settlement on his land while sailing up the Ouse and promised to put in a word with the king. William made Benedict an abbot and gave him the land on which to build the abbey. The site had been a place of worship since 1070, when Benedictine monks led by Benedict of Auxerre moved from their wooden church on the River Ouse and began building the abbey around 1100.

THE TOM BROWN INN, YARM

Private Tom of the 3rd Hussars (the Blands Dragoons) was born at Kirkleatham near Redcar on June 25th, 1710. Tom showed conspicuous courage at the Battle of Dettingen in 1743 in Bavaria during the War of the Austrian Succession. The thrilling citation for his resulting knighthood reads as follows:

> 'He had two horses killed under him, two fingers of his bridle hand chopped off and, after retaking the standard from a gentleman at arms, whom he killed, he placed it between his legs and the saddle and made his way 80 yards through a lane of the enemy, exposed to fire and sword of the enemy in the execution of which he received eight cuts in his face, hands and neck, 2 balls lodged in his back, 3 went through his hat, and in this hacked condition he rejoined his regiment, who gave him three huzzas on his arrival'.

At Dettingen, King George II became the last English monarch to lead his army into battle. The heroic

Tom Brown was the last man to be knighted (as a Knight banneret) on the battlefield. Tom was buried in Yarm in 1746 in St. Mary Magdalene's Church where his grave is marked with a replica of a Commonwealth War Graves Commission headstone, presented by the Queen's Own Hussars in 1968. A banneret was 'a commoner of rank who led a company of troops in battle under his own banner; the military rank of a knight banneret was higher than a knight bachelor (who fought under someone else's banner), but lower than an earl or duke.

THE TOMMY WASS, LEEDS
In 1927 this Beeston pub was known as **The Alice Doidge Refreshment Rooms**, but the place dates from the late 19th century when it was a farmhouse on a 64-acre farm run by the eponymous Thomas Wass.

THE TRUE BRITON, WILBERFOSS
The first recorded alehouse here was licensed in 1729, later accompanied by up to four others later in the century. In 1823 there were **The Horseshoes** or **The Blacksmith's Arms** (demolished to make way for the bypass), The True Briton, and **The Waggon & Horses**. The True Briton became **The Oddfellows Arms** around 1840 and The Waggon & Horses closed before 1872.

THE UNICORN, RIPON
Tom Crudd, alias Thomas Spence or Old Boots, worked at this coaching inn as boot boy greeting travellers on the stagecoaches and private carriages. He was something of a star, offering entertainment as well as boot-jack or boot-pull and slippers; his star turn was holding a coin (proffered by a guest) between his nose and chin. Tom kept the coin.

THE VERMUYDEN HOTEL, GOOLE
Named after the Dutch civil engineering expert Cornelius Vermuyden from Zeeland. On instructions from Charles I, in his 1629 Dutch River project, he diverted the Dutch River, or River Don, northwards to join the River Ouse and thereby drain the marshland of Hatfield Chase, a favourite hunting ground of kings. A more lucrative benefit for the port was that it made the lower Don navigable for small barges, bringing coal to Goole from the South Yorkshire Coalfields for transfer to seagoing vessels.

THE VICTORIA, HUDDERSFIELD
Known locally as The Bum-Royd. The official name is after the nearby Victoria Tower on Castle Hill: a tavern was built on the hill in about 1810 to cater for visitors and patrons of the bowling green, bare-knuckled prize fights, dogfights and cockfights. The Victoria was converted in 1935 from a suburban house.

THE WAKEMAN, RIPON
Named after the ancient office of the Wakeman. The Curfew Horn, unique to Ripon, has been blown each night by the Wakeman since the 13th century to 'set the watch'. The ceremony still takes place at the four corners of the obelisk and at the mayor's house. It was originally blown at the mayor's house and then the town hall, but reversed in 1913 so that spectators might catch the 9.29 pm to Harrogate. The Wakeman also hired constables to help keep order in the city. The office of Bellman dates from 1367, and ever since he can be found ringing his bell at eleven o'clock every Thursday morning in Market Square to open the now defunct corn market. He was empowered to levy a toll on each sack sold (the Market Sweepings), to start the Quarter Sessions and inflict whippings on law-breakers. All householders had to contribute to the cost of this service — twopence for each outer door of their house per annum.

WETHERSPOONS WINTER GARDENS, HARROGATE
Concerts were a popular attraction here with bands like Cecil Moon's Palm Court Trio making regular

appearances to packed houses. In the 1930s, the Municipal Orchestra played every morning throughout the year, with free admission for the patients of the baths. The Gardens opened in 1897 and were demolished in 1936 when the Lounge Hall and Fountain Court were built to replace them. All that remains are the original stone entrance foyer and staircase. The days of such top-class classical entertainment by the likes of Britten, Segovia, du Pré, and Menuhin are over.

TH' WHIG MUG HOUSE, HULL
Mug houses were, and still are, pubs in which your personal mug was hung over the bar or in the window to await you. This was in Whitefriargate but there were others in Trinity House Lane and Low Gate.

THE WILD MAN, NEAR TADCASTER
Notorious as haunt of thieves and highwaymen it was possibly originally called **The Bush** or something similar if the depositions of York Castle in 1675 are to be believed: Abraham Ibbotson of Leeds was charged with stealing horses, the felonious act being plotted at an ale house in Street Houses *"in the way betwixt Tadcaster and York where there was a bush as a signe."* The bush was associated with the Roman god Bacchus who was often depicted as a wild man on account of his characteristic state of frenzy and intoxication; the two symbols have become virtually synonymous. Legend has it that the almost life-size sign was covered up when Queen Victoria passed by *en route* to York with white calico *"so that the Queen might not be shocked at the sight of so hairy (and naked) a man"*. It is now the Aagrah, a Kashmiri restaurant and provides refreshment of a more exotic nature.

THE WILLIAM DIGHTON, HALIFAX
See the Dusty Miller, Mytholmroyd.

WHITELOCKS ALE HOUSE, LEEDS
Grade II listed Whitelock's Ale House first opened its doors in 1715 as **The Turk's Head** in, fittingly enough, Turk's Head Yard. The pub was ideally placed to cater for the traders and customers thronging Briggate market. It is Leeds' oldest surviving pub.

In 1867 John Lupton Whitelock, a flautist with the Hallé and Leeds Symphony Orchestra, was granted the licence of the Turk's Head. The Whitelock family bought the pub in the 1880s and in 1886 completed a refurbishment which has left us with the elaborate décor we can still see and enjoy today, including the long marble topped bar, etched mirrors and glass.

In the mid-1890s the pub was rebadged as **Whitelock's First City Luncheon Bar** and in 1897 John Lupton Whitelock installed electricity, including an exciting new revolving searchlight, at the Briggate entrance to the yard. Trick beer glasses in which a sovereign was placed ensured the punter got, not the money, but an electric shock.

Prince George (1902-1942), later Duke of Kent, threw a party there in a curtained-off section of the restaurant. In those days a doorman ensured that men wore dinner jackets; women were not allowed at the bar, so waiters served drinks to the women where they sat.

John Betjeman described Whitelocks as *"the Leeds equivalent of Fleet Street's Old Cheshire Cheese and far less self-conscious, and does a roaring trade. It is the very heart of Leeds."* It figures in *Great Bars of the World* rubbing shoulders with the Long Bar in Shanghai's Peace Hotel and Harry's in Venice.

THE WOMBWELL ARMS, WASS
The Wombwell Arms was constructed around 1620 as a granary, probably using stone from nearby Byland Abbey. The historic building became an ale house in about 1645. Originally called **The Stapylton Arms** after the Stapylton family who owned the village of Wass, the name was changed to

The Wombwell Arms in 1896 when the village was purchased by Sir George Wombwell of Newburgh Priory near Coxwold. Sir George was a member of the same family that owned land near Barnsley in South Yorkshire on which the town of Wombwell is now built. In 1924 the village, including The Wombwell Arms, was sold in various lots at auction. Ownership of The Wombwell Arms then passed to Russells Brewery of Malton and subsequently to Camerons of West Hartlepool. In 1987 the freehold of The Wombwell Arms was sold off by Camerons and the pub remains a freehouse to this day.

THE WUTHERING HEIGHTS, STANBURY NEAR HAWORTH
Brand Brontë (or Kate Bush).

THE ZETLAND, MIDDLESBROUGH
Now closed, but was built in 1860 to serve the railway station opposite as a pub and hotel. Glories included the mosaic floor at the entrance and the cast iron columns on the frontage; in 1893 a magnificent tiled and mirrored back lounge was added with ornate ceiling. It is named after Lawrence Dundas, 3rd Earl of Zetland (1844–1929) who was made Marquess of Zetland in 1892. Zetland is an archaic spelling of Shetland. From 1889 to 1892 he was Lord Lieutenant of Ireland and was made Earl of Ronaldshay, in the County of Orkney and Zetland, and Marquess of Zetland. The family seat is still Aske Hall near Richmond.

THE ZETLAND HOTEL, SALTBURN
The hotel is the oldest railway hotel in the world (it opened in 1863) and had its own railway halt for the exclusive (and weather proof) use of its clients.

Some Lost Pubs of Yorkshire

O Yorkshire, Yorkshire: Thy Ale is so strong
That it will kill us all if we stay long:
So they agreed a Journey for to make
Into the South, some Respit there to take.
George Meriton 1684, *The Praise of Yorkshire Ale*

York

Artichoke, Micklegate
Barefoot, Micklegate
Barleycorn, Coppergate and Bedern
Blue Bear, Castlegate
Bird in Hand – demolished to make way for
   Exhibition Square
Black Dog, High Ousegate
Bowling Green, Groves Lane;
   there is still a bowling green nearby
Cattle Market, Fawcett Street
Coach and Horses, Jubbergate.
   The sign depicted the coach and horses but the
   writing made no such reference, saying instead
   Saynors after the family which ran it. **The
   Coach and Horses** in Nessgate was known as
   Big Coach; that in Micklegate as **Little Coach**.
Cooper,
   the **Barrell Churn** and the **Barrell** in the late
   18th century and the **Mail Coach** after that
   for 140 year; now the **Roman Bath**.
Cricketers Arms, Tanner Row
Cygnet, Nunnery Lane
Eagle and Child, Shambles
Ebor Vaults, Church Street
Elephant and Castle, Skeldergate
Fighting Cocks, Walmgate
Fortunate Tar, North Street
Froghall Tavern, Layerthorpe
Garricks Head, Low Petergate
George, Bootham Bar
Glassmakers Arms, Fawcett Street
Gallows House, Tadcaster Road
Globe, Shambles
Golden Barrel, Walmgate
Greyhound, Spurriergate
Ham and Barrel, Walmgate
Ham & Firkin, Walmgate

Hand & Heart, St. Sampson's Square
Hand & Whip, Castlegate
Haymarket, Haymarket
Hole in the Wall, next to the Chapel of
   St. Sepulchre where the Minster Library is now
Imperial, Crichton Avenue
Jacob's Well, Trinity Lane
Jolly Bacchus, High Ousegate
Leeds Arms, Peasholme Green,
Leopard, Coney Street
Lion & Lamb, Blossom Street
London Hotel, Davygate
Londesborough Arms, 52 Low Petergate
Lottery, St. Nicholas' Place
Magpie, Penlys Grove Street
Neptune, Micklegate
Newcastle Arms, George Street
Old Malt Shovel, Walmgate
Old Turk's Head, King's Square
Pack Horse, Shambles
Pack Horse, Skeldergate
Railway King, George Hudson Street
Reindeer, Penlys Grove Street
Sanctuary, 68 Gillygate
Ship, 5 King's Staith
Sportsman, Hungate
Spotted Dog, Walmgate
Talbot, Church Street
Three Cups, Walmgate
Three Jolly Butchers, Church Street
Trinity House, Trinity Lane
Trumpet, Town End Street
Turf Tavern, Thanet Road
Turk's Head, St. Andrewgate
Unicorn, Tanner Row, and Lord Mayor's Walk
Whale Fishery, Carmelite Street

Leeds

The Gamecock (Pudsey)

Pineapple Inn (Hunslet) first recorded in the High Street in 1871. There were four Pineapples in Leeds at one time.

Black Dog (East Leeds)

City of Mabgate (East Leeds)

This pub is shrouded in mythology. Apparently there was a tunnel from the nearby parish church linking the Palace pub and the cellar of the Mabgate pub. This was allegedly to have built by the priests so they could clandestinely visit prostitutes in secret, and no doubt down a few pints at the same time. The Mabgate area of the City was a notorious red light district - the name 'Mab' was an insult in Shakespeare's day - it was synonymous with a prostitute.

The Punch Clock (Beeston) – after the clocking in time machine, at the **Crooked Clock**.

Hark to Rover (Kirkstall)

The Whip

Star and Garter

The Cobourg

The Haunch of Venison

The Horse and Trumpet

Amongst the 200 or so dwellings in High Street we learn from directories that in:

1854 John Swale had a beer house at 120 High Street

1861 William Maxwell had a Beerhouse at No. 2; William Anderson had a Beerhouse at No. 47; Sarah Swale had a Beerhouse at No. 121

1866 George Murfin now had No. 47; Sarah Swale had moved to No. 118

1871 William Maxwell was now at No. 1; John Stewart had started a Beerhouse at No. 32; George Murfin was now at No. 95; Thomas Ackroyd was at No. 97

1872 H. Cockshott was at the Brokers Arms at No. 1; J. Stewart was at the Pine Apple Inn at No. 32; George Naylor a fully licensed victuallar was at the Hop Pole at No. 51; George Murfin had the Swimmers Arms at No. 95; Thomas Ackroyd had the Lisbon Tavern at No. 97; George Parfitt a full licensed victullar was at the Golden Fleece at No. 103/5

1876 T. Kidney had the Swimmers Arms at No. 95;

1877 Samuel Stead is now at the Swimmers Arms; John Birch is now at the Lisbon Tavern;

1881 Henry Cockshott is at the Brokers Arms; John Stewart at the Pine Apple Inn; Richard Goodhind at the Hop Pole; Matthew Mann at the Swimmers Arms; John Birch at the Lisbon Tavern

1891 William Smith is now at the Brokers Arms; George Horsfall is at the Pine Apple Inn; Walter Ormerod is now at the Hop Pole; Terence Tolan is at the Swimmers Arms now 91 High Street; George Brewster is at the Lisbon Tavern now 93 High Street

1894 Joseph Glendenning now has the Pine Apple Inn; Abraham Castellow is at the Hop Pole now 47 High Street; Edward Merritt is now at the Swimmers Arms; William Foster is now at the Lisbon Tavern

1901 Fred Ayres is now at the Brokers Arms; Pat Ivers is now at the Swimmers Arms; William Elliott is now at the Lisbon Tavern.

If nothing else this clearly demonstrates what a transitory, incestuous and unpredictable business running a beer house or pub was at the end of the 19th century. The rapid turnover and changes of tenancy may be indicative of failure to keep the pledges relating to disorderly behaviour, short measures and watering down, and maybe liver disease and other drink-related illnesses.

Sheffield city centre

Ball Inn
Barleycorn
Barrow Boys
Birmingham Arms
Brave Old Oak
Buccaneer
Ceylon Inn
Claymore
Cossack
Domino
Matilda Tavern
Mulberry Tavern

Museum
Paradise Inn
Phoenix
Pump
Raven
Rock Tavern
Runaway Girl
Sun Tavern
Three Cranes
Wapentake
Yorkshire Grey

Hull

Bowling Green Tavern
Builders Hotel
Burns Head
Cartmans Arms
   this was also the North Myton Soup Kitchen in the early 1860s; the name probably originates from a previous tenant, Atkinson Miller, who was listed here as a Hackney Cartman in the 1861 census.
Citadel Hotel
Crystal Hotel
   the Crystal was demolished in the early 1970s as part of a compulsory purchase order which razed this whole district, taking with it the **Sculcoates Arms, Burns Head, Mechanics Arms, Pacific Hotel** and others.
Dover Castle and **Dover Castle Hotel**
Drum & Cymbals
   fittingly on Sibelius Road - closed in 1956, when the licence was surrendered for the granting of a full licence to **The Old English Gentleman**.
Edinburgh Packet
Ferryboat Tavern
   a beer-house around 1842 which gets its name from the many boats which were used in the area to transfer workers from the Groves on the east-side of the river, to work in the factories on the west. From ca.1873 to 1876 it was known as Tiger No.5, as John Stephenson (landlord of the Tiger No.1 in Waterworks Street) had bought several inns and given them all the name Tiger and a number. The practice

did not last long, however, and the pubs soon reverted back to their original names.
Full Measure
Highland Laddie
   listed from 1803 as the **Golden Fleece**, victualler. From 1826 it became known simply as **The Fleece,** until 1907 when it was re-named the Highland Laddie.
Lily Hotel
Lord Londesborough
   originally known as the **Anchor**, and later the **Paul Pry**, it was re-named the Lord Londesborough around 1863 in honour of the colonel (honorary) of the First East Yorkshire Rifle Volunteers. In 1864 the Hull Rifle Corps were allowed to re name the street (Waterworks Street), which was home to their Rifle Barracks, as Londesborough Street.
Marrowbone & Cleaver, Fetter Lane
   Fetter Lane got its name from the fetters that prisoners were held in while at the 'House of Correction'. This dingy building stood opposite this pub within Fetter Lane from ca.1796 until the 1820s, when a combined Gaol and House of Correction was built in Castle Street.
Mechanics Arms
   named after Rose's iron foundry nearby
Monument Tavern
   may have been known as the **Cross Keys** or **Turks Head** before 1778 until 1817 when it was re-built. From the 1820s it was the **Old Andrew Marvel**, but later owners changed it to the **York Tavern**, and then the **Wilberforce**

Wine Vaults, before it became known as the Monument Tavern around 1851. The latter names both refer to the monument erected in honour of Hull M.P. and abolitionist William Wilberforce.

Myton Tavern

closed after damage following an air raid on 8 May 1941. Before closure, it was known as **Freddie Fox's** after a landlord.

Nags Head

in the late 18th century – it was the **Summergangs New Inn** – but known as the Nag's Head by 1810, and sold that year as part of the estate of bankrupts Thomas Railey and James Hunt, brewers at the George Yard brewery; other pubs of theirs sold were the **Sir Ralph Abercromby**, High Street; **Kings Arms**, Witham, and **Opening of the Doc'**, Blanket Row. Worthington's purchased all the freehold licensed property in 1922, from William Smith ex-brewer of the Victoria Brewery. The £70,000 he paid got him the Nag's Head; **Kingston Arms**; **Druids Arms**; **Buck Inn**, Beverley; **Highland Laddie**; **Station Hotel**, Howden; **Number One**; **Moulders Arms**, Beverley; **Crown Inn**, Paull; **Newbegin Arms**; **Four in Hand**; **Blue Bell**, Ellerby; and the **Kings Head**, Nafferton.

Neptune Arms

first recorded in 1817, and known locally as **Little Neppy**. Owned by the Hull & Barnsley Railway Co. Brewers Kendall & Gruby re-named it the **Exchange Brewery** in 1876, the brewery was next to the **Portland Arms** in Porter Street. In 1892 Worthingtons bought the brewery, and the estate of 24 pubs which included **Railway Tavern**; **Queen's Head**; **South Myton Tavern**; **Shipwrights Arms**; **Reefer**; **Crown & Cushion**; **Land of Green Ginger**; Neptune Tavern; **Oriental**; **Cromwell Hotel**; **Plumbers Arms** in Dagger Lane; **Juno**; **The Queen**, Charlotte Street; **Norwood Arms**; **Mason's Arms**; **Red Lion**; **Linnet & Lark**; **Dog & Gun**; **Earl Cardigan**, Fish Street, **Alexandra** and the **Albert Hall** in Midland Street.

Old Greenland Fishery, Wincolmlee

converted from houses in the early 1820s, its name refers to the Arctic whaling ships, many of which were built and sailed from the Greenland Yards in the area. The 'Old' was added around 1882, to distinguish it from another pub of that name in Bridge Street.

Ordnance Arms

ironically given its name, this pub received a direct hit on 9th May 1941, and what was left was demolished soon after. The licence was eventually transferred to the **Star of the West**.

Oriental Hotel

got its first licence in 1881, when the **Brotherton Tavern** closed down. 'Oriental' was a reflection of the varied nationalities of its clientele, many of whom would have been foreign seamen from ships in the docks.

Punch Hotel

was at the back of the present Punch Hotel in Queen Victoria Square from 1845. In 1894-95 the original Punch Hotel the old Punch was demolished, and rebuilt by the Hull Brewery Co. The new pub opened in 1896, and is still open today.

The Rampant Horse

This, in Mytongate, was originally known as the **Full Measure**, but by 1826 it had become known as the Rampant Horse. The name Rampant Horse may have been taken from the coat of arms of a previous owner of the property, or the use of the land on which it stood. The opening to the left of the bar led to Dinsdales' Entry, which contained livery stables and was named after the Dinsdale family who ran the pub for more than 30 years. There was another **Rampant Horse** on the rampage in Paisley Street from about 1867.

Sculcoates Arms, Charles Street

The 'Scully Arms' boasted one of the most attractive pub fronts in Hull and was a tragic loss. The property was been built between 1838 and 1842, and was known '**by the sign of The New Inn**', when sold in 1849. It had its own brewing facilities then. The pub was refurbished in the 1890s, when its famous ceramic tiled exterior was added. Inside the bar was finished in white glazed tiles; women were *verboten* and had to sit in the Snug – entered by a side door. During the 1930s the pub was known locally as '**Smokey Joe's**'. It had a brass pixie which had a permanently lit flame for smokers, and a stove in the corner with a pan of peas warming on the top.

Sculcoates Commercial Hotel, Wincolmlee
This was situated from 1838 within warehouses on the east side of Wincolmlee. In June 1937 the rear outbuildings – which had just been rebuilt following damage by a moored ship – collapsed into the river.

Seedcrushers Arms
Sculcoates was the centre of Hull's most important industry; oil seed crushing and many of the workers in the oil crushing mills would have lived near this pub in Sculcoates.

The Ship's Hold, Wincolmlee
The Ship's Hold in Wincolmlee was first recorded ca.1822. It was re-built in 1904, when the tiled frontage was added. The door on the left of the building led to the Bottle & Jug area, and the door to the right to a very small bar.

Shipwright's Arms, Marvel Street
Another ship-related pub which was originally built ca.1810 as two shops, one of which later became this beer-house around 1826.

St. Leger Hotel
Originally known as the **Druids Arms**, from 1863, and was later re-named after the horse race. Latterly it has been known as the **Kingston Tavern**.

Stag Inn
Previously a grocers and tea dealers shop. It was first recorded as a beer-house about 1862.

Star of the West, West Street
Originally a three-storey house built around 1788, with a small front garden. The name was probably a seafaring reference, as a nod to the many sailors who lodged in the area. Or, it may just be because it was in West Street.

The Theatre Tavern, Dock Street
Was first known as the **Norwegian Tavern**, from c.1806. Its name changed to the Theatre Tavern in 1893, to mark the opening of the Grand Theatre in nearby George Street.

The Tigress
On the corner of Blaydes Staithe, opposite the **Highland Laddie**. The inn is recorded in deeds of 1734 and was first known as the **Blue Ball** – the first of many names which included

the **Ball**, the **Full Measure**, the **Corn Exchange Tavern**, the **New Exchange Tavern**, and finally the Tigress Inn around 1867.

Wheatsheaf Hotel, King Edward Street
Originally called the **Mill Inn** after the 18th century windmill which stood on the corner of what is now King Edward Street and Waltham Street, known as Waltham's Mill – giving Waltham Street its name. By 1822 the Mill Inn became known as the **Wheatsheaf Inn**; a sheaf of wheat was popular as an inn sign, and was commonly associated with the baking trade, although also linked with agricultural trades. Around 1840 Charles Searby, a bricklayer and builder took over and changed the name to the Wheelrights Arms, reverting to the Wheatsheaf Inn ca.1851. It was popular with the Merchant Navy radio officers, who when in port, called it **The 2182 Bar,** a reference to the radio-telephone calling frequency of 2182 kilocycles.

Windsor Hotel, Waterworks Street
Built in the late 1700s on the corner of Chariot Street, it was first mentioned in Clayton's directory of 1803 as the **Tiger** public house, with Mrs Sarah Mercer as victualler. Around 1826 the Tiger became known as **The March of Intellect** and locally as **The Sweeps** due to its unusual inn-sign.

Zoological Hotel, Beverley Road
The building that later became the Zoological Hotel (the **Zooey**) appeared in the *Hull Advertiser* newspaper in July 1815 as '**the house of Mrs Dunn - known by the sign of the Ship**'. In 1840 the **Ship** was re-named as the Zoological Hotel, taking its name like the **Polar Bear** and the **Botanic** from the short-lived Zoological Gardens on Spring Bank that opened that year, or the earlier zoological collection held in the original Botanical Gardens on the Anlaby Road.

A fitting place to end: the Zooey was my local when I lived in Harley Street, while the Polar Bear was my local when I lived in Sunny Bank.